Managing and Visualizing Your BIM Data

Understand the fundamentals of computer science for data visualization using Autodesk Dynamo, Revit, and Microsoft Power BI

Ernesto Pellegrino

Manuel André Bottiglieri

Gavin Crump

Luisa Cypriano Pieper

Dounia Touil

BIRMINGHAM—MUMBAI

Managing and Visualizing Your BIM Data

Group Product Manager: Pavan Ramchandani

Publishing Product Manager: Kaustubh Manglurkar

Senior Editor: Hayden Edwards

Content Development Editor: Aamir Ahmed

Technical Editor: Saurabh Kadave

Copy Editor: Safis Editing

Project Coordinator: Rashika BA

Proofreader: Safis Editing

Indexer: Subalakshmi Govindhan

Production Designer: Shyam Sundar Korumilli

First published: November 2021

Production reference: 1251021

Published by Packt Publishing Ltd.

Livery Place

35 Livery Street

Birmingham

B3 2PB, UK.

ISBN 978-1-80107-398-1

www.packt.com

To my partner in life, Vanessa De Vivo, and my sister, Alessia Pellegrino, for their love and support.

– Ernesto Pellegrino

Contributors

About the authors

Ernesto Pellegrino has background experience in computer science, start-ups, and web application development. He graduated in architecture from Roma Tre University. During the last 5 years, companies such as Microsoft and Autodesk have recognized him for contributing to their R&D projects. Also, Ernesto has been a speaker at national events dedicated to design technologies several times. The connection between computer science and academic knowledge has led to him being head of R&D in one of the most well-known Italian architecture and engineering firms, La SIA SpA. With BIM expertise and computer science skills, Ernesto is working on several projects implementing top-notch digital processes and technologies.

I want to thank the people who have worked closely with me and supported me during the book's development. Starting with the Packt team, Aamir, Kaustubh, Hayden, and Divij, who guided and advised me the whole time, thank you guys for your precious help. Vanessa De Vivo and Alessia Pellegrino, my partner in life and my sister. They overviewed the entire project from the beginning, helping me every time I needed it. Manuel, Luisa, Gavin, and Dounia, thank you all for your participation and support. Without all of those people, the book couldn't have been completed. One more thing, if you liked the illustrations in the book, you can get in touch with Vanessa on Instagram @sparkle_rabbit_art!

Manuel Andrè Bottiglieri is a full stack BIM developer at Lombardini22. Having graduated in architecture, he works as BIM developer and system integrator in the research and development team at Lombardini22. He deals with information modeling, custom APIs, cloud services, and full stack development to process, analyze, and share data through digital models. He is an enthusiast of coding, IoT, big data, and business intelligence, and is a member of the BIM User Group Italy (BUG Italy).

Gavin Crump is the owner of, and a BIM consultant at, BIM Guru. Having worked in many architectural firms over the past 10 years as a BIM manager, Gavin opened his BIM consulting firm, BIM Guru, at the start of 2020. Launching off the back of his YouTube efforts on the Aussie BIM Guru channel, his focus has shifted toward educating all levels of AEC professionals about software-based workflows, computational design, and how they can navigate the industry from a BIM perspective.

Luisa Cypriano Pieper is BIM manager at CES – Contracting Engineering Services. She is an Italian-Brazilian architect with a passion for automation and process improvement. Luisa has worked in offices in various sectors in Brazil, Italy, Belgium, and Spain. She was previously a BIM manager and BIM consultant before recently becoming head of the BIM management team. In this position, her responsibilities are implementing innovations and managing workflows across the multinational company CES, always looking from a BIM perspective.

Dounia Touil is an architect and design technology specialist at NSW Arkitektur. She leverages BIM and design technology to provide professionals with methods and practices to improve project outcomes. With a background in architecture, she has worked in France and Norway in all phases of building design and construction. Over the years, she has been part of large and complex projects in the commercial, residential, office, and transportation sectors. Her current focus is on design automation, data visualization, and software interoperability.

About the reviewer

Jisell Howe is an experienced technologist with expertise in CAD/BIM management, data visualization, software support, process management, and project management. Howe has a hybrid manufacturing and design background where communicating the data story is imperative for success with various stakeholders and clients. She holds a Bachelor of Science degree in applied management and an Associate of Applied Science degree in architectural drafting and estimating from Dunwoody College of Technology in Minneapolis, MN.

Table of Contents

3
Warming Up Your Data Visualization Engines

Section 2: Examples and Case Studies from Experts around the World

4
Building a Data Bridge between BIM Models and Web-Based Dashboards

5
Getting Started with Autodesk Dynamo and Data Gathering

6
Importing Revit Plans in Power BI Using Shape Files

7
Creating a Revit Model-Check Dashboard Using Dynamo and Power BI

Section 3: Deep Dive into Autodesk Dynamo

8

Deep Dive into Dynamo Data Types

9

Using Dynamo to Place Family Instances

10

Gathering a Revit Model's Data from Multiple Models at Once

11
Visualizing Data from Multiple Models in Power BI

12
Having Fun with Power BI

Other Books You May Enjoy

Index

Preface

The book aims to give practical skills to those working in the AEC field who want to learn data visualization skills. Each chapter will focus on a specific subject to help you to master the use of Autodesk Dynamo and Power BI to gather, manage, and visualize BIM data. Along the way, we will talk about various IT subjects that are fundamental to understand for you to grasp what is going on behind the scenes.

The book is divided into three sections. The first one is a bit more theoretical. The second one showcases examples from colleagues worldwide of how to manage and visualize a model's data. The third section is all about creating scripts and visualizing data. Throughout the book, you will also see a lot of memes that have been hand-drawn by myself and my partner in life, Vanessa De Vivo, who works as a freelance illustrator. Those memes will break up the book's seriousness from time to time and hopefully make you smile while learning.

Who this book is for

The ideal reader is a professional working in the AEC field with a background in BIM processes and modeling. I am talking about BIM managers, BIM coordinators, BIM specialists, design technology professionals, and all professionals who want to start analyzing the data of their projects. You will learn about how to approach the data management side of BIM, the most common workflows, and the best tools available, both online and offline.

What this book covers

Chapter 1, Introducing Units of Digital Information, starts by providing information on the history of digital data units of measurement. The chapter focuses on introducing you to the world of digital data without talking about BIM, talking instead about data in general. I will refer to other industries and describe why everyone is digitizing and why digital information is so valuable.

Chapter 2, Understanding Data Centers, talks about everything to do with data centers. Cloud technologies, data structures, and data centers: what are they, and why are there are more and more data centers being built worldwide every year? Then, I'll talk about two exciting projects. One is the Switch data center, which is the largest globally, and then I'll talk about Project Natick, which is interesting because it will be built beneath the ocean! After this overview on data centers, I'll talk about how to get started with Microsoft Power BI, giving you just a bit of theory and a well-organized exercise to familiarize yourself with the data analysis tool.

Chapter 3, Warming Up Your Data Visualization Engines, introduces you to some of the most common chart types. We will explain what they are, how they are used, and how to achieve the best results. After that, I'll talk about the benefits of analyzing BIM data, giving a general introduction to the subject. Toward the end, we'll get back to some practical exercise with Power BI, this time with a new, more complex dataset. The goal is to allow you to develop, using Power BI, the chart types discussed at the beginning of the chapter.

Chapter 4, Building a Data Bridge between BIM Models and Web-Based Dashboards, continues on the last subject of the previous chapter, real-time data. This chapter is perfect for continuation because it shows an excellent example of real-time streaming data from a BIM model made with Autodesk Revit to a Power BI dashboard. The goal is to build a simple Revit plugin using Visual studio. You will learn more advanced computer science topics. Even if you don't want to learn programming in the future, you still need to use such skills to develop other, more complex Autodesk Dynamo scripts.

Chapter 5, Getting Started with Autodesk Dynamo and Data Gathering, is dedicated only to understanding the fundamentals of Autodesk Dynamo. I wrote this one with Luisa Cypriano Pieper. We first cover the theory, introducing you to the world of visual programming and giving you a bit of history and context. Then, we deep dive into the core features of Autodesk Dynamo, exploring the UI, the library, the menus, and other options. Next, we will create two scripts in Autodesk Dynamo. The first one will export data from the Revit model to an Excel spreadsheet. The second one will import an updated version of that data back into the Revit model.

Chapter 6, Importing Revit Plans in Power BI Using Shape Files, focuses on Power BI and how to import a Revit floor plan. Having learned the basics of Autodesk Dynamo, you will now be ready to go another step up on the Dynamo skills ladder. You will follow a step-by-step guide to create a script in Dynamo that enables the use of Revit floor plans inside Power BI. This is an advanced workflow, and it aims to show you that mastering Autodesk Dynamo BIM is fundamental nowadays in our AEC industry. This workflow will help many of you stand out and offer something extraordinary and advanced to your colleagues and managers. By the end of this chapter, you will be a lot more confident using Autodesk Dynamo.

Chapter 7, Creating a Revit Model - Check Dashboard Using Dynamo and Power BI, is the last chapter written by the experts. Here, Dounia will showcase a workflow on creating an auditing model dashboard using Revit, Dynamo, and Power BI. These kinds of dashboards are helpful to check a model's integrity and issues. You will follow a step-by-step guide to create a Dynamo script that gathers all the necessary data from the Revit model. Next, you will learn how to make a dashboard and take advantage of that data. As in the previous chapter, we use some additional packages inside Dynamo to create shape files to visualize and interact with the Revit model view in Power BI.

Chapter 8, Deep Dive into Dynamo Data Types, is all about the more complex Dynamo data types. It is a computer science subject, a fundamental one, and relatively simple to learn. I will pick up from the topics in *Chapter 5, Getting Started with Autodesk Dynamo and Data Gathering,* where we introduced primitive data types, such as strings and integers. Then, we will continue that subject by adding more complex data types. I am talking about lists, variables, objects, arrays, and others. Along the way, I'll give examples and references to make sure you are comfortable with the subject. This is important to help you build more complex scripts using Autodesk Dynamo.

Chapter 9, Using Dynamo to Place Family Instances, is a fun chapter. After a bit of theory and hands-on experience, now is the time to create a script using what you will have learned in all previous chapters, especially *Chapter 8, Deep Dive into Dynamo Data Types,* where you will have learned how to start working with strings, variables, and `if` statements. In this chapter, you will create a script that places family instances (digital objects such as doors, chairs, or lamps) inside a Revit model. The script we will develop will automatically calculate a point in the XYZ coordinate space, and it will use that point to place the chosen object. This is a fun chapter for all readers, from beginners to intermediate users. Other than working with lists and strings, you will see how to automatically place objects inside a Revit model, which is quite a good goal to reach.

Chapter 10, Gathering a Revit Models' Data from Multiple Models at Once, will show you how to extract data and automatically place objects inside a Revit model. You will be ready to learn how to collect data from all families from multiple Revit models. This chapter will be divided according to three main learning goals. The first one is the data gathering part, where you will learn how to manage lots of lists of data. The second part will focus on preparing that data for Microsoft Excel. The last part will be related to using data to visualize everything inside Power BI, including a map showing the location of each Revit model. Each piece will be written as a step-by-step guide, using screenshots when needed.

Chapter 11, Visualizing Data from Multiple Models in Power BI, continues from where the previous chapter left off. In *Chapter 10, Gathering Revit Models' Data from Multiple Models at Once*, you will have created a script to collect multiple models' data. Here, you will focus on Power BI, visualizing multiple models' data. You will learn how to manage an extensive dataset coming from multiple Revit projects. I will talk about organizing data, formatting data, and creating and filtering charts. Also, you will learn how to show the location of a model using a map inside Power BI. Toward the end of the chapter, you will also learn how to customize the map to show data in different colors and shapes.

Chapter 12, Having Fun with Power BI, is the last chapter of the book. The book's primary goal is to give you data visualization skills. The previous chapter was a deep dive into Power BI. Here, I will let you have fun connecting Power BI to a Google form that pushes data in real time. This chapter will guide you in creating a dashboard using live data generated by you. I will explain the workflow to connect Google services and Power BI to stream data and populate our charts continuously.

To get the most out of this book

This may be obvious, but I think you should underline, highlight, and annotate everything that helps you fix a concept in your head. Repeat until the idea is well impressed. Also, you could read the book with a colleague, so you can help each other with the exercises, or maybe you could compete and have a fun challenge from time to time.

Software/hardware covered in the book	Operating system requirements
Autodesk Revit 2019 or higher	Windows
Autodesk Dynamo BIM 2.4 or higher	Windows
Microsoft Power BI Desktop	Windows
Microsoft Excel	Windows or macOS

If you are using the digital version of this book, we advise you to type the code yourself or access the code from the book's GitHub repository (a link is available in the next section). Doing so will help you avoid any potential errors related to the copying and pasting of code.

Download the example code files

You can download the example code files for this book from GitHub at `https://github.com/PacktPublishing/Managing-and-Visualizing-Your-BIM-Data`. If there's an update to the code, it will be updated in the GitHub repository.

We also have other code bundles from our rich catalog of books and videos available at `https://github.com/PacktPublishing/`. Check them out!

Download the color images

We also provide a PDF file that has color images of the screenshots and diagrams used in this book. You can download it here: `https://static.packt-cdn.com/downloads/9781801073981_ColorImages.pdf`.

Conventions used

There are a number of text conventions used throughout this book.

`Code in text`: Indicates code words in text, database table names, folder names, filenames, file extensions, pathnames, dummy URLs, user input, and Twitter handles. Here is an example: "Now, we should start with the table's name as a string without any symbols or special characters. So, please type `table_levels`."

Bold: Indicates a new term, an important word, or words that you see onscreen. For instance, words in menus or dialog boxes appear in **bold**. Here is an example: "When you have everything selected, please click on **Format as Table**."

> **Tips or important notes**
> Appear like this.

Get in touch

Feedback from our readers is always welcome.

General feedback: If you have questions about any aspect of this book, email us at `customercare@packtpub.com` and mention the book title in the subject of your message.

Errata: Although we have taken every care to ensure the accuracy of our content, mistakes do happen. If you have found a mistake in this book, we would be grateful if you would report this to us. Please visit www.packtpub.com/support/errata and fill in the form.

Piracy: If you come across any illegal copies of our works in any form on the internet, we would be grateful if you would provide us with the location address or website name. Please contact us at copyright@packt.com with a link to the material.

If you are interested in becoming an author: If there is a topic that you have expertise in and you are interested in either writing or contributing to a book, please visit authors.packtpub.com.

Share Your Thoughts

Once you've read *Managing and Visualizing your BIM Data*, we'd love to hear your thoughts! Scan the QR code below to go straight to the Amazon review page for this book and share your feedback.

https://packt.link/r/1-801-07398-8

Your review is important to us and the tech community and will help us make sure we're delivering excellent quality content.

Section 1: Overview of Digitalization and BIM Data

In this part of the book, you will develop a good overview of what is happening in relation to digitization in general and why analyzing BIM data is so important. The first three chapters will explain background IT subjects that are fundamental in terms of reaching the book's goal: managing and visualizing BIM data. For example, we will learn how series of ones and zeros create digital content on the screens of our devices, along with how much digital data we produce every day, what types of digital data there are, and how our job falls inside the category of hybrid jobs. These are just some of the subjects we will cover during the first three chapters.

This section comprises the following chapters:

1
Introducing Units of Digital Information

Welcome to the world of BIM data and digitalization!

Before we start digging into the core of digitalization in the **Architecture, Engineering, Construction (AEC)** industry, BIM data visualization, or management with Autodesk Dynamo and its business intelligence tools, I would like you to know *why* every business on earth is becoming a data-driven business. If you look around, every type of company, small or large, non-profit or governmental, is walking through a digital transformation, implementing and applying ones and zeros to every process they can. However, in the end, all that matters for company owners is that their company has to adapt to the new business model. It will take time for all of us to go fully digital, but we all will, whether it takes 10 months or 10 years; we are all already in that queue.

Even though this book's aim is to give you some knowledge on BIM data visualization and management, in the first chapter, we will start talking about data. Though we will set BIM aside for now, we will return to it later on, once we get more comfortable with digitalization and basic computer science concepts. We are going to learn about the events that started our digital era, and how modern devices use binary code to represent things such as pictures and videos. Then we will talk about types of digital data and about all of the data that surrounds us, all the time, everywhere (that's why they call it big data, right?!). Finally, we will explore so-called hybrid jobs.

But don't worry, I won't go too much into technical details, although we will cover some technical notions when it comes to Dynamo, data manipulation, and databases. So, get a cup of coffee and if you can, get an Italian one (even better if it's Neapolitan), and meet me in the first chapter!

Figure 1.1 – Say "big data" one more time meme!

In this chapter, we will cover the following topics:

- Exploring the beginning of the digitization era
- Learning how simple digital data is
- Getting to know types of digital data
- Understanding how much data we produce
- Learning about hybrid jobs

Exploring the beginning of the digitization era

Lots of companies across the globe started **the digital transformation** process around the 1950s, when Dr Presper Eckert and Dr John Mauchly invented the UNIVAC, the Universal Automatic Computer, after receiving funds from the Census Bureau. This computer was the first commercial computer for business and government applications! The real leap, though, when things started to become super-duper serious, was in the 1990s, due to the diffusion of the world wide web. If you think about it, ever since then, shopping, banking, working, health, education, and so on, *changed forever!*

I remember when I was a kid at the end of 1990s; during weekends, my family and I used to go to the shops. There, like everyone else, me, my twin brother, my sister, and our parents bought new clothes, groceries, or new games for the PC (which was my and my dad's favorite!). At that time, no one thought that one day you would be able to buy groceries using your PC or your smartphone. For example, while I'm writing this book, my partner and I are also moving to a new house and have bought a new sofa and a few other pieces of furniture online.

In the following graph, you can have a look at the growth, from 1996, of two of the biggest e-commerce companies – Amazon and eBay:

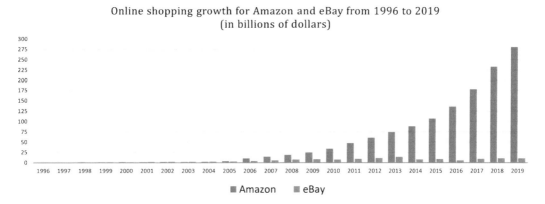

Figure 1.2 – Growth of Amazon and eBay online shopping from 1996 to 2019

The important thing here that I would like you to understand is that since the 1990s (more or less), the impact of digitalization has been huge for every field, not only for e-commerce. Things such as paper and photographs have been transformed into binary code, the ones and the zeros of computer storage.

Let me ask you this question: *Why is data so valuable?*

The short answer is that, today, *data is profitable.* Google and Facebook, for example, built an empire by collecting and analyzing people's data, and today, advertisement companies can even predict what you'll buy tomorrow, literally. When I'm talking to friends and colleagues about this subject, I like to ask them a question, so I want to do the same with you: *Do you remember what you were doing or searching on the internet in May 2009, for example?* No? Well, Google does. The data we provide to those companies is so vast that they found a new name for it: **big data!**

But to better understand this sea of data, to use that information to upgrade a company process or find possible mistakes, or even predict something somehow, companies needed to turn it from raw data into well-organized information. And once they did that, they could give advertisers, for example, a set of tools to target their potential customers with astonishing precision. At this point, with all of the data turned into useful information, they needed to build something technologically advanced to analyze and categorize everything deeply, and use that information to make future predictions. That's where **Artificial Intelligence (AI)** comes to the stage. To give you an example, let's look at the social media platform Facebook. Instead of merely offering advertisers the ability to target their users using data such as demographics, gender, or consumer preferences, they instead provided the ability to target them based on *what they will think*, *how they will behave*, and *what they will buy*. Facebook, back in 2016, revealed an AI engine with self-improving capabilities that could predict all of those things!

And as insane and frightening and unique as it may sound, this is not the only prediction engine out there. In my opinion, I hope that governments will better regulate those systems because they raise more and more questions every day, especially ethically speaking. Think, for example, about Cambridge Analytica, the Facebook scandal of early 2018. Without going into too many details, Cambridge Analytica was implicated in a massive data breach. They used almost 90 million people's private data without their consent. That's massive. And the final goal was to create customized and targeted ads to address your vote for the upcoming political election. Again, like everything else, AI can help our society in many ways, but this is a clear example of how dangerous those systems may be in the wrong hands.

In this section, we just scratched the surface, introducing the events that started the digital era. Coming up, we will cover quite a curious subject: how digital content comes to life on the screens of our devices, starting from a series of ones and zeros.

Learning how simple digital data is

My life and your life are full of data. When you commute to work, for example, you could be scrolling through Twitter, looking at friend's pictures on their social networks, buying groceries from your favorite online store, or streaming music. Everything represented by computers is made of ones and zeros; it is that simple. But how is that possible? How did pictures, videos, and songs start from a simple series of ones and zeros?

Although the answer could be a lot more complex and technical, we will stick to the basics to understand the general concepts. Essentially, to do that, we need to learn things from the point of view of a computer, something that you use all of the time and probably take for granted. This concept is essential to understand when it comes to learning computer science theory. Each one or zero stated in a single **switch** is called a **bit**, the smallest piece of data a computer can store. Just one circuit board can handle billions of switches, and computers are now able to use billions of bits to represent more complex data, such as text, songs, and images.

So, speaking of switches, an electrical current flows through switches, and when it does or does not travel through a switch, the switch goes on or off. To give you more context, imagine only using words to describe every note of your favorite song, or every scene of your beloved TV show. That is exactly what a computer does! Our devices use binary code as a language to create digital content we all know.

Here is a simple example of the electrical current that flows through switches:

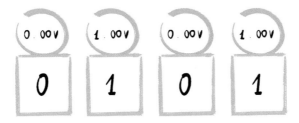

Figure 1.3 – Example of electrical flow that lets switches go on or off

Before going forward with the bits and the switches thing, you need to remember that in the past, we had analog electronics. All of those older electronics, including televisions, used analog signals with variable wave height to represent sounds and images. The problem was that those wave signals were really small and the waveforms could be interrupted by interference caused by any other signals (and nowadays we are surrounded by signals). This caused snow visuals and static sounds, for example. During the last 30 years, analog technologies have all been digitized. Using bits instead of waveforms reduces the interference dramatically.

Fortunately, neither you nor I have to learn binary code to use Word, Photoshop, or Revit! Let's take an image, for example. Every image on a computer screen is made up of dots that we call pixels, and I'm not talking about object-oriented graphics, of course (vector artworks); let's keep it simple. Anywhere between a few hundred to a few billion pixels can constitute an image, and each pixel is made up of one color, which is coded with decimal values or hexadecimal code. Those decimal values and code have been transformed by the computer, starting from a series of ones and zeros, which started from the flow of electrical current into billions of switches.

Now that we know how computers process binary code, we are ready to talk about digital data types, which is fundamental to understanding more complex subjects, such as data manipulation and databases.

Getting to know types of digital data

Let's go straight to the point. To group or classify the data out there, three major groups have been defined: **unstructured**, **semi-structured**, and **structured**.

To give you a simple example, it is possible to compare these types of data to vegetation. I've used three pictures, one for each data type. Take a look at them in the following paragraphs. Data can be represented as trees, leaves, and branches; *unstructured data* is like a wild and *uncultured forest or jungle*, with all the nature that creates beautiful chaos. We can imagine *semi-structured data* as *forest paths*, where the path is a bit difficult, but not as difficult as the wild and uncultivated forest. The last one is *structured data*, which is represented by a very *well-organized field* that it is possible to walk easily through.

So, let's take a look at each of these data types in more detail.

As the name suggests, the *unstructured data type* is data with an unknown form. It can be a combination of images, text, emails, and video files, and it can create value only when it is processed, analyzed, and well organized.

Figure 1.4 – Unstructured data is like an uncultured forest or jungle

Some of the main characteristics of the unstructured data type are as follows:

- It does not have any particular format or sequence.
- It does not follow any rules or semantics.

- It does not have an easily identifiable structure.

- It cannot be stored in a spreadsheet-like form (that is, based on rows and columns).

- It isn't directly usable or understandable by a program.

So, basically speaking, *anything that isn't in a database form belongs to the unstructured data type.*

> **Important note**
> Gartner estimates that unstructured data constitutes 80% of the world's enterprise data.

Figure 1.5 – Semi-structured data is similar to a forest with paths

The *semi-structured type,* in contrast, is a type of data that can be processed using metadata tagging, which will help us to catch useful information. With this type of data, it is difficult to determine the meaning of the data, and it is even more challenging to store the data in rows and columns as in a standard database, so even with the availability of metadata, it is not always possible to automate data analysis. To give you an example, please take a look at the following email structure:

```
To: <Name>
From: <Name>
Subject: <Text>
CC: <Name><Name>
Body:<Graphics, Images, Links, Text, etc.>
```

Those email tags are considered a semi-structured data type, and similar entities in the data will be grouped in a hierarchy. For each group, there could be a few or a lot of properties, and those properties may or may not be the same. If you read the email structure again you can immediately see that tags give us some metadata. Still, it is almost impossible to organize the data of the body tag, for example, because it will almost certainly contain no format at all. So, let's take a look at the most common features of the semi-structured data type:

- Attributes within the same group may not be the same.
- Similar entities will be grouped.
- It doesn't conform to a data model, but it contains tags and metadata.
- It cannot be stored in a spreadsheet-like form, that is, based on rows and columns.

There are lots of challenges here, too, to better manage, store, and analyze semi-structured data. The computer science community seems to be going toward a unique standard format for storing semi-structured data. All you need to know, for now, is that there is a format that is hardware and software independent, which is **XML**, an extensible markup language, which is also open source and written in plain text. This XML format is more or less the alter ego of the **Industry Foundation Classes (IFC)** for BIM models!

The third data type is the *structured data type,* which is a database of systematic data that can be used by companies for direct analysis and processing. It consists of information that has been both transformed and formatted into a well-defined data model. Without going too much into the technical details, remember that this type of data is mapped into predesigned fields that can later be read and extracted by a relational database. This way of storing information is the best one out of the three types, and even though the relational model minimizes data redundancy, you still need to be careful because structured data is more inter-dependent, and for this reason, it can sometimes be less flexible.

Figure 1.6 – Structured data looks like a well-organized field

So, some of the most important features of the structured data type are as follows:

- It conforms to a data model.

- Similar entities are grouped.

- Attributes within the same group are the same.

- Data resides in fixed fields within a record.

- The definition and meaning of the data is explicitly known.

At this point, I would like you to understand that we will have to carry out different tasks to transform our raw data into structured information, whether we are dealing with unstructured, semi-structured, or structured data.

As you probably already understand, data is becoming a fundamental tool for knowing and understanding the world around us. Simply put, we can think of data as a way to "approach" problems and to "solve" them in the end. And at this point, I would like to introduce you to the **Data, Information, Knowledge, Wisdom (DIKW)** pyramid, also known as the **DIKW** model. The pyramid helps us by describing how raw data can be transformed into information, then knowledge, then wisdom. Take a look at the following image. As we move up to the top of the pyramid, we look for patterns, and by imposing structure, organization, classification, and categorization, we turn data without any particular meaning into knowledge, and finally wisdom.

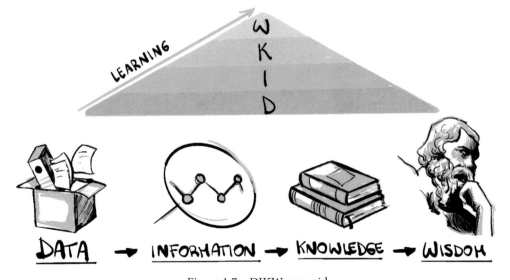

Figure 1.7 – DIKW pyramid

To better fix the concept in your head, I would like to give you a simple yet practical example of the DIKW pyramid by talking about the weather! Imagine that it is raining; this is an objective thing and has no particular meaning, so we can associate raining with **data**. Then, if I tell you that it started to rain at 7p.m. and the temperature dropped by 2 degrees, that is **information**. Continuing on that path, if we can explain why this is happening, like saying that the temperature dropped because of low pressure in the atmosphere, you're talking about **knowledge**. And in the end, if we get a complete picture of things such as temperature gradients, air currents, evaporation, and so on, we can statistically make predictions about what will happen in the future – that's **wisdom**!

Although we didn't go into the technical details, I would like you to remember that businesses and organizations all around the world use processes such as the one described here, the DIKW pyramid, when it comes to organizing their data.

Here, we've learned some fundamental concepts, such as types of digital data and their differences. We've also learned about the DIKW pyramid. Next, we will talk about how much data we produce every 60 seconds!

Understanding how much data we produce

In this section, we will dive into a little bit of computer science, learning about *digital data measuring units*, but we will also talk about a curious subject. I'm talking about **the data we produce every 60 seconds: it is unbelievable!** So, first of all, let's talk about measuring units.

One byte consists of 8 bits, and since computers deal with ones and zeros, which means that they deal with math of base two instead of decimals (math of base ten), all increments in data storage units have to equate to the power of two, rather than the power of ten, like we all are used to. Consequently, one **kilobyte (KB)** consists of 1,024 bytes or 2^{10}, and not 10^3 as you probably expected.

Now, let's see some real-world examples:

- 1 hour of social network page scrolling will consume around 120 MB of data.
- 1 hour of streaming music will consume about 150 MB of data.
- 1 hour of watching full HD YouTube videos will consume approximately 1,500 MB (or 1.5 GB) of data.
- 1 hour of high-definition streaming on Netflix will consume more or less 3,000 MB (or 3 GB) of data.
- 1 hour of Skype calls with five or six colleagues will consume up to 4,000 MB (or 4 GB) of data.

Another example is that *the entire original Super Mario Bros game consists of 32 KB, which is roughly 0.03 MB!* There is an unbalanced proportion between the game's size, which is incredibly small, and the amount of happiness it brought people of any age from all over the world!

Now that we've got some understanding of the measuring units, let's talk about something more fun: data exchanges of the online services we all use, every day. We will also build, later on, a few Power BI charts using the data I am going to show you right now. We will create those charts to get some familiarity with this powerful business intelligence tool and discover some of its basic commands and features.

Have you ever wondered how much data we generate every 60 seconds?

The amount of data we generate is insane. Think, for example, of a quite simple thing that we do over and over every day: Google searches. We even invented a new verb for it, *"googling"!* It has also become synonymous with the internet. Anyway, we all are curious about everything all the time. People like me and you are always thirsty for information, and that's why we use Google all day long. The famous search engine is so dominant in the search engine market because it provides free access to information in a blink of an eye. But, of course, Google didn't become a giant overnight. Back in the days before Google or Facebook, the absolute king of the internet was named Yahoo, a tech company founded in 1994 that, today, still, handles 5% of web searches. A few years later, in 1999, the company was worth $125 billion, but unfortunately, the giant made some wrong moves and started to lose users. Probably the most significant wrong move was to refuse to acquire Google. Yes, in case you didn't know, Google's Larry Page and Sergey Brin approached the Yahoo CEO in 1998 and asked for the small amount of $1 million. You can deduce the end of the story; **Yahoo refused*. But this wasn't the only mistake made by Yahoo. Yahoo declined to buy Google again in 2002 for an amount of $5 billion, and in 2008 refused to be acquired by Microsoft for $44.6 billion, but that is another story. Anyhow, Google today has passed $1 trillion in market value, which is astonishing.

Back to the data! At Google, nowadays, they process something like 5.4 billion searches per day! Breaking it down, you get 3.8 million searches per minute. Insane. The giant search engine now dominates the market with almost 93% of total internet searches.

But this is not the only crazy number of online services we are going to talk about. You might be wondering about LinkedIn, Amazon, Netflix, YouTube, Instagram, and so on. Earlier, I told you that we would be talking about what happens every 60 seconds. Well, if you go back a few lines, you'll see a sign with two asterisks right next to the phrase **Yahoo refused*. I counted how long it takes to read the text from the *"**Yahoo refused."* to now, and guess what, *it takes more or less 60 seconds to read those lines!*

Here, I have listed a few things that happened in that timeframe:

- Amazon shipped between 6,000 and 7,000 packages.
- Users scrolled more or less 350,000 times on Instagram.
- 55,000 users, approximately, logged on to Microsoft Teams.
- Netflix users streamed about 100,000 hours of video.
- 2,000 new Reddit comments were created.
- LinkedIn gained 120 new professionals.
- 4,500,000 videos were watched on YouTube.

Figure 1.8 – Data everywhere!

These are just a few of the things that happen every 60 seconds on the internet, and even if it seems overwhelming, we, as humankind, just started the ladder of digitization. During the last 10 to 20 years, thanks to the spread of the internet, we saw a rapid evolution of the business landscape. In this short period, the digitization era has left us with a very eventful time.

In the next section, we will talk about a less technical yet quite interesting subject: hybrid jobs!

Learning about hybrid jobs

Today, because of the large amounts of data we produce and collect, companies from every industry are looking for new types of employees. Nowadays, an increasing number of professionals are developing IT skills that make them the perfect candidates for many companies that have invested in digital transformation. This interesting factor occurs in any field: financial, medical, engineering, hospitality, and so on.

I would like you to understand this concept because if you would like to apply for a new job, you probably would have a better chance if you have learned some coding or data science skills! This is why. People working in HR call them **hybrid jobs**. According to *Burning Glass Technologies,* a company that specializes in analyzing trends, skills demand, and job growth, *one of every eight job postings asks for candidates with hybrid skills,* no matter the field.

Employers indeed are requesting coding and data analysis skills, other than a degree in their business area. Here, we are talking about a mix of skills from different domains. For example, marketers rely on big data or data science abilities to coordinate their advertisement campaigns. At the same time, increasing numbers of architects and engineers need to work with data systems and robotics. Take the engineering field as another example; it is a common practice that students take computer science classes. So, we see a significant increase in the computer science skills demand from employers in various industries and sectors.

Figure 1.9 – A woman with hybrid skills!

Some of those hybrid jobs are as follows:

- Data scientists
- Business intelligence managers
- Virtual reality architects

- Visual data scientists

- Web analytics managers

These roles are just a few among all of the new jobs that our *digital economy* is demanding. We also, as professionals in the AEC industry, have seen the spread of new roles in the last few years, such as design technology professionals, computational design specialists, developers with an architectural or engineering background, and so on.

Anyhow, we can say without any doubt that every company, no matter what the field is, is becoming little by little closer to a tech company. That's the reason why we will have to adapt to this change, and we all have to learn computer science by learning the logic of how software is created. You can't merely learn how to use a few pieces of software and use them your whole life! In our ever-changing world, we should learn the logic underneath the tools, and not the tools themselves.

Machines and algorithms will be our next best friends/colleagues! Nevertheless, we, as professionals in the AEC industry, have to do the same as other colleagues in other sectors are already doing. We're doing nothing special here. We need to increase our knowledge and work hard to overcome our next challenges, which will let us better understand, manage, and analyze our processes and model's data!

We just learned what hybrid jobs are and why IT and computer science skills are becoming more and more critical for all types of businesses. If you aren't yet, get ready to acquire new hybrid skills in the upcoming months or years. And, by the way, by the end of the book, you'll already have started that path. So, stick with me and follow the book without skipping any parts! You know the saying, *"No pain, no gain!"*

Summary

In this chapter, we have learned why every company is moving toward a data-driven business model. Then, we discussed how series of ones and zeros create digital content. Also, we started to explore the three types of digital data, unstructured, semi-structured, and structured, and how the DIKW pyramid helps us to organize our data into useful information. Next, we discovered how much data we produce every 60 seconds, and it is unbelievable that those numbers keep growing every month! Finally, we discussed how data science skills have become vital for so-called hybrid jobs.

In the next chapter, we are going to deep dive into the world of data centers: when the first data center came to be, what they are now, and why are they so important for businesses and organizations worldwide. Then we will talk about two of the most significant data center projects, and finally, we will take a first look at Power BI's core functionalities.

2
Understanding Data Centers

Welcome to the second chapter! I want to introduce you to the world of data centers. This is an essential subject because before learning data science or programming skills, you should know everything about how data flows. You need to precisely understand where and how files and information are both stored and retrieved, and you need to understand the types of environments in which data resides. Here, we will learn the importance of data centers and the most common data center types that companies use to support their IT infrastructures. We will also talk about The Citadel and Project Natick, two of the most promising and advanced data centers worldwide. At the end of this chapter, we will be introducing Power BI by analyzing an exciting yet straightforward dataset, the World Happiness Report!

Today, we know that companies and organizations worldwide have IT systems that need to be managed, updated, and monitored. And that is how data centers come into play. They are used to guarantee the continuity of businesses' IT infrastructures. Their primary tasks are recovering and backing up data, as well as networking. Everything we do on our devices goes to or comes from a data center somehow. We can say without any doubt that times have changed, and the information demand is increasing month by month. Probably 90% of what we do every day travels from one server to another in the blink of an eye. And all of those networking activities are managed and hosted by data centers:

Figure 2.1 – "The cloud" is just someone else's computer!

In this chapter, we will cover the following topics:

- Understanding data centers
- Getting started with Microsoft Power BI

Understanding data centers

A data center is a facility that contains networking and computing equipment. Its purpose is to collect, distribute, process, and store large amounts of data. It can consist of just one server or more complex systems with hundreds or thousands of servers on racks (frameworks for holding or storing hardware). *So, every organization, no matter what its size is, needs one.*

Data centers are mainly divided into two prominent families:

- **Traditional data centers**: Always physically accessible
- **Cloud data centers**: Always accessible through the internet

Although those two types are so different from each other, it is difficult to find a facility that is *only physically accessible* or *only accessible through the internet*. Usually, traditional data centers are rooms or buildings directly owned by a private organization for internal use only. The majority of data centers are a combination of both worlds. Companies such as Amazon and Microsoft provide cloud data center services. I want you to keep in mind that **cloud computing** and **cloud storage services** are booming these days.

With traditional data centers, you need to purchase several things, from the server hardware to the networking hardware. You also need to hire a technical team dedicated to the maintenance of the system. Other than that, you have to design and buy the infrastructure to provide an uninterruptible power supply, a cooling system, backup generators, and so on. You would probably only choose to have a traditional data center if you have lots of money to invest, or if your company is named Amazon or Google!

However, if you are a company owner and are about to buy or switch to a cloud solution, please keep in mind that the *human factor is as important as the others*, or maybe more. People with IT-related skills are essential here. For example, if you've got the budget to sustain the initial investment to buy the hardware and the software needed, but you have no clue who to hire and what their skills must be, take a step back! Talk to IT managers when you get the chance, or at least some HR professionals who work with IT professionals. Even better, hire someone like a design technology manager or an IT manager who will not only help you out during the initial phases of planning, but will be the pillar of all your future IT decisions.

Software/hardware are just tools. People determine the success (or not) of the process.

So, let's get started and look at the different types of data centers.

Learning the different types of cloud solutions

I want to start by sharing my personal experience about the first time I came into contact with *the cloud*. In 2013, I was working as a freelance teacher in London, UK. I gave some private lessons to engineers and architects who wanted to learn and improve their Autodesk Revit skills. My typical day was going around London on the tube, with my laptop and an external hard disk in my backpack. At that time, I did not want all my stuff to be on the cloud. My hard disk was a good one, quite expensive, and I thought it would never break. A few months later, though, after a few sudden moves, my external hard disk failed, and I lost almost everything. It was a very tough day, both financially and psychologically, because I had to create everything from scratch: PowerPoint presentations, Word docs, Revit files, templates, and families. All lost. After a couple of days, I decided to try one of the most well-known cloud storage services, and I must say I found it helpful. For instance, if tomorrow my laptop burns (hopefully not), I would not lose all my files because everything is secured online. Even if a data center shut down somehow, you would not lose your stuff because many copies of your files can be found elsewhere.

Figure 2.2 – Everything is in the cloud!

This is why the cloud is so important today! Now let's take a look at the different types of clouds:

- A **private cloud**, meaning that software and hardware are dedicated solely to you, and the infrastructure is maintained on a private network.

- A **public cloud**, meaning that the cloud resources, storage, and servers are operated by a third-party cloud service provider and delivered through the internet. This kind of solution is the most widely used worldwide, mainly because of the lower costs.

- Or a **hybrid solution** that uses both the cloud and the traditional data center features. A hybrid cloud, in many ways, combines the best aspects of each solution. If you think about it, *you don't need to have the same privacy or protection level for all of your data and business applications.* To give you an example, you could benefit from a mixed environment like so: all your financial and sensitive information might be located on-premises, meaning on a data center situated directly at or close by your office; then you could have your HR application, employee information, and your supplier's data running on a private cloud; and as a third environment, you could have information dedicated to R&D and all of your application testing on a public cloud. Probably this is the best solution in terms of performance, scalability, and maintenance costs.

Anyway, we now know that there are different types of cloud solutions to choose from. But what about the security levels of those services? What if we need to create a BIM model of a sensitive building and provide our client with a secure platform to share and store data?

As you can see, when it comes to our data, security is something significant to consider. Think, for example, about a bank's transaction data, politicians' emails, or a BIM model of an airport. All of these things need to be super secure because we are talking about sensitive information. Today, thousands of companies offer cloud storage solutions, but not everyone can provide a super-secure system. If you decide to pick one, choose carefully, and possibly select something that's *compliant with the BIM security protocols*!

With BIM becoming more collaborative and more complex, it is *imperative* that the BIM management fully understands the cloud's security systems and protocols. To give you an example, the **British Standard Institution (BSI)**, which is the organization that regulates UK National Standards, published in mid-2020 the new international standard **BS EN ISO 19650-5:2020** (this is a specification for security-minded information management). This is only one among all of the standards and protocols that countries worldwide are introducing. Think about BIM models of airports, ports, governmental facilities, and so on. Those standards aim to reduce the risks associated with sensitive information. Indeed, if a sensitive building's data was compromised, it could impact those environments' security and safety. I suggest you find a cloud service that complies with your own country's BIM security standards.

At this point, we've learned what private, public, and hybrid clouds are. We also learned that to pick the right service, you need to choose something that's compliant with BIM security standards, such as the BS EN ISO 19650-5:2020. In the next section, I want you to learn how everything started: how old data centers developed into the systems that every company worldwide is using right now.

Introducing the first data center in history, ENIAC

In the 1950s, the same two engineers who developed the UNIVAC also developed the first hardware that resembled modern data centers, whose purpose was to store US Army codes: **Electronic Numerical Integrator And Computer (ENIAC)**. This so-called "giant brain" was enormous, and it needed a room over 170 sq meters (1,800 sq ft). Despite its significant size, ENIAC could store 1,000 words, 12 characters each. They soon started to work on two new projects: **Electronic Discrete Variable Automatic Computer (EDVAC)**, which was the ENIAC's successor, mainly because it had a binary-based system; then, the **Universal Automatic Computer (UNIVAC)**, the first commercial computer for business, which we mentioned in the first chapter.

It's very curious that because of the UNIVAC's commercial nature, they started a considerable campaign trying to sell it to companies and organizations all over the US. It must have been a colossal challenge for the two engineers because, if you think about it, commercial electronic devices did not exist until that point. In a certain way, those electronic computing machines are the grandfathers of our modern devices!

Look at the following image, which shows the first sales brochure ever published for an electronic digital computer:

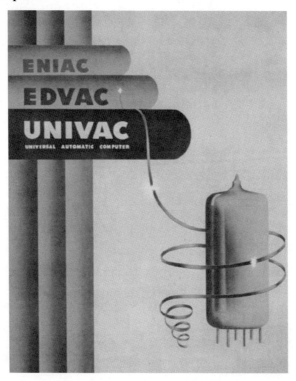

Figure 2.3 – First sales brochure ever published for an electronic digital computer

In addition to the brochure marketing campaigns, to reach out to a large number of customers and increase public awareness of computing technology, the UNIVAC was promoted through television channels and radio programs. Consequently, the UNIVAC was sold to various governmental organizations and businesses that could afford such an expensive machine. At the time, the price was around $150,000 ($1,500,000 in today's money), and some of the organizations who bought the computer were the US Navy, the US Air Force, and General Electric.

Today, modern data centers are everywhere, and they consist of more significant and complex facilities, made of one building or several, ranging from 500 to 50,000 sq meters (roughly 5,300 to 530,000 sq ft), and some of them are even being built under the ocean, such as Project Natick! According to `statista.com`, there are 8.4 million data centers all over the world. To attain the level of technology and efficiency of today's data centers, lots of implementations and improvements happened over the last 70 years, starting with the ENIAC project.

Now that we understand that ENIAC is considered the first data storage device in history and that cloud storage solutions are spreading worldwide, we can introduce The Citadel and Project Natick, two of the most advanced data center projects worldwide.

Learning about The Citadel and Project Natick

Did you know that every human generates around 1.7 MB of data each second? I didn't know that, but tech companies know it, so they found a solution: building data centers everywhere.

Here, I would like to introduce you to two of the most advanced data centers in the world. I picked these two projects because their main focus is being powered by 100% renewable energy. In 2021, if you're building such an advanced structure, but you don't think about environmental impacts, *you can't be on the "top players" list* (or, at least, my list).

The first one is the biggest data center in the world: **The Citadel**. This unique facility is the size of a city, and it is owned by a company named **Switch**.

Figure 2.4 – The Citadel by Switch, the data center the size of a city

The facility is in Reno, Nevada, US, in the same industrial area as Tesla's Gigafactory. As suggested previously, the Citadel is powered completely by renewable energy, and it purchases *587 million kWh (kilowatt-hours) per year!* And for that reason, the company Switch received a Green Power Leadership Award in 2019 from the Environmental Protection Agency. The colossal data center is about 680,000 sq meters (72,000,000 sq ft); with that size, the area could host 34 Roman colosseums (roughly 20,000 sq meters each)! To protect their customers' data, the Citadel is protected by a team of security agents that works like the US Army, and its campus is surrounded by 6-meter (20-foot) concrete walls. The Citadel is so secure that it surpasses the standard data center security levels.

Now let's look at **Project Natick**, a data center project from Microsoft, built and tested under the ocean. Natick is a research project aiming to develop a modular data center system that lives near the users, close to the coast. Instead of having a colossal facility like The Citadel, Project Natick consists of containerized blocks. To reduce energy consumption, Microsoft's R&D team found an attractive solution. Each container is deployed in deep water, and by using the cold temperature of that depth, they can optimize and reduce the overall power consumption.

In a nutshell, organizations such as Google, Amazon, and Apple are becoming more and more efficient in powering their facilities, but Microsoft is testing a new kind of data center, one that will be located underwater and that will require less energy to run, regardless of its source. Data centers on land need lights, oxygen, and humans to work correctly, while this underwater data center doesn't. In this way, you can limit heat production, which needs to be measured and controlled. But they didn't stop here.

Figure 2.5 – One module of Project Natick's containerized underwater data centers

They are also testing a unique tidal turbine that will generate electricity using the water's movement around the container!

Microsoft believes that Project Natick data centers can survive for up to 5 years, after which they need to replace all hardware and computers on board with new ones. The container will last up to 20 years. After this period, the entire box will be retrieved and recycled and have a new life. The company's vision is to place many of those modules near the world's largest cities' shorelines. In this way, all businesses that need real-time data will benefit from this system's low latency. Project Natick, other than using 100% renewable energy to power the modules, also uses recycled materials to build all the containers.

Unlike The Citadel, Project Natick is a research project in its early stages of development. It is too soon to determine whether or not the underwater data center will succeed, but so far, it is very promising!

Now that we've explored these two impressive and exciting projects, I recommend you Google them if you want to find out more. Now, let's jump to a hands-on section by introducing Microsoft Power BI and showcasing a couple of simple dashboards to warm up the engines. Let's find out more in the next section!

Getting started with Power BI

Before we start, I would like to answer the following questions for you:

- What is Power BI?
- Where can you find datasets to start practicing yourself?

To put it simply, **Power BI** stands for **Power Business Intelligence**, and it's software that provides users that have no programming skills with a set of tools for visualizing, reporting, and sharing data. The user interface is pretty intuitive for users who already have a little bit of experience with Excel. Power BI is often used to find insights within our organization's data. It can help us to connect different datasets and create engaging visuals and graphs. One of the most exciting ways to use the software, in my opinion, is to tell a story using charts by examining the *what-if* scenarios.

Important Note

In the following chapters, we will mainly use Power BI as our data visualization tool because it is well known in the AEC community. However, I would like to make it clear that you could use similar platforms as well; the core purpose of everything here is visualizing data, whether you do it with Microsoft Power BI, Tableau, Qlik, or Looker.

To answer the second question, you can search online for free and open datasets, and you will probably find platforms such as **Google Dataset Search, Datahub.io**, and **Earth Data**. I've chosen to use **Kaggle**, and here I found the **World Happiness Report** dataset. I encourage you to open one of the previously mentioned platforms and search for a dataset that you find of particular interest, whether it is about Game of Thrones, crime rates, dogs, or anything else. Just pick the one you like the most and start practicing with Power BI (I mean after you've completed this chapter!). *You won't believe how easy it will be to manage BIM model data after a week or two of practicing with Power BI.*

Setting up Power BI and exploring the World Happiness Report

To use Power BI, you need a Power BI account. If you haven't already, you should open the Power BI website and sign up with your organizational account (`yourname@ yourcompany.com`). Remember that Power BI, as a business tool, doesn't allow registration from consumer emails, such as Gmail or Outlook. Once you've created an account, you should get a welcome email from the Power BI team. You should also confirm your account by clicking a link inside the Power BI welcome email. Please create the account and come back.

For your information, you should know that Power BI comes with different license types. Long story short, the free account has a 10 GB data capacity limit, 1 GB as the maximum size of a data model, and some other limitations when you want to share your dashboards or interact with apps. Anyhow, for our purpose, we can use the free license without any issues. I've created a link to the final report that is accessible by guest users who don't have a Power BI account: `https://cutt.ly/ejGxc6y`.

When you open the link, you should see a web page that looks like this:

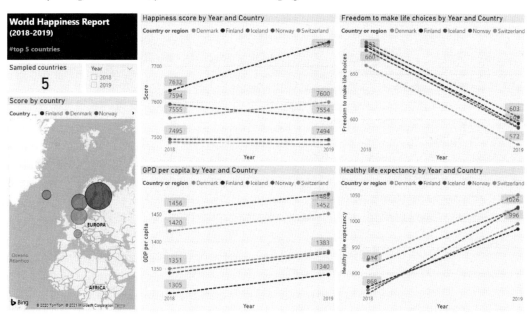

Figure 2.6 – World Happiness Report screenshot from the Power BI dashboard

When you open up the web page, you can explore the data, filter the results, and check the correlation between the happiness score and other metrics. Click on the right arrow at the bottom of the web page to move to other pages. You can find data about the GPD per capita for each of the listed countries, data about the freedom to make life choices, and much more. Please note that I've created two simple dashboards. The first one contains data from the top five countries. The second one relates the first place and the last four positions.

Creating your first dashboard

Let's see how you can create a dashboard with this dataset. Even if you're already a Power BI advanced user, I recommend you follow along, as you may discover some new ways to manipulate data, even if this is a relatively simple dataset. To start, we need to import the **Comma Separated Values** (**CSV**) files. To do this, follow these instructions:

1. Firstly, to download the Kaggle dataset, open up the Kaggle web page and register for a free account. You can use this link to open the Kaggle signup page: `https://cutt.ly/Nkr2VEd`.

2. Once you have registered a Kaggle account, use the following link to download the World Happiness Report dataset: `https://cutt.ly/HjGxLaB`.

3. You should get a ZIP file that contains five files. Please keep in mind that for simplicity purposes, I've used the 2018 and 2019 files only. I want you to do the same for now. Later on, if you wish, you can use more data by importing and manipulating all other files.

4. Open Power BI and log in. Then we can import our datasets. You can import as few or as many datasets as you want. The business intelligence tool can import almost every type of dataset, and in this example, I will be using CSV files. Please take a look at the Power BI website to see the complete list of all the supported file formats. The first screen you should see at startup is as follows:

Add data to your report

Once loaded, your data will appear in the **Fields** pane.

| Import data from Excel | Import data from SQL Server | Paste data into a blank table | Try a sample dataset |

Get data from another source →

Figure 2.7 – Power BI start screen (it may vary in future versions)

5. Once you're on that screen, please click on **Get Data** on the **Home** tab. You should see an icon with a white cylinder and an Excel-like table.

6. Now select the **Text/CSV** format to tell Power BI what type of file we want to import, and then click **Connect** in the bottom-right corner of the screen.

7. A new window will pop up. Here, we need to select what files to import. Please choose the previously downloaded files. *Remember to choose the 2018 and 2019 CSV files only.*

After importing the CSV files, you need to manipulate the data to let Power BI understand the relationships between tables, columns, and values. You can do that using **Power Query Editor**, which pops up after completing the import process. If you have missed it, no worries; click on **Get data** and import the second CSV file first anyway.

When you're done, let's start using **Power Query Editor**:

1. Click on **Transform Data** on the same **Home Tab** where we just found the **Get data** button. Depending on your dataset or datasets and your report's goals, the steps needed to manipulate the data can vary. For example, you may want to format a column that has been recognized as simple text in date/time. Or you may want to add a custom column to insert a label that will separate tables with the same values.

    Once you've imported the 2018 and the 2019 files, you should see the data in the **Fields** section. Please take a look at the following screenshot:

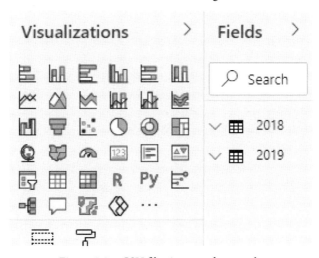

Figure 2.8 – CSV files imported correctly

The 2018 and 2019 CSV files will be listed here. Inside Power BI, those imported files are called **tables**.

2. Now, let's click on **Transform data** to edit those tables. You will see a new Power BI editing environment. This is called **Power Query Editor**. This editor plays an intermediary role, where you can edit the data before creating the graphs.

3. From here, I decided to create a new table by combining the data coming from the two imported CSVs. To do so, inside **Power Query Editor**, click on the little black arrow on the right of the **Append Queries** button and select **Append Queries as New**. You will find this button on the **Home** tab of **Power Query Editor**:

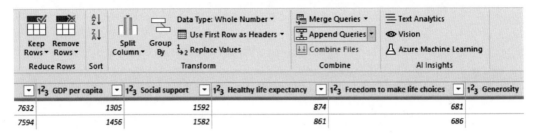

Figure 2.9 – Power Query Editor and the Append Queries button

4. A new window will pop up. Here, Power BI is asking you to choose the tables that need to be combined. Please select **2018** as the first table and **2019** as the second one, as shown in the following screenshot:

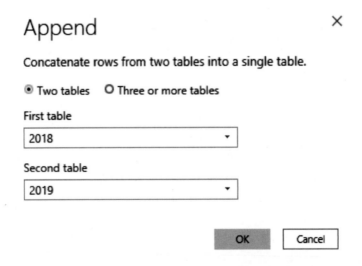

Fig 2.10 – New window where we can select the two tables

5. Click **OK**. A new table will appear on the left side of **Power Query Editor**.

6. Right-click on that new table and rename it. I've renamed it 2018+2019.

At this point, if you scroll down, you will see all of the data from the two combined tables. But we're not done yet. We have quite a big problem here. How can you tell what row belongs to what table? I mean, how can you know if row 45, for example, belongs to table 2018 or table 2019?

To address that, we need to do something that helps us solve this problem. All we need is an extra column for each of those tables, a column such as Year or Belongs to or something like that. So, let's create these columns:

1. On the left side of the screen, you should see three tables, **2018, 2019**, and the one we just created on the left pane. Click on **2018** to select it, then click on the **Add Column** tab and select the **Custom Column** button. This button should be the second one from the left.

2. I will type Year in the **New column name** text field in the new window. At this point, Power BI wants to know the custom column formula, but we don't need one here. We want each row of the **2018 table** to show **2018**. In this way, when we combine the two tables, we reference what data belongs to what table. So, type 2018 in the **Custom column formula** box and click **OK**.

3. Now we need to do the same for the **2019** table. Repeat every step until you have created a new custom column for the **2019** table.

4. When you're done, click on the **2018+2019** combined table and go to the far right. You should see the **Year** values displayed correctly for each of the tables, as shown in the following screenshot:

376	0.144		2018
200	0.444		2018
83	0.064		2018
270	0.097		2018
224	0.106		2018
218	0.038		2018
149	0.076		2018
153		393	2019
252		410	2019
271		341	2019
354		118	2019
322		298	2019
263		343	2019

Figure 2.11 – Now, each table has the reference we needed

If you scroll down, you can now clearly see where table 2018 ends and where table 2019 begins. We need a couple more steps to confirm our data modeling operations. First, we need to be sure that Power BI knows that the values 2018 and 2019 are recognized as whole numbers. We can't set them as date/time values because we would need to add the days and the months, but we don't have this kind of information in this example. So, let's make sure the values 2018 and 2019 are recognized as whole numbers and not just text. Please do the following:

1. While you are on the new combined table, click on the second tab at the top of the screen, **Transform**.

2. Then we need to select the header of the new column, **Year**. To do so, make sure to scroll to the right of the table. You'll see the **Year** column is the last one because it's the last one we've created. Now, click on the header of that column. Once you've clicked, you'll see the background color changing for the entire column.

3. While the **Year** column is selected, go to the **Any column** section on the previously opened **Transform** tab. Here, we can click on the button showing **Data type: Any** to see a full list of data types. Instead, I want you to click on the button just below this one, **Detect Data Type**, as shown in the following screenshot:

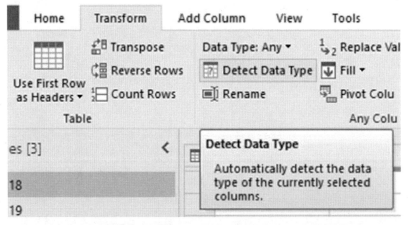

Figure 2.12 – The Detect Data Type button can be found on the Transform tab

As the values 2018 and 2019 are not full date/time objects, Power BI will recognize those as the whole number data type, and that is what we want. We are all set now.

4. We need to confirm our data modeling operations by clicking on the **Close and Apply** button on the **Home** tab. At this point, Power BI needs a few seconds to apply our changes.

Before creating graphs, please check the **Model** view and look at the automatic relationships between the tables. On the left of the screen, you can see three little boxes. If you hover over each one, you can see three different types of view:

- **Report**: Used to create charts
- **Data view**: Used to see the raw data and for editing
- **Model view**: Used to let Power BI understand the relationships between tables

Click on the **Model** view. It should look like this:

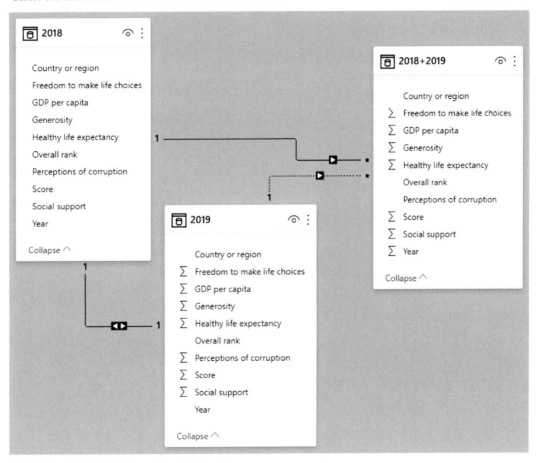

Figure 2.13 – Power BI's Model view

Each line represents a connection between tables. For example, Power BI automatically understood that the **Overall Rank** column of the 2018 table shows the same data as the 2019 table, and their relationship is 1:1. Again, as this is not a book on Power BI, we won't go into too much detail. We will stick to general and basic concepts. *I recommend you learn more using the Power BI official community forum or any other learning platform.*

Customizing and filtering the chart

OK, now for the fun part. At this point, we've organized all of the data and we are ready to create some cool graphs. Go back to the **Report** view. Now, for example, let's create a pie chart like so:

1. Click on **Pie Chart** in the **Visualizations** pane, right next to the **Fields** pane.

2. In the **Fields** pane, click on the **2018+2019** table and drag **Country or region** to the pie chart's **Legend** property.

3. Next, drag the **Score** values into, well, the **Values** property. You will see the most chaotic pie chart ever:

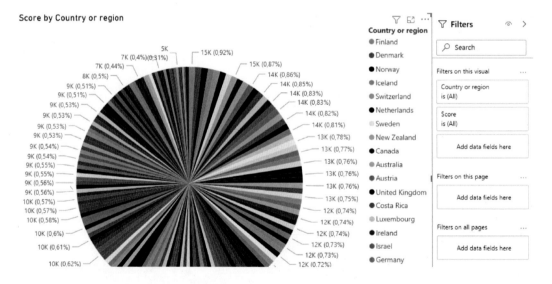

Figure 2.14 – Messy pie chart

It's not the pie chart's fault; it is just showing us what we asked. We asked to show all of the countries, with all of the scores, for both the 2018 and 2019 tables.

4. To create a more understandable chart, we need to filter the data. And we can do that by using the **Filters** pane, right next to the **Visualizations** and **Fields** panes. Here, you can decide to filter data only on this visual, meaning only on this pie chart, or you can filter data on this page or, instead, on all pages. As we want to create understandable charts for the entire page, I want to add a filter to the **Filters on this page** section. I want to show just the first five countries on this page, for example. So, let's drag **Score** from the **Fields** pane to the **Filters on this page** section of the **Filters** section.

5. For **Filter Type**, we can choose **Advanced filtering**. Then, select **is greater than** and type 7487 right below that.

> **Important Note**
> Depending on your region and computer settings, you may need to enter 7.487 or 7,487 to let Power BI understand that this is a number in the order of thousands.

6. Now click **Apply filter** to complete the operation.

You will see an updated version of the pie chart, showing only the first five countries with the highest overall happiness score.

One more thing: we don't want the pie chart to show just percentage values and scores. We want to add more helpful information to the chart. Let's do that by selecting the chart and clicking on the **Format** button, right below the **Visualizations** pane's 30-ish chart icons:

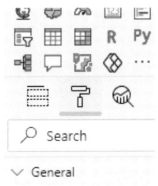

Figure 2.15 – Format button

This is the place where we can customize the design of the charts. Let's go to the **Detail label** property and select **Category, data value** from the first drop-down list. You can customize each chart's fonts, backgrounds, and colors using all of the **Format** section's properties.

Now that you understood how to create a chart, insert data, and customize it, it's your turn to make some cool charts! I want you to explore Power BI and discover its functionalities. No worries, though, if you feel stuck or you can't do what you want. You will learn more and more in the next chapters! When you're done with the Happiness report, try to find a new dataset that interests you and do some Power BI experiments.

Summary

In this chapter, you learned why cloud storage services are crucial for every organization and the difference between private, public, and hybrid cloud solutions. You also discovered two of the most interesting data center projects worldwide, and you learned when and how the first data center in history came to life. We introduced one of the most powerful data analysis tools, Microsoft Power BI, and you created your first graph.

In the next chapter, we will talk about the benefits of analyzing BIM data. We will go through a list of what I think are the most significant advantages of doing BIM data analysis. I am talking about having better overall project control, improving collaboration by improving communications. Let's find out more in the next chapter!

3
Warming Up Your Data Visualization Engines

In this chapter, we will have an exciting talk about what data visualization is and what some of the standard chart types are. We will also discuss why BIM data analysis is essential and why companies move toward a data-driven business model. Last but not least, we will explore some of the Microsoft Power BI charts.

Figure 3.1 – Carl, should I follow the data?!

In this chapter, we will cover the following topics:

- Getting started with data visualization
- Why analyzing BIM data is important
- Exploring Microsoft Power BI charts

Getting started with data visualization

Using images and pictures to tell stories is as old as human existence. The first appearance of a pie chart was in the early 1800s. And of course, later on, when computers came out, data visualization reached a whole new level. So, what is **data visualization**?

In a nutshell, *data visualization is the graphical representation of data or information.* You can easily imagine that trying to find patterns and trends on an infinite spreadsheet is way more complicated than looking at a cool chart. Whether you work in design, music, or marketing, you need to visualize data. No matter what your job is. We've already mentioned that in a previous chapter. Data visualization is important because it provides a quick and easy-to-understand way to communicate information. No matter your language, data visualization speaks in numbers, percentages, parts, slices, groups, and more. So, it is fair to say that *data visualization is a universal language.* We see graphs and pies every day, and we almost don't notice them. Have you ever used a weight tracking app? Have you ever looked at a weather forecast app? Those services, among many others, use charts and graphs to communicate information.

Anyhow, data visualization is quite popular these days. *And if you've paid attention to previous chapters, you should already know why* data visualization is becoming more and more popular worldwide. One of the main reasons is that there is a lot more data available. Today we are surrounded by data! That, of course, makes it easier to create charts and graphs if you have lots of datasets at your disposal. Another important reason is that we have removed the "hardware" barriers with cloud computing and cloud storage services. We no longer need to use our own "limited" machines to store large amounts of data. We can use dozens or even hundreds of PCs' computing power altogether while we are on "the cloud."

The following list shows a few key points on why data visualization is so important:

- Visual charts are a universal language.
- Data on graphs, pies, or charts is easier to understand and remember.
- We increase knowledge by visualizing data; seeing is believing.
- Visuals are way more effective than simple text.

Figure 3.2 – Cool-looking charts are more attractive than boring spreadsheets!

With so much data available, it is necessary to choose what kind of chart we need to use, whether it is a pie, a bar, or a map chart. Let's see some of the most common chart types:

- Scatter plot chart
- Bubble chart
- Bar graph
- Stacked bar graph
- Column chart
- Stacked column chart
- Pie chart
- Map chart
- Line graph
- Radar chart

And many, many others.

Each one of the previously listed chart types is useful for a specific goal. For example, if you want to visualize the adoption of electric cars by year and country, you probably want to use a bar graph or a column chart. Instead, if you want to visualize the relationship between the number of ingredients and the difficulty level of recipes, you want to use scatter plots or bubble charts.

Let's explore the different types of data visualization now.

Scatter plot

The **scatter plot** (or **scatter chart**) is a mathematical diagram of two different numerical values. It uses Cartesian coordinates to display the relationship between values. *The values are usually represented as dots, and their distance from the horizontal and vertical axis indicates the value of that specific data point.* Also, if the dots can vary in shape, size, or color, we can display additional information. If that's the case, this type of chart is often known as a bubble chart. And by the way, you don't have to use only dots or squares or similar shapes to represent values; you can get creative too if you want!

For example, take a look at the following figure, which is a scatter plot chart showing the relationship between the difficulty of a recipe and the number of ingredients:

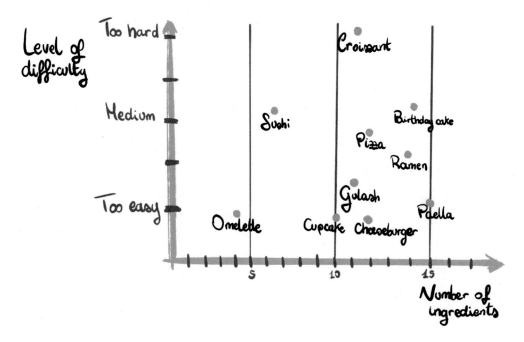

Figure 3.3 – Scatter plot example (number of ingredients and level of difficulty)

Column chart

This is probably one of the most common types of charts, perhaps because, at some point, all of us used column charts at school.

The column chart uses Cartesian coordinates to show values on the *x* and *y* axis. You could use it to visualize weight loss/gains over time. Or you could use it to show how many electric cars have been sold by country.

You could also use it to show data coming from a BIM model of a hotel. For example, you could show how many rooms there are per floor, what the total area per room type is, and so on. The following figure, as an example, shows the number of rooms by floor, using the column chart:

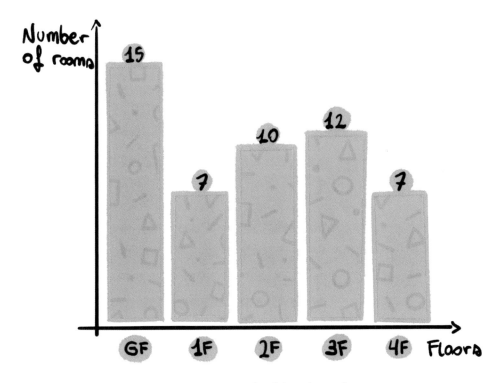

Figure 3.4 – An example of the column chart

Bar chart

The bar chart is very similar to the column chart. The main difference, though, is its orientation. The bar chart, unlike the column chart, displays values on the horizontal axis. Here, the horizontally placed rectangles are called bars, as the name suggests. And the longer the bar, the higher the value. This type of chart is also ideal for comparing data of the same category. Think, for example, about a music store that ships instruments in the European Union and wants to analyze how things are going. With the sales data, the store could create a bar chart like the following:

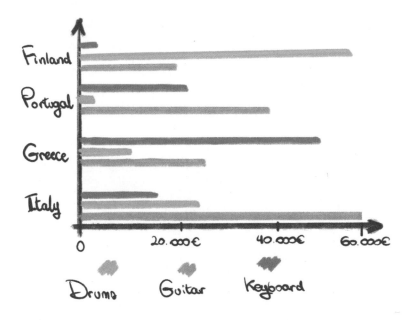

Figure 3.5 – An example of the bar chart

Here, we used the horizontal axis to show profits, while the vertical axis shows the countries and the group of instruments. In this way, we can immediately see what instruments did better and where. However, this isn't a common use of the vertical axis. Generally, the bar chart's vertical axis is used to indicate time ranges. The following is a list of a few other examples in which the bar chart could be helpful:

- Which salesperson did better in the last 6 months?
- What's your website traffic composition?
- What are the top-paid jobs in your country?
- What is an electrical system's power consumption?
- What is the total paintable wall area by wall type?

Now that we have looked at the column chart and bar chart, let's now have a look at a stacked bar chart.

Stacked bar chart

The column chart and the bar chart are, in a way, simpler versions of the stacked column and the stacked bar charts. We already know that the bar chart is a horizontal version of the column chart. Let's take a closer look at the stacked bar chart.

The **stacked bar** chart uses rectangles to show data and uses Cartesian coordinates to place information. The difference from a standard bar chart is that each rectangle consists of two or more segments. For example, you can create a stacked bar chart like in the following figure, using the same hotel data we showed before in the column chart. This time though, we will use the stacked bar chart to show how many door types there are per floor:

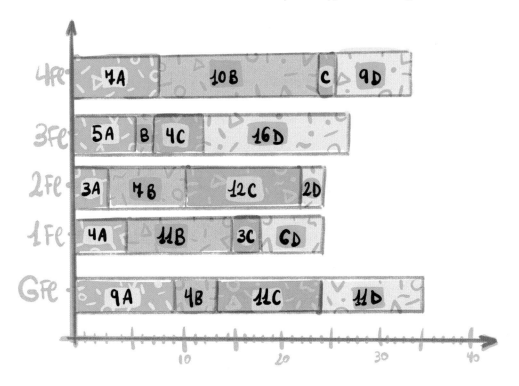

Figure 3.6 – Stacked bar chart example

The preceding figure shows that on the third floor, we have 5 doors of type A, 2 of type B, 4 of type C, and 16 of type D. We now understand that the stacked bar chart (or the stacked column chart) helps show the parts of *multiple totals*. Instead, if you're going to show parts of *one total*, you want to use the simpler versions, the bar chart or column chart.

Line chart

This is one of the easiest chart types to understand, but at the same time, it is one of the most powerful. Indeed, this type of chart is often used to emphasize the changes in value over time for one variable. Also, you could use it to show multiple variables and compare their differences in value by adding multiple line segments. Line graphs use points to display data. *Those data points are connected with line segments in a "dot-to-dot" fashion.* The *x* axis usually indicates time progression, such as days, weeks, months, and so on. At the same time, the *y* axis suggests a range of values, such as revenue in euros, pounds, or any other currency. Later on, we will use a line chart to display information about cryptocurrency price variations. However, even though the line chart's best use is to display revenue/loss over time, it can also be used for the following:

- To show variations of the number of subscribers by week, maybe having one line for each gender.

- To display how many users are actually using your Dynamo scripts over time.

- To indicate the number of clash detections by a system over time.

- To control whatever needs to be controlled, over time!

Using a line chart, this example shows the revenue changes for Toyota, Ford, and Tesla, starting from 2014:

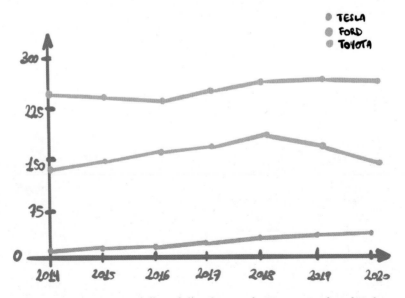

Figure 3.7 – Revenue in billion dollars by year for Toyota, Ford, and Tesla

I've decided to use those three car makers because I think their revenues are quite interesting. Toyota is bigger than Ford and way bigger than Tesla. On the other hand, Ford's revenues are five times bigger than Tesla's. But if you compare the starting and ending points of each, you get the following income growths:

- *Toyota: +7%*

- *Ford: -11%*

- *Tesla: +888%*

Again, charts like that show insights we couldn't have imagined just a few years ago. And the exponential growth of Tesla will promote the company to one of the industry leaders in 5 to 10 years. Information is telling this story, not my opinion.

Even though a line chart is awesome to create and use, you should be careful when plotting too many lines! *Things will get messy in no time if you add, for example, 10 or more lines* all together. Maybe, if you need to compare lots of categories of data values, you should use another type of chart!

Pie chart

The **circle graph** or **pie chart** consists of a circular chart that displays different values of a given variable or summarizes a set of categorical data. This chart can be divided into a series of "slices." Each slice shows data of a particular category. If you add up the values of each slice, you will get 100 percent of the data.

In short, a pie chart gives us a quick and easy-to-understand snapshot of how a group is broken into smaller subgroups. A variant of the pie chart is the donut chart, which has a hole in the center and uses arcs to display each subcategory value. So, the pie chart is best to use when you want to compare parts of a whole. It is not good when you want to show changes over time.

The following figure shows an example of a pie chart; in this example, I've used the chart to indicate the number of lighting fixtures by area:

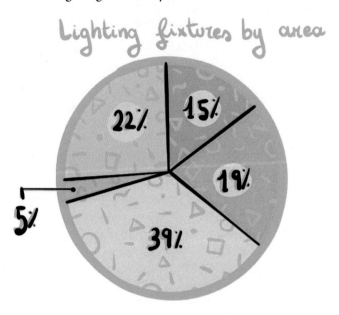

Figure 3.8 – Pie chart example

Radar chart

This is one of my favorites. Radar charts are a simple, yet powerful, type of chart when it comes to communicating information. The **radar chart** (also known as a spider, web, or polar chart) is used to visualize multiple quantitative variables. Take a look at the following figure:

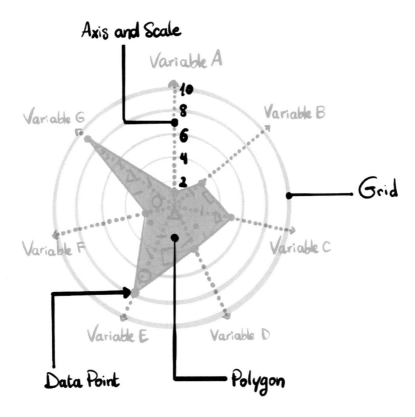

Figure 3.9 – Radar chart elements

The Radar chart consists of four elements: the grid, the axis and scale, the data point, and the polygon. Each data point is placed onto an axis that starts from the center. Each axis represents a particular variable. The grid lines are used for the axis-to-axis connection and provide a helpful guide. The scale values typically start from 0 at the center and 10 at the grid's edge.

As you can see, it is the ideal type of chart if you need to show performance and can also contain multiple polygons to compare multiple datasets. Take a look at the following figure:

Figure 3.10 – BIM competency radar chart

The chart displays skills and knowledge for typical BIM roles. At a glance, you can immediately see that the BIM manager has more skills in training and implementation than the BIM specialist. Also, the BIM coordinator is the role responsible for model audit and coordination, and for this reason, has higher skills in those fields than the BIM manager, and so on. I would like you to know that this type of chart has some limitations too. *For example, you don't want to place more than three or four polygons because it will quickly become harder to read.* You don't want to add lots of axes for the same reason.

Waterfall chart

This chart has too many names. I use always waterfall chart, but if you search on the internet, you will see names such as the following:

- Cascade chart
- Bridge graph
- Flying bricks chart
- And even Mario chart, due to the resemblance to the famous game!

Despite the confusion with the name, this chart is very popular within sales departments because it can provide quick insights into negative/positive trends of a value, by year, month, and so on. One key thing, oftentimes underestimated, is that this chart does not only display changes over time but also provides information about a previous timeframe or milestone. Its beauty, in my opinion, lies in the effortlessness of construction, even though you're dealing with complex datasets. To give you a few examples, this chart can be used for the following:

- Price changes
- Cash flows
- Inventory analysis
- Subtotals of **HVAC (heating, ventilation, air conditioning)** systems by category

The following figure, for example, shows the revenues and costs of a company during 2020:

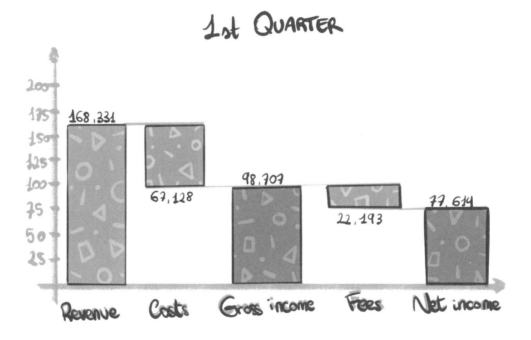

Figure 3.11 – Revenue and cost analysis using the waterfall chart

We have analyzed some of the most used chart types, and up to now, we've learned what data visualization is and why it is a universal language of communicating information. We've also discovered the most common types of charts and talked about some of those, such as the column chart, the stacked bar chart, and the radar chart. Now let's find out what the reasons to visualize and analyze BIM data are.

Why analyzing BIM data is important

As AEC industry professionals, we already know the definition of **Building Information Modeling (BIM)**. Although not everybody agrees on the same "shade" of definition, we can say that BIM is a process to manage building data. Everybody agrees on that. But, what about the data-driven business model? How can BIM fit into this new type of business? We already know that, worldwide, companies and organizations are implementing a data-driven business model. And the reasons behind that are related, of course, to profits and cost reductions. Yes, it has been proven by various research institutes, such as BARC and McKinsey Global, that *businesses that gather and analyze data increased their earnings by 8% and reduced costs by 10%*. And those are facts based on numbers, not opinions.

Until now, we all, in different ways, have implemented BIM processes to design, manage, and control our projects. However, *the most significant change that is happening now, is the transition from a design-driven BIM to a data-driven BIM*. Today, we are in the golden age of gathering and analyzing data, and we will use that data to improve our BIM processes. But there is a problem. A large amount of our construction data is unstructured. You now know that by "unstructured data," we are talking about PDFs, emails, and documents. And almost every day I read on social networks that AEC companies are implementing machine learning to transform data from unstructured to structured. I don't know if I am missing something here, but the truth is that *unstructured data is not machine-readable*. We need to develop different types of algorithms or systems to do so. The AEC industry should make decisions on numbers and facts to move forward. But that is my own opinion. We will see how it goes.

Now, in order for us to transition from a design-driven BIM to a data-driven BIM, we need to organize and categorize our model's data. Think, for example, of clash detection. In case you don't know, **clash detection** is the technique of identifying overlapping parts of a building. If we continuously collect data on clash detection and then *add BIM analytics tools to it, we are taking data analysis a step forward*. By visualizing data on clashes, week after week, we will start to find patterns and clash relationships early in a project's design phase. Consequently, we will begin to reduce them significantly and much, much quicker than before.

Other than clash detection, by analyzing BIM data, we can also see the following advantages:

- Increased revenues and reduced costs

- Reduced clashes by spotting clash relationships

- Real-time control over project costs, schedules, and standard compliance

- Improved collaboration by sharing real-time information

- Less time wasted reading emails and reports

- Improved processes by analyzing data

As you can see, by creating charts using software such as Power BI, we can share and distribute information to our colleagues and project partners so everybody has a complete overview of what is going on in real time. Think, for example, about using automated dashboards regularly in project meetings. *In this way, everybody is more engaged in solving issues than wasting time reading emails, reports, or even worse, boring spreadsheets!*

Besides, all of the colleagues who are not yet "into Revit" or other parametric software used in a BIM workflow can benefit from BIM dashboards. They can quickly and easily check for issues, **RFIs (requests for information)**, project estimates and costs, or any other construction data that requires their participation.

At this point, we've learned that information is power. BIM data analysis provides us with information and insights we couldn't imagine just a few years ago. I hope you now want to transition from a design-driven BIM to a data-driven BIM and see data as a strategic asset. Leveraging data analytics will help us overcome the following industry challenges!

Figure 3.12 – Information is power!

Next, we will explore some of the most used Power BI charts, including when and how to use them. In later chapters, we will learn a lot more about BIM data analysis from experts and industry professionals, who will showcase their BIM data workflows and techniques. Stay tuned!

Exploring Microsoft Power BI charts

As seen in the previous chapter, Power BI provides us with lots of charts to create appealing dashboards. In this section, we will explore some of them by making a couple of dashboard pages. *The goal here is to push you to use various charts and understand how to customize them using the available software tools.* Power BI can also import other types of graphs that are not available out of the box. Here, though, we will not cover this feature because we want to focus on the software's default ones. Later on, in *Chapter 6, Importing Revit Plans in Power BI Using Shape Files*, we will also learn how to download and import more complex types of charts.

To create our first dashboard, we will use a new open dataset from the Kaggle platform. The dataset I've chosen this time refers to a cryptocurrency that is becoming very popular these days, Dogecoin. *The Dogecoin project began in 2013 as a joke, but nowadays, it isn't a joke anymore.* This crypto was developed by an Adobe software engineer, Jackson Palmer from Sydney, Australia, and an IBM software engineer, Billy Marcus, from Portland, US. The currency, since 2013, has gained popularity, with impressive trading volumes since then. In January 2021, the fun currency caught Elon Musk's eye, the famous entrepreneur, after almost 8 years. The Tesla and SpaceX CEO started to tweet about Dogecoin at the end of January 2021, and the crypto skyrocketed.

Figure 3.13 – Dogecoin logo

Now, let's start to explore this dataset with Power BI using the Dogecoin dataset!

Downloading and importing the dataset

In this section, we will follow a few steps to import the Dogecoin dataset inside Microsoft Power BI. We will use the Kaggle platform to find and download our dataset. Kaggle is the same open data platform we used before, so you don't need to waste time signing up to a new service.

Let's get started:

1. The first thing to do is to download the dataset. You can find it at the following link: cutt.ly/2kZDXle.

2. Then, as we've seen before, we need to click on **Get Data** inside the Power BI **Home Tab** and select **Text/CSV**.

3. When you've imported the **CSV** file, click on the **Data view** button to switch to the **Data view** page. You should see something like the following screenshot:

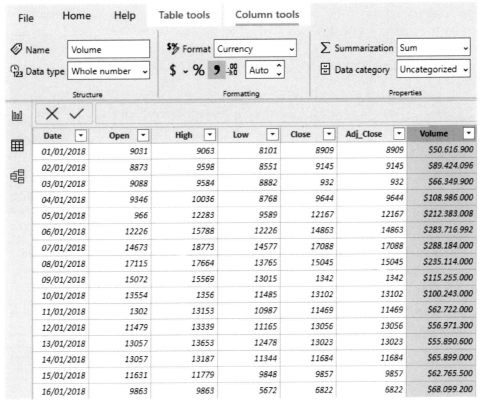

Figure 3.14 – Screenshot of the Data view

4. If you don't see those column names and values, please repeat the steps from the beginning. At this point, we need to check the values to see if the formatting is correct. As you can see in the preceding screenshot, I've already selected the **Volume** column and assigned the **Currency** formatting option. Please go ahead and do the same.

Now that we have imported, manipulated, and organized our data, we are ready to perform some more complex operations. Indeed, we want to format our values and address some of the errors that may happen when working with numbers and decimals.

Formatting the other values

Now we need to set up the formatting for the other columns as well. Let's start with the **Open** column, which is the currency's value at the opening of that specific date. The number shown is incorrect, and we need to address that. We want to show the correct value of **0.009031** dollars instead of **9031**. *If on your PC, you already see the valid value of* **0.009031**, *you can skip these steps. It may depend on the OS regional settings.*

On the contrary, if you see the value of **9031**, you may want to follow the following steps to display the correct decimal values. To do that, we want to use the **Power Query Editor** and create a few custom columns. This time, instead of adding simple strings as we did in the previous chapter with "2018" or "2019," we want to perform a division for each row. Let's see how to do this:

1. Open up the Power Query Editor by clicking on **Transform Data** from the **Home** tab.

2. Inside the PQE, let's go to the **Add Column** tab (it's the third one starting from the left).

3. As we did previously, click on the **Custom Column** button to open the **Custom Column** window. Here, we want to rename the column inside the **New column name** textbox. I've renamed it USD Open.

4. Below, we can find the **Custom column formula** textbox. Here, we will write our formula instead of putting just the values "2018" and "2019" as we did in the previous chapter.

5. Go ahead and type this formula: ([Open] / 1000000). If you are familiar with Microsoft Excel, this is something very similar – we are dividing each value in the **Open** column by 1 million to show the correct USD value of almost 1 penny (**0.009031**) on the date January 1, 2018.

6. Once done, click **Ok** at the bottom right to confirm. If you did it correctly, you should see something like the following screenshot (check the row for January 1, January 2018 – it should display the value 0.009031):

ABC 123 USD Open
0,009031
0,008873
0,009088
0,009346
0,000966
0,012226

Figure 3.15 – Screenshot of the newly created column, USD Open

7. Once you've completed the previous steps correctly, please go ahead and do the same for all of the other columns. The following screenshot shows the final result; hopefully, you can see the same corrected values on your screen too:

ABC 123 USD Open	ABC 123 USD High	ABC 123 USD Low	ABC 123 USD Close
0,009031	0,009063	0,008101	0,008909
0,008873	0,009598	0,008551	0,009145
0,009088	0,009584	0,008882	0,000932
0,009346	0,010036	0,008768	0,009644
0,000966	0,012283	0,009589	0,012167
0,012226	0,015788	0,012226	0,014863
0,014673	0,018773	0,014577	0,017088
0,017115	0,017664	0,013765	0,015045

Figure 3.16 – All custom columns completed

8. Now, let's check the formatting of each new column. Just select the column by clicking on the header, then go to the **Transform** tab and click on the **Detect Data Type** button. You will see that Power BI, above the **Detect Data Type** button, has selected **Decimal Number** as the data type. If you don't see **Decimal Number**, please select that from the **Data Type** button's drop-down window.

9. Please repeat the previous step with all the other new columns.

10. To complete our task, we need to do one last thing. As we will show the average values on a column chart, we want to create one more **Custom Column**. So, create a new one. The formula to use this time is: (([USD High] + [USD Low]) / 2). The result will indeed be the average value. Check the result on January 1, 2018. It should be **0.008582**.

11. Before creating the actual graphs, we need to confirm every step we have done until now. You can check all of the steps on the right side of the PQE, inside the **Query Settings** pane. If you don't see the **Query Settings** pane, you can always activate it by going to the **View** tab and clicking the **Query Settings** button on the far left of the tab.

12. Every step we just completed needs to be confirmed before closing the Power Query Editor. So, let's confirm our steps by clicking on the **Close & Apply** button from the **Home** tab.

Awesome, we are now ready to create our first chart. So far, we have learned how to address issues that may arise with our datasets. We understand how to format values and create custom formulas to manipulate our data. And we also understand that we need the Power Query Editor to do that. Let's now begin the development of the first chart.

Creating the column chart

Let the fun begin! At this point, we have completed the boring (but fundamental) part of formatting and organizing data. We now want to create our first chart. The chart's goal is to show information about the currency price variation over time, from January 1, 2018 to the beginning of February 2021. Let's see how to do this:

1. First of all, open the **Report** view, then go to the **Visualizations** pane and click on the **Stacked column chart** icon as shown in the following screenshot.

Figure 3.17 – Stacked column chart icon on the Visualizations pane

You will see a gray chart box is displayed on the canvas. No data will be shown at this point because we need to drag our values into the chart's parameters, right below the chart's icons.

> **Important Note**
>
> To avoid confusion here, let me point out something. I know we previously learned that the column and the stacked column are two different chart types, and that is 100% true, but Power BI has one button to create both of them: **Stacked column chart**. So, depending on the data and the field's customizations, you can make both the column and the stacked chart.

2. Now drag the **Date** field from the **Fields** pane into the **Axis** parameter of the **Stacked column chart** that we just placed.

3. Next, drag the **USD Average** field we calculated before into the **Values** parameter. If you don't get the intended result, please go back to the *Formatting the other values* section. You may have missed some of the required steps.

4. Now, let's check the **USD Average** you just dragged into the **Values** parameter. If you click on the pointing down arrow, you want to have **Sum** selected, as shown in the following screenshot.

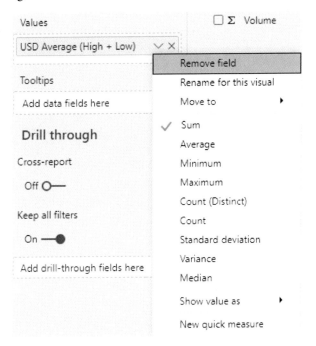

Figure 3.18 – Click on the arrow and select Sum from the drop-down list

5.   You'll see the chart starts to display some data. If you grab the right and left handles (located at the edges of the chart box), you can resize the chart according to your needs. I've stretched the chart from the left side to the right. In this way, we can see the whole dataset without having to scroll with the mouse.

6.   Now, we want to transform the **Date** values into a **Date Hierarchy** object. To do that, let's go to the **Axis** parameter and click on the down arrow right next to the **Date** values, then select **Date Hierarchy** from the drop-down window. Power BI indeed has out-of-the-box functionalities that will change date values into a drillable hierarchy of year, quarter, month, and so on. This is a pretty nice feature because we can dynamically explore different views of the data over time. The following screenshot shows you where to find the **Date Hierarchy** selection.

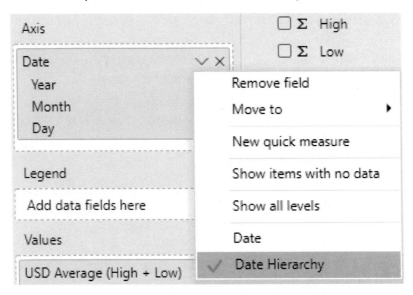

Figure 3.19 – Click on the arrow and select Date Hierarchy from the drop-down list

7.   When you click on the **Date Hierarchy** option, you will see four new parameters showing underneath the **Date** parameter: **Year**, **Quarter**, **Month**, and **Day**. You can remove one of those parameters if you don't want that drillable option on your chart (I usually remove **Quarter** as I am not used to working with it).

At this point, you should see four rectangles. Each rectangle represents the sum of the **USD Average** price per year, from 2018 to 2021. But we don't want that; we want to see the variation of the currency price every month.

8. All we need to do is to drill down and find our monthly visualization. Pay attention to the top right of the chart box. There are seven icons. Starting from the left, you have four icons for drilling up or down. Click on the fourth icon on the left; if you hover over it, a white bubble should appear stating **Expand all down one level in the hierarchy**:

Figure 3.20 – Screenshot of the fourth drill-down button to click

When you click on it, your chart will look like the following screenshot:

Figure 3.21 – Monthly visualization of the chart

Don't worry about the graphics; we will address those in a minute.

9. For now, I would like you to take a few minutes and use the **drill-down** and **drill-up** arrows to understand what they do. This will come in handy when you create your first charts at work. You could create a chart like this to show how many families have been placed inside the Revit model by day, week, or month. Or you could show how many MEP systems have been placed on a construction site, and so on.

10. Let's switch to the **Format** pane (you can find it right next to the **Fields** pane button, underneath the chart icons). The **Format** pane can be accessed by clicking on the paint roller icon as shown in the following screenshot.

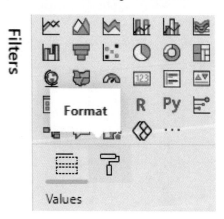

Figure 3.22 – Format pane icon

Here, there are lots of options to go through. I will not explain every detail of each parameter because I think they are pretty straightforward and easy to understand. Instead, I will write what my settings of choice are.

11. So, expand the *x*-axis parameter and set these values:

- **Font Family**: **Cambria**
- **Minimum category width**: **50**
- **Maximum size**: **20%**
- **Inner padding**: **20%**
- **Concatenate labels**: **Off**
- **Title**: **Off**
- **Gridlines**: **Off**

12. Now let's move to the *y*-axis parameters. Leave everything as the default, but change the following:

- **Font family**: **Cambria**
- **Stroke width**: **2**
- **Line style**: **Dashed**

13. Do not expand the **Zoom slider** parameter; just turn it on.

14. We will now change the color of the rectangles. I've chosen the color orange as it resembles the Dogecoin logo, but you, of course, can choose whatever you like. So, expand the **Data colors** parameters and modify the **Default color** option.

15. Next, turn **Data labels** on and set the **Position** parameter to **Inside End**.

16. All we need to do now is to change the background color. Jump to the **Background** parameter and turn it on if it isn't already. Expand the options and set these options:

- **Color**: **black**

- **Transparency**: **98%**

17. The following screenshot shows the result:

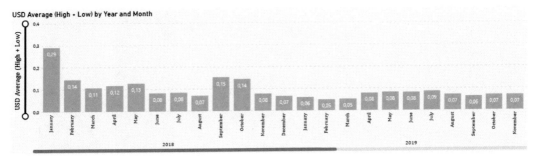

Figure 3.23 – Customized column chart

18. Perfect! We've completed the creation of the column chart. We learned how to convert a **Date** object into a **Date Hierarchy** object and use the drilling options to change time visualization. Also, we changed the graphics of the chart by customizing fonts, shapes, and colors. Next, we will place a few more charts to complete our dashboard.

Creating a waterfall chart

Now that we have displayed the currency price variation over time with the previous column chart, we want to analyze the volume's increase or decrease. The volume variation of a currency is simply the total amount of coins traded at that particular date. We want to use the waterfall chart to see, over time, how the volume became what it is today. Indeed, waterfall charts are often used to visualize how a starting value becomes the final value through intermediate steps; those steps represent the volume increase or decrease over time. Let's take a look at the following figure:

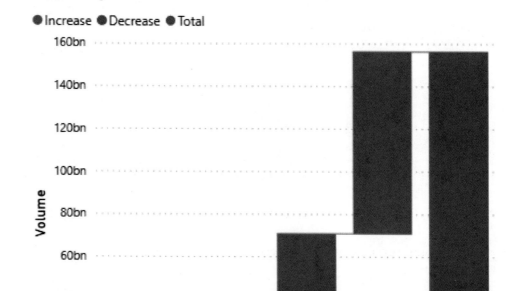

Figure 3.24 – Waterfall chart of Dogecoin volume by year

Using this type of chart, we can immediately see that 2020 and 2021 combined consist of more than 70% of the total volume. It is impressive that just by placing the correct parameter onto the right chart, we can quickly get incredible insights! Let's now create this chart and customize it:

1. To place the waterfall chart, click on the chart icon from the **Visualizations** pane. If you can't find it immediately, you can always mouse over each icon; a little white box will appear, indicating the name of the chart.

2. Once you've placed it, use the handles on the edge of the chart box to resize the chart as you would like.

3. Now, let's drag **Date** to the **Category** field and **Volume** to the **Values** field. Remember to transform the **Date** object into a **Date Hierarchy** object as well.

4. We are all set with the parameters of the chart. Now click on the **Format** button to customize the graphics and appearance.

5. First of all, let's turn off the **Legend** option (this isn't necessary, but it is just something I don't want us to see in this case).

6. Now expand the *x* **axis** and set the following parameters like so:

*   **Font Family**: **Cambria**
*   **Inner padding**: **20%**
*   **Title**: **Off**

7. For the **y axis**, we want to set the following:

*   **Font Family**: **Cambria**
*   **Title**: **Off**
*   **Stroke width**: **2**
*   **Line style**: **Dashed**

8. Turn on the **Data labels** options, and set the following options:

*   **Position**: **Auto**
*   **Font Family**: **Cambria**

9. Change **Sentiment colors** in any way you like (I've used a range of blue colors).

10. Leave the **Title** option on (it should be on by default). In this way, when we drill up or down, the title will change accordingly.

11. The last thing to do is set **Background color** to **black** and **Transparency** to **98%**, as we did for the previous column chart.

12. Now, let's drill down on the column chart we created previously until we see days instead of months.

13. At this point, try to select one of the days available. The waterfall chart will change relative to the volume of that particular day. Please check the following figure showing the completed waterfall chart:

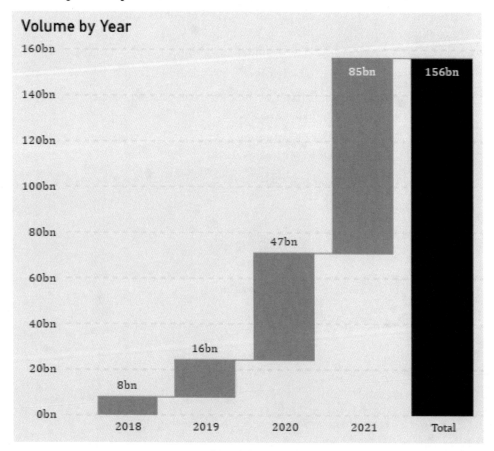

Figure 3.25 – Screenshot of the completed waterfall chart

Pro tip!

To select more than one value simultaneously, please hold *Ctrl + Left mouse* click (*Cmd ⌘ + Left mouse* click on a Mac) and choose, for example, four different days from the stacked column chart.

The following figure shows the charts in both states, unselected and selected. On the left, there is no selection, and the chart shows the total values of all the time ranges imported. On the right, I've selected the last 3 days using *Ctrl + Left mouse* click, and the charts updated accordingly.

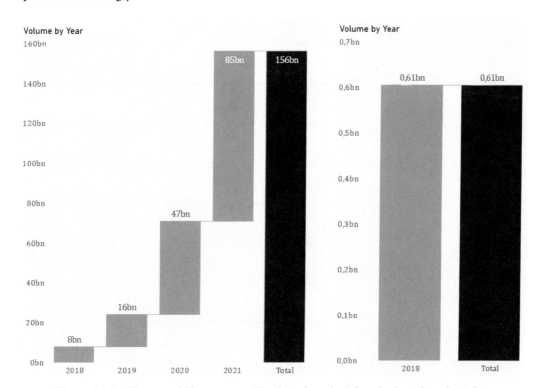

Figure 3.26 – Charts in different states. Unselected on the left and selected on the right

We have now created a fantastic waterfall chart that shows us the currency's total volume and its growth by year. Also, we continued practicing formatting fonts, shapes, and colors. Next, we will create a line chart and use it to display changes in currency value over time.

Creating a line chart

It is now time to create a line chart. We will use this to see how the highs and lows of currency prices are related to each other. The line chart is also known as a line plot or line graph. It uses line segments, starting from the left of the graph. The chart's goal is to display changes in value over time. This chart uses Cartesian coordinates, and most of the time, the horizontal axis indicates a progression in time, while the vertical axis displays one single unit of measurement. In this example, the vertical axis will show the currency value range. If we add more than one field to the vertical metrics, we could compare two or more lines and determine how they relate to each other. Let's create the chart:

1. Mouse over the icons until you find **Line chart**, then click on the icon to place it on the Power BI canvas.

2. As we did previously, drag the handles to resize them as you would like.

3. Now drag **Date** to the **Axis** parameter, then **USD High** and **USD Low** to the **Values** parameter.

4. Awesome! You should see the two lines appearing on the chart. Now let's customize the graphics.

5. Open the **Format options** by clicking on the **Format** button (right next to the **Fields** button).

6. Make sure to turn the **Legend** and **Zoom slider** options on.

7. On the *x* **axis**, set these options:

   Font Family: Cambria

   Title: Off

8. On the *y* **axis**, set these options:

   Font Family: Cambria

   Title: Off

   Stroke width: 2

   Line style: Dashed

9. As we aren't using the secondary values, make sure the **Secondary values** parameter is turned off.

10. Expand the **Data colors** parameters and choose the colors you would like to use (I've selected a dark blue for **Highs** and a light blue for **Lows**).

11. Now let's move to the following parameter. Expand **Shapes**, and set the options like so:

- **Stroke width**: **3**

- **Show marker**: **On**

- **Marker size**: **5**

- **Customize series**: **Off** (This is used if you want different styles for each line value, but in this case, it isn't necessary.)

12. Now let's complete the chart's appearance by customizing **Background** with the color black and setting **Transparency** to **98%**.

13. The final result should look like the following figure:

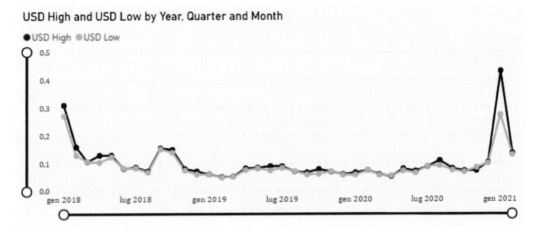

Figure 3.27 – Line chart showing USD High and USD Low currency price variation

We need one last thing to complete our dashboard: a title! So, let's go back to Power BI and place the title by following these instructions:

14. Click on the **Insert** tab (right next to the **Home** tab on top of the Power BI menu).

15. You'll see five distinct sections: **Pages**, **Visuals**, **AI visuals**, **Power Platform**, and **Elements**. From the **Elements** section, click on **Text box**.

16. Add the title **Dogecoin dashboard** and resize it using the edge handles, as we have done previously.

17. Now customize the text font and color as you prefer.

18. Finally, download the logo found here: `cutt.ly/XkN54JT`.

19. Add the logo to the canvas by clicking on the **Image** button from the **Elements** section.

20. Customize the background of the logo (if you want) by using the **Format** pane.

21. You can find the final result at this link: `cutt.ly/vkMwr4T`.

At this point, we have completed our dashboard with three excellent charts and a fantastic logo! I want to point out that we used static datasets in this example and in the previous one, the Happiness World Report. As mentioned in an earlier chapter, Power BI can connect to almost any kind of dataset. *The last two examples are static because the data itself can't be updated in real time.* After all, it is stored in a CSV file on our computer.

Anyway, the Microsoft business intelligence tool can connect to live data through Power Platform, for example, or to a database. And speaking of real-time data, the next chapter will show us exactly that, using a plugin that we are going to develop together. In this way, every time we refresh the page, we see new data on our dashboards, and that is *BRILLIANT!*

Summary

In this chapter, we covered quite a lot of things. We learned what data visualization is and that visuals are way more effective than simple text. *After all, seeing is believing!* Then we discovered some of the most common chart types and analyzed some of them. Besides that, we understood why analyzing BIM data is so important, and we learned that businesses worldwide have increased their incomes and reduced their costs by doing so. *Finding patterns and getting insights from data is like having superpowers!* Then, we learned how to create some of the "out-of-the-box" charts in Power BI, customize them, and have an overview of the fantastic and fun Dogecoin currency.

At this point, I want to introduce you to the subjects of the following four chapters. From *Chapter 4, Building a Data Bridge between BIM Models and Web-based Dashboards* to *Chapter 7, Creating a Revit - Model Check Dashboard using Dynamo and Power BI,* we are going to learn a lot of new things. These chapters show some examples of managing and visualizing data by some of the most brilliant minds in our industry; each one of them will teach us particular workflows for data analysis.

As we previously talked about real-time data, the first example I want to show you is from Manuel Andrè Bottiglieri, an old friend of mine and a colleague I have learned a lot from over the years. Manuel is an architect and works as a full stack BIM developer at Lombardini 22, one of Italy's most renowned architectural firms. Manuel will show us how to develop a Revit plugin with Visual Studio to connect Power BI to the model's data in real time.

Next, we have Luisa Cypriano Pieper, an architect who works in Spain as a BIM manager for CES, a Belgian multinational company specializing in engineering and sustainable development. She will teach us the fundamentals of Autodesk Dynamo BIM for Revit and follow us in developing two scripts. The first one will help us export data from the Revit model to Excel, while the second will do the opposite, updating the data on Excel and importing it back to Revit.

Then we have the architect Gavin Crump. He is the founder of, and a consultant at, BIM Guru, a BIM consulting company in Australia. He describes a terrific workflow on visualizing Revit floor plans inside Power BI. This is an advanced workflow that will teach us how to use Power BI to include Revit floor plans in our dashboards. And, of course, we are talking about interactive floor plans.

To close the loop, last but not least, we have a chapter from Dounia Touil, an architect and design technology specialist from NSW Arkitektur in Norway. She is involved in a variety of projects, from concept to construction, leading research activities and providing computational design solutions. A note worthy of attention is that Dounia, other than producing an excellent chapter on managing and visualizing BIM data, also gave birth to a beautiful boy during the development of her chapter. So, double applause for her!

Now let's move on, and I'll see you later.

Section 2: Examples and Case Studies from Experts around the World

In this part of the book, you will receive an overview of the tools and processes for managing and analyzing data by reading examples from experts worldwide! These brilliant colleagues will teach us various subjects, starting from building a C# plugin to streaming data from Revit to Power BI. In addition, you will learn how to create Autodesk Dynamo data-gathering scripts, how to import Revit plans in Power BI and link them to charts, and how to create a model check dashboard to obtain an overview of model issues.

This section comprises the following chapters:

- *Chapter 4, Building a Data Bridge between BIM Models and Web-Based Dashboards*
- *Chapter 5, Getting Started with Autodesk Dynamo and Data Gathering*
- *Chapter 6, Importing Revit Plans in Power BI Using Shape Files*
- *Chapter 7, Creating a Revit - Model Check Dashboard Using Dynamo and Power BI*

4

Building a Data Bridge between BIM Models and Web-Based Dashboards

This chapter is written by Manuel André Bottiglieri

Manuel André Bottiglieri, as mentioned previously, works as a BIM full-stack developer at Lombardini22. In 2011, I met him at the Architecture University in Rome. Since then, we have studied and worked together on a variety of projects. Among those, I remember that we developed a workflow using Microsoft Azure services to update the Revit model's data from the web, just by overwriting values from an Access database. That, almost 10 years ago, was crazy to me back in 2012. Today Manuel works mainly in the development of web applications to manage assets and clients' data. Now, Manuel will teach us about a fantastic workflow on streaming real-time data from the Revit model to Power BI. Enjoy reading. Speak to you later!

This chapter will dig into the Revit environment, showing how to mix project data with users' info, taking advantage of **C# scripting** to catch data through event-driven activities. *C# can be read as C sharp*. It is a Microsoft programming language, a son of the C programming languages family, introduced in 2002. Since that year, C# has been updated and implemented several times. Today, C# is one of the most used programming languages around the world. Indeed, many programs and games we use are written using a combination of the C programming family languages. Autodesk Revit, for example, written in C++ and C#, is one of them.

You will be able to collect additional information from your Revit projects without adding complexity or tasks for your team members. We will start developing our first **Revit plugin** with the Visual Studio IDE to build the data bridge between Revit models and our **Power BI** environment. In the end, you will be able to deliver project insights to your collaborators to make it easier to track project info, file size, and user activities.

In this chapter, you will learn about the following:

- The fundamentals of creating your first Revit plugin
- Understanding how to set up the environment and configure frameworks and libraries
- Preparing Microsoft Power BI for the real-time dataset stream
- Exploring how to set up custom measures in Power BI to build additional KPIs on top of your raw data
- Publishing your final report to the Power BI cloud service

Before we start, please check the following technical requirements.

Technical requirements

The examples used in this chapter can be found at `https://github.com/PacktPublishing/Managing-and-Visualizing-Your-BIM-Data/tree/main/Chapter04`.

It is not required to have a basic understanding of any scripting language. However, knowledge of the Revit APIs and the methods used to communicate through the HTTP protocols will be of benefit.

The working sample provided in this GitHub repository is supposed to be a starting point, hoping to give you a new perspective, highlighting the benefits of taking advantage of Revit APIs.

To manage this project, you need to have access to Revit 2020 or higher versions (licensed or student subscription), Power BI (a free subscription), and Visual Studio 2019 Community (a free subscription). So, if you haven't already, please download this software from the official websites and come back! Following are a couple of useful links to help you download Visual Studio and MS Power BI:

- `https://visualstudio.microsoft.com/downloads/`
- `https://aka.ms/pbidesktopstore`

Please read the following instructions to install Visual Studio Community 2019 properly.

Installing Visual Studio Community

Visual Studio Community 2019 is a powerful tool that developers worldwide use to build a wide range of applications. When it comes to installing the software, there are lots of modules to choose from. No worries if you've already installed it; you can always integrate new modules anytime. Following are two guides to cover the new installation and the integration of the .NET module if you have Visual Studio already installed and didn't install the module.

New Visual Studio installation

If you have Visual Studio already installed, then, you can skip the following guide and go to the Integrating a .NET module section. Please read the following step-by-step guide:

1. Download the software from the previously provided link under the *Technical requirements* section.

2. Execute the installer and click **Ok** until a new configuration window pops up, as shown in the following screenshot:

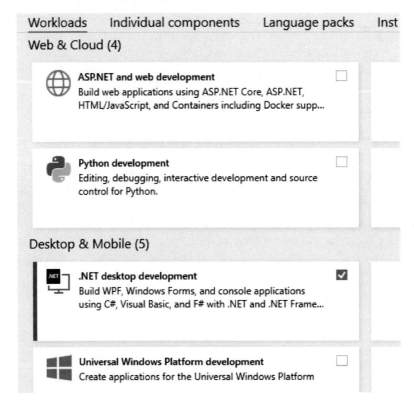

Figure 4.1 – Select the .NET desktop development option

As you can see from the previous screenshot, you have to check the **.NET desktop development** option. This module will allow us to develop our custom plugin.

3. After checking the .NET option, go to the right side of this installation window and scroll the available options until you find **.NET Framework 4.8 development tools**. Once you find it, check the box and click **Install** at the bottom right of the window. The following screenshot shows where to find .NET Framework to install:

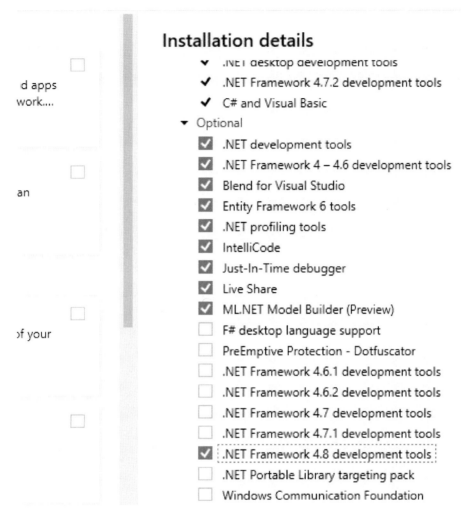

Figure 4.2 – Check .NET Framework 4.8

If you can't find .NET Framework 4.8, please mouse over the available solutions to read the full title.

Perfect! That's all we have to do to set up our environment. The installation process could take a while to download and install all of the required packages. Please don't use your PC during the installation. In the meanwhile, you can go on and read the following sections.

Integrating a .NET module

To install additional modules, please read the following steps:

1. Close Visual Studio if you have it open, and download the installer if you don't have it anymore. The link to download the installer is as follows:

    `https://visualstudio.microsoft.com/downloads/`

2. Once downloaded, run the installer and click on **Modify** as shown here:

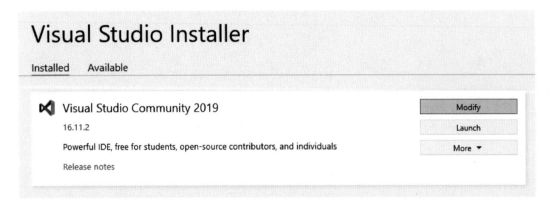

Figure 4.3 – Click on the Modify button of the installer launch screen

3. When you click on **Modify**, a new window will pop up. From here, please go back to *Figure 4.1*, under the *New Visual Studio installation section*, and follow the guide to add the required module.

At this point, your Visual Studio is equipped with .NET Framework 4.8. Now we can focus on the process and the problem we aim to solve.

Identifying the problem

When speaking about BIM projects, our attention is usually focused on compiling updated schedules or drawings to better comply with technical project deliveries. Of course, these scopes are all essential steps to achieve in our professional environment. Still, in this case, we will set ourselves the goal of expanding (with no maintenance costs) our level of digital data management skills.

Taking advantage of our digital environment, we will build a monitoring system on top of our BIM models, focusing our attention on usage, performance, and activities related to our project files.

After this quick introduction, let's go straight to the environment setup. First, we will need to configure Visual Studio to import the required Revit APIs. Also, we will check and install some other frameworks and libraries as these are necessary for the plugin to work. Enough talk here. I'll see you in the next section.

Creating your first Revit plugin

Our scope is to focus the activities on building a **data connector** from Revit to Power BI. According to this, we are going to use our basic template provided with the GitHub repository. The template gives you a new, ready-to-use Revit toolbar with four sample commands. It's not important how to build that project from scratch, but if you are interested in learning more about Revit plugin fundamentals, I suggest you start with the official documentation at the following URL:

```
https://knowledge.autodesk.com/support/revit-products/learn-
explore/caas/simplecontent/content/lesson-1-the-basic-plug.html.
```

At this point, the first thing to do is to set up the environment. This is fundamental in any development software such as Visual Studio. We need to know how to let Visual Studio import the Revit API required to complete the plugin. Let's go.

Understanding the environment

How can we implement software capabilities? How does a plugin work? What are the basic steps to develop one? This project aims to simplify answering these questions as much as possible and help us understand the functioning of a development process, recognize the schemas, and the relationships between the parts. Do not be scared! It all seems so complex, but let's unveil what's behind it. Soon, everything will seem much more intuitive.

Let's start by saying that a **plugin** is nothing more than a .dll file loaded by the program during the startup process. Each file consists of a library of commands that will modify its characteristics and user interface. Please take a look at the following figure:

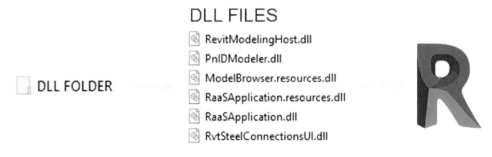

Figure 4.4 – Revit .dll folder

The figure shows a simplified flow of information between the **DLL FOLDER**, containing all of the plugins that Revit will load on startup and Revit itself. Basically, every time we start Revit, the program will look inside that particular folder and load every file inside, no matter what version. Every loaded .dll file will "bring" some new functionality to Revit.

Revit has to check another type of file, the so-called manifest file, to load the plugin correctly. At each start, Revit looks at its plugins folder and loads the various libraries following the instructions on each manifest.addin file in this folder. Manifests are text files in XML format with the identity information of each plugin: name, ID, and the path of the relative .dll file.

At this point, it seems clear that all we need is to generate our custom .dll and manifest.addin files and save them in the Revit plugins folder. In this case, to achieve that, the scheme is simple. We start from a list of C# classes (built on top of Revit APIs) to extract our final plugin through Visual Studio as a couple of files: .dll and .addin. The following diagram shows what happens when we create the Revit plugin:

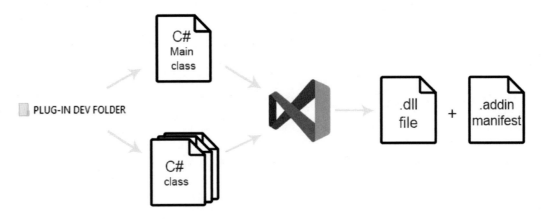

Figure 4.5 – Plugin development

As you can see, Visual Studio has to load the Revit APIs to let developers use classes and all the built-in functions and objects. When we complete the plugin, Visual Studio will generate those files, .dll and .addin. C# files are divided into individual classes, each designed to implement specific functions of our new library. Nothing complex – do not worry. For the purpose of this project, you don't need to script any code. Everything is ready and organized in our template.

Now that we better understand the environment and the process of generating a plugin (.dll file), we know how to load it on Revit (manifest.addin). We just have to use Autodesk's APIs to insert our toolbar into Revit with custom functionality to read and send data to our preferred business intelligence service (in this case, Microsoft Power BI). The following diagram shows the flow of the data that our plugin will perform:

Figure 4.6 – Sending data to Power BI

Once ready, the plugin starts sending information from the Revit model, packing all of the data inside a text file (in this case, a JSON file), then Power BI receives that file and we can use it to create our unique dashboards. Here, we learned what files are fundamental to develop our first Revit plugin. Indeed, we understood that the DLL files contain the plugin's logic and the manifest addin file includes the instructions to execute it. Next, we will deal with the installation of .NET framework and other libraries.

Configuring dotnet framework and PresentationCore. dll

Once Visual Studio is installed, open it from the start screen and click on **Open a project or solution** as shown in the following screenshot:

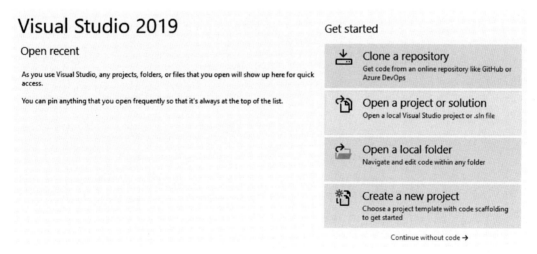

Figure 4.7 – Visual Studio 2019 start screen

Next, a new window will pop up. Now let's navigate to the folder where you previously downloaded the GitHub repository. Select the file `packt-my-revit-plug-in.sln` and click open. After a few seconds, if this is your first time installing Visual Studio, you may see a message window pop up. If the message is related to a missing .NET library framework, please go ahead and install it. When ready, start with the following instructions to complete the application environment setup:

1. Inside Visual Studio. On the **Solution Explorer** panel (you should see it on the right side of the screen), you need to expand **References** under **myApp** to check if the required libraries are available, as shown in the following screenshot. If you don't see **Solution Explorer**, click on **View** from the top menu and select **Solution Explorer** to activate it, or type the shortcut *Ctrl + Alt + L*.

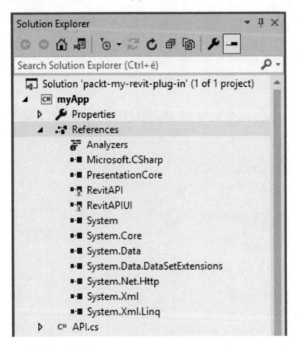

Figure 4.8 – Solution Explorer in Visual Studio 2019

As you can see, **RevitAPI** and **RevitAPIUI** have a small yellow triangle on their left, and those icons tell us that something is missing from those libraries. We will fix that in a few steps. We need to configure the framework first.

2. The framework we have installed is **.NET Framework 4.8**. To see if everything is okay, we should check a few things. Please navigate to the following folder:

```
C:\Program Files (x86)\Reference Assemblies\Microsoft\
Framework\.NETFramework\
```

Inside that folder, you should see a bunch of other folders. Scroll through them and check whether there is one named **v4.8**. If the answer is yes, please skip the following steps, and go to the *Installing the Revit dll section*. If you don't have such a folder, keep following the next steps.

3. Once you find **Solution Explorer**, right-click on **myApp**, then select **Properties**.

4. A new window will pop up. You should already be in the **Application** section. If you aren't, please select **Application** from the buttons on the left side of the window.

5. Here, you need to select **Install other frameworks...** from the drop-down list, under the **Target framework** option, as shown in the following screenshot:

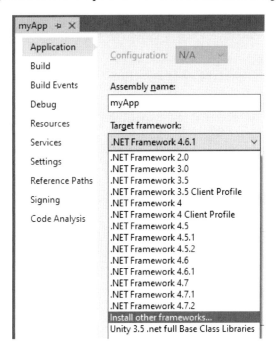

Figure 4.9 – You can find Install other frameworks… under the Target framework option

6. At this point, you should see a new website open up. It is the **dotnet** library website that Microsoft has made available for developers around the world.

7. Scroll down to search for **.NET Framework 4.8**, as shown in the following screenshot:

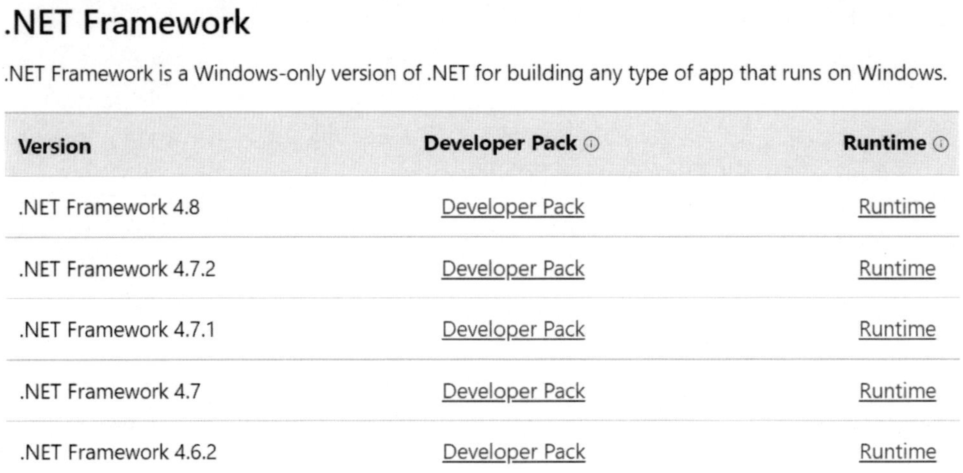

.NET Framework

.NET Framework is a Windows-only version of .NET for building any type of app that runs on Windows.

Version	Developer Pack ⓘ	Runtime ⓘ
.NET Framework 4.8	Developer Pack	Runtime
.NET Framework 4.7.2	Developer Pack	Runtime
.NET Framework 4.7.1	Developer Pack	Runtime
.NET Framework 4.7	Developer Pack	Runtime
.NET Framework 4.6.2	Developer Pack	Runtime

Figure 4.10 – Screenshot of the dotnet website to download the library .NET Framework 4.8

8. As you can see from the previous screenshot, you have two options to choose from. Please select the **Developer Pack** link to download the required .NET Framework 4.8.

9. The download of the executable file may take up to 30 seconds to complete. Once the download is complete, navigate to the download folder, and install the library.

10. The installation process is quite simple. You only need to accept the privacy policy and click **Ok**.

Now that the framework has been correctly installed, let's double-check everything is okay. Please navigate to the following:

```
C:\Program Files (x86)\Reference Assemblies\Microsoft\
Framework\
```

At this point, you should see, among all folders, one named **v4.8**. That means the installation has been successfully completed. Do not close that folder. Instead, scroll among the available files, and find the one named `PresentationCore.dll`. If you still do not see the folder or the file, a problem might have occurred during the installation of .NET Framework. You may want to go back to *step 3* and re-install the library. In this section, we introduced the Solution Explorer of Visual Studio, and we learned how to search for and install the dotnet framework. Next, we will install the Revit dll library files and make sure Visual Studio imports them correctly.

Installing the Revit dll

Next, we need to check another two dll files. Those two files are RevitAPI.dll and RevitAPIUI.dll, and they come with the default Revit installation. We don't need to download a new executable here. Navigate to the following folder and check that they are there:

```
C:\Program Files\Autodesk\Revit 2020\
```

Okay, we've completed the setup of the required dll libraries. Now go ahead and close and reopen the project with Visual Studio 2019. As we are developing a Revit plugin, we need to tell Visual Studio to switch to **Debug mode**. Debugging, in a nutshell, means that Visual Studio will highlight any errors in the code. Developers use debugging features of software such as Visual Studio Community or Visual Studio Code to know exactly where code breaks, so they can debug (resolve bugs in) their code. Anyhow, to switch to **Debug mode**, please do the following:

1. As we already did before, go to **Solution Explorer**, right-click on **myApp**, and select **Properties**.

2. Now open the **Debug** section and select **Start external program** under the **Start action** options.

3. If the Revit.exe file does not show up inside the textbox, click on **Browse** and navigate to the file Revit.exe. Make sure to select the **Revit 2020** directory path, as shown in the following screenshot:

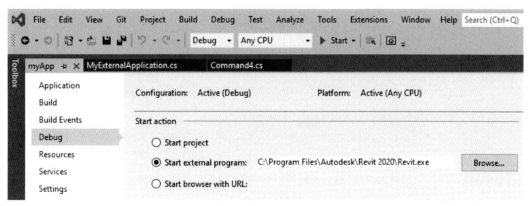

Figure 4.11 – Screenshot of myApp properties to switch to Debug mode

Once this step has been completed, we have a couple of things left.

4. Please now select **Build** from the left menu.

5. At the top of the window, right after the **Configuration** option, click on the drop-down list and select **Debug** as shown in the following screenshot:

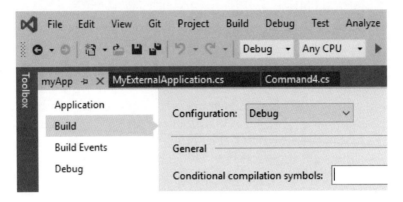

Figure 4.12 - Debug option

6. Next, at the bottom of the same window, we need to check that **Output path** is correct. Please take a look at the following screenshot:

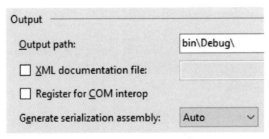

Figure 4.13 – Output options from the Build section

7. If you don't see the path bin\Debug\ written after the **Output path** option, please go ahead and type it in. Do not forget the ending **backslash** (\).

    Alright, I know that this part might be a bit boring, especially if you've never done something like that, but stick with me. It's absolutely worth it! The good thing is that we need to do that only once.

8. Once you've completed all of the previous steps, click on **File** from the top menu and then click **Save All** as shown in the following screenshot:

Figure 4.14 – Save all settings in Visual Studio 2019

Now you're done with the debugging mode, you're ready to move on to the following configuration steps.

Updating your local repository

The next thing to do is *edit a file inside the GitHub folder* that was previously downloaded. In case you missed it, the folder can be downloaded from here:

```
https://github.com/PacktPublishing/Managing-and-Visualizing-
Your-BIM-Data/tree/main/Chapter04
```

But before opening such a file, we need to download a text file editor. I suggest you use something such as **Notepad++**, which can be downloaded from here:
```
https://notepad-plus-plus.org/downloads/v8/.
```

> **Important Note**
>
> Notepad++ is a free text editor that we will also use later on in the book. Indeed, we need an editor like Notepad++, especially in *Chapter 6, Importing Revit Plans inside Power BI Using Shape Files*, by Gavin Crump. However, if you prefer to use other types of editors, feel free to do so. It is not mandatory to use Notepad++. Once you've downloaded **Notepad++**, please install it and restart your computer if necessary.

If you already use another text editor, skip the first two steps and jump to *step 3*:

1. Open up the GitHub folder previously downloaded for this chapter.

2. Inside that folder, open **myApp**, and scroll down to find `myApp.manifest.addin`.

3. At this point, right-click the file and select **Edit with Notepad++** as shown in the following screenshot:

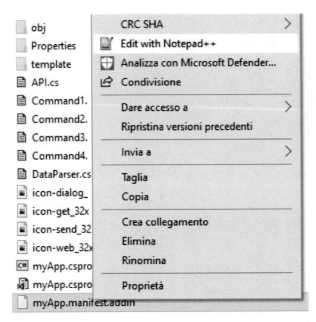

Figure 4.15 – Click on Edit with Notepad++ after right-clicking the file myApp.manifest.addin

4. When Notepad++ opens the file, let's take a look at *row 5*.

   We need to replace the default path with one that matches your PC path.
   The following row is what needs to replace row 5:

   ```
   <Assembly>C:\[YOUR_PATH_FOLDER]\packt-my-revit-plug-in-
   master\myApp\bin\Debug\myApp.dll</Assembly>
   ```

5. Now, you need to copy that path and paste it inside Notepad++, on row 5. Also, pay attention to the `Assembly` tags. Make sure you do not accidentally remove them. You can recognize those tags because of the opening and closing horizontal arrow symbols. When you're done, also make sure that the path ends with the following:

   ```
   ...\myApp\bin\Debug\myApp.dll</Assembly>
   ```

6. Now click on **File** from the top menu and select **Save**. Then close the file.

At this point, the editing of the manifest file is complete. We now need to copy it into the Revit plugin folder. The standard installation path should be found at the following:

```
C:\ProgramData\Autodesk\Revit\Addins\2020
```

Please go ahead and paste the file myApp.manifest.addin inside that folder. We have now completed the update of the manifest addin file. We need to do the same thing to a C# file, but this time, inside Visual Studio 2019.

Updating the RibbonBar.cs file

As we did for the manifest addin file, we have to update a couple of directory paths, but this time, on a C# file. Without further ado, please open up Visual Studio 2019, navigate to the **Solution Explorer** and find the RibbonBar.cs file as shown in the following screenshot:

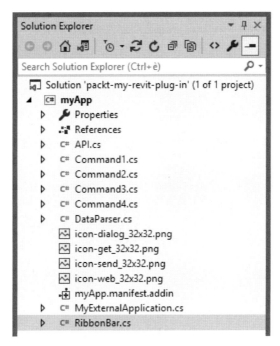

Figure 4.16 – RibbonBar.cs file found from the Solution Explorer panel

At this point, please follow the following steps to update the C# file:

1. Click on the `RibbonBar.cs` file to open the Visual Studio editor.

2. Navigate to line **23**. Here, you will find the path that needs to be updated, as shown in the following screenshot:

Figure 4.17 – Line 23 of the RibbonBar.cs file

3. From here, you need to replace this with the following path: `"C:\[YOUR_PATH_FOLDER]\packt-my-revit-plug-in-master\myApp\bin\Debug\icon-dialog_32x32.png"`.

4. Select the first part of the string and replace it with your GitHub project folder previously downloaded for this chapter.

5. Once you paste the path and update the one at line **23**, please do the same at lines **24**, **28**, and **29**.

6. After pasting your local path to each line, please click on the **File** menu and click **Save All**. You could also use the shortcut *Ctrl + Shift + S*.

Well done! Now we are ready to test the plugin startup.

Testing the plugin startup

Now we need to do one last thing before starting and testing the solution. Open up Visual Studio 2019 and expand **References** from **Solution Explorer**. You can find **References** right below the **myApp** project file, as shown in the following screenshot:

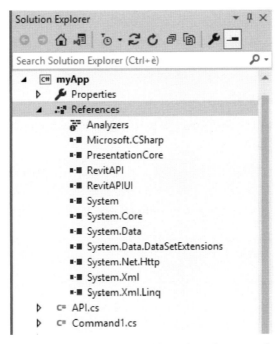

Figure 4.18 – References can be found from the Solution Explorer panel

Once **References** has been expanded, you should see a bunch of libraries. Please check that **RevitAPI** and **RevitAPIUI** do not show a yellow triangle with an exclamation mark. If you do see a yellow triange, it means you probably missed one or more configuration steps. Please go back and start again from the beginning.

If you don't see the yellow triangles, it means that you are finally ready to test the plugin. First, open up Visual Studio Community 2019, select the **Debug** mode (**1**), and click **Start** (**2**) to start the solution as shown in the following screenshot:

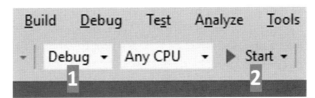

Figure 4.19 – Select Debug and click Start from the toolbar at the top of the user interface

At this point, you will see an **Output** panel show up at the bottom of the Visual Studio interface and, of course, Revit 2020 loading. Congratulations – now that we have completed the configuration of the initial settings, we can move on to Revit.

Exploring the toolbar

The first time you start the solution, Revit will display a warning message like the one shown in the following screenshot:

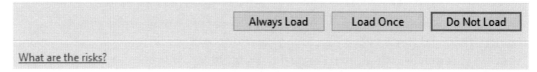

Security - Unsigned Add-In   ✕

 The publisher of this add-in could not be verified. What do you want to do?

Name: packt-my-revit-plug-in
Publisher: Unknown Publisher
Location:
C:\Users\aiten\Downloads\packt-my-revit-plug-in-master\myApp\bin\Debug\myApp.dll
Issuer: None
Date: 2021-06-12 16:42:15

Make sure that this add-in comes from a trusted source.

| | Always Load | Load Once | Do Not Load |

What are the risks?

Figure 4.20 – Warning message from the Revit start screen

As you can read in the previous screenshot, the warning message says: **The publisher of this add-in could not be verified. What do you want to do?** The message is a warning from Revit, and the reason is that the plugin has not officially registered yet. This is normal in the early phases of development. However, for simplicity, we will not cover the code to register Revit add-ins in this chapter. You can ignore that message, and select **Load Once** or **Always Load** if you don't want to see that message anymore. After you click on **Load Once** or **Always Load**, Revit will start loading your custom dll file! Give it a few seconds to complete.

At this point, you should see a message like the one shown in the following screenshot:

Figure 4.21 – Plugin successfully loaded

Great! This means that all of the previous steps have been successfully completed. Well done!

To give you an example, this message comes from the plug-in itself, and it says, *hey I am ready!* Displaying messages is one of the most straightforward tasks to achieve with the Revit APIs.

Indeed, the previous message was developed with literally one line of code. If you want to play around with it, please go ahead to *line 16* of the `MyExternalApplication.cs` file and update the string with one of your choices. Although, I won't tell you how to find the `MyExternalApplication.cs` file, as you should now be able to find it on your own. Make sure to update only the string part of the code as follows:

```
TaskDialog.Show("Revit", "my plug-in successfully loaded");
```

If you change the first string containing `"Revit"`, you update the window's title. Meanwhile, if you change the second one, you update the message itself. Give it a try!

> **Important Note**
> Remember to remove this line of code before building your final solution. Otherwise, you will face annoyed colleagues who are forced to see that message each time they launch a Revit session!

Now that we have completed the plugin startup, each time you launch Autodesk Revit 2020, your plugin will start as well. This is because we have copied the plugin `dll` file inside the Revit add-in folder. Besides, after opening a new Revit project, or an existing one, you can finally see the homemade toolbar. This new interface is organized with four distinct buttons. Each one, of course, runs a specific action. *We want to find a way to communicate with the user using an external service and exchange real-time data.*

Please open up Revit. Both a new file or an existing one will work. Once Revit has loaded, navigate to **My Custom Toolbar**. You will find it on the right-hand side of the Revit ribbon. After clicking on **My Custom Toolbar**, you will see a bunch of icons show up, like the ones shown in the following screenshot:

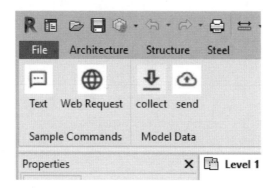

Figure 4.22 – Buttons of the custom toolbar

Each of those buttons performs a specific task. Starting from the left of the previous screenshot, the following list provides a description of each one:

- **Command 1 – Text**: Sends a message to the user using the TaskDialog API from the Autodesk library `Autodesk.Revit.UI`, previously loaded when we imported the DLL libraries.

- **Command 2 – Web Request**: Uses the `WebRequest` API from the Windows library `System.Net` to communicate with an external service through a web request. As soon as the command receives a response from that service, it will display the related message to the user.

- **Command 3 – collect**: We use this to collect specific Revit project data, such as username, software version, document path, size, and name.

- **Command 4 – send**: This is the most important one. Indeed, this button's task brings together all the previous functions, sending the collected data to our Power BI service through a web request.

I've placed the word *Command* before the buttons' names because each has been developed using separate C# classes. If you don't know what a C# class is, don't worry, there is no need to know that at this point. In the future, if you would like to develop one of your own, you may want to learn some more advanced concepts of computer science. But, for now, you can find each button's code in separate files, as shown in the following screenshot:

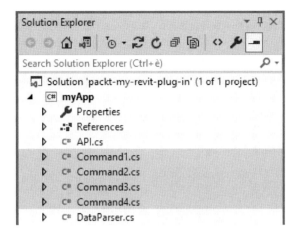

Figure 4.23 – Corresponding files to each button of the toolbar

Congratulations, you have completed the environment setup for your first C# Revit plugin.

In this section, we learned what Visual Studio options to configure to allow communication between Visual Studio and Autodesk Revit. We also learned that this is fundamental for debugging purposes. Without debugging, we wouldn't be able to identify errors in our code. Also, we understood how to configure dotnet framework and how to import the required API. Finally, at the end of the section, we understood how to test our solution using Visual Studio and customize the startup message strings.

Next, we will move on to Power BI. The following section will cover fundamental configuration steps to let Autodesk Revit push the model's data to Microsoft Power BI in real time. Let's go.

Preparing Microsoft Power BI

Looking back at our initial purpose, we would like to deliver a simple new functionality to enhance data collection without increasing any efforts by our Revit users. That's why we choose to take advantage of their daily activities by setting the software to listen at Synchronizations event to trigger *Command 4 automatically*. As soon as someone syncs their model with the central one, we will collect new data and deliver it to the Power BI service.

In our class `MyExternalApplication.cs`, there is a pre-defined method named `application_DocumentSynchronizingWithCentral` at *line 33*. This method has been added to the list of functionalities, and it will be triggered every time on document synchronization (*line 20* of the same file).

Now that every configuration step has been completed, our flow works better, but our puzzle still needs one last piece. We have to set up the web service on which our plugin should collect and send data.

To get started, please open the browser and navigate to `https://app.powerbi.com/`. Authenticate your Power BI account and go to your preferred workspace. Remember that you can access those spaces with a free Power BI subscription.

So, let's start by doing the following:

1. Open the **My workspace** area from the web **Power BI** application as shown in the following screenshot:

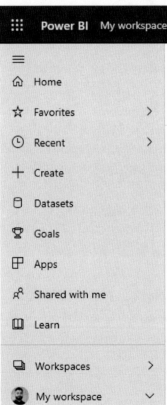

Figure 4.24 – Power BI web application menu

You can find the **My workspace** button at the bottom of the list.

2. Once you click on that button, you should see a button named **New**, with a plus icon to its left. Please take a look at the following screenshot and click on this button to create the new workspace:

Figure 4.25 – Click on the New button to create a new workspace

3. At this point, a drop-down list will show up. Please click on **Streaming dataset** as shown in the following screenshot:

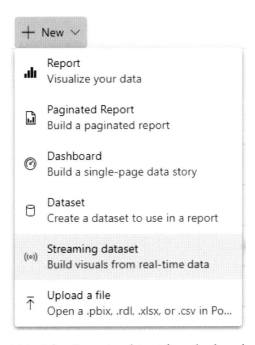

Figure 4.26 – Select Streaming dataset from the drop-down list

4. Once you click on that, you'll see a side window show up. The side window contains three web service icons. Select the first one, **API**, and click on **Next**.

5. The new streaming dataset side window will ask you for two things:

    a. A **Dataset name**: I've used My_dataset, but you can choose the name you want.

    b. Then, we need to provide the name of the attributes that Power BI will receive and their data type. Let's proceed in order.

6. As the first attribute name, please go ahead and type `user` inside the **Values from stream** field. Then select **Text** from the drop-down list on its right. As you type, you'll notice a new box showing underneath those fields. As we enter more attribute names, you'll see that data is formatted using square and curly brackets inside this new box. This type of formatting is called **JSON**, and it is a standard for sending and receiving data using API services. The following screenshot shows this step:

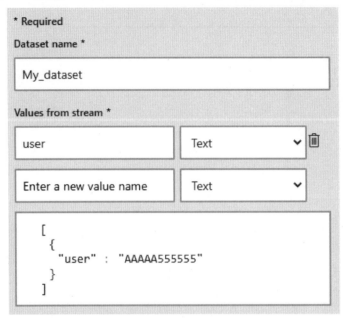

Figure 4.27 – JSON formatted attributes inside the new streaming dataset

7. Now, as we just did with **user**, go ahead and type:

    a. `software`

    b. `project`

    c. `path`

    Those attributes must be of the **Text** data type, like the **user** attribute.

8. Next, we need to insert:

    a. `size` as a **Number** value

    b. `date` as a **DateTime** value

    c. `dateTime` as a **DateTime** value

9. One last thing to do is to enable **Historic data analysis** by turning on the button at the bottom of the same window. We want to use historical data to create our final report. Please take a look at the following screenshot. It contains all of the attributes and data types we need to enter:

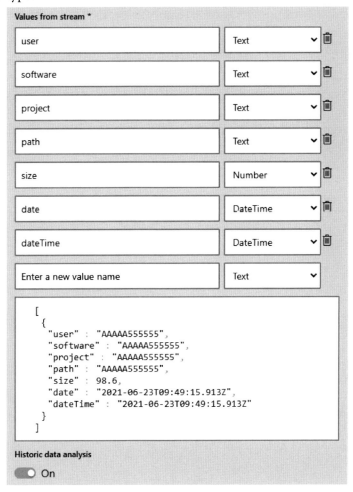

Figure 4.28 – All of the attributes and data types to insert

If everything is correct, please click the **Create** button to complete those last steps.

At this point, we have told Power BI what structure we want to use for our data. The web application now shows a final page where it says **Streaming dataset created**. From here, you can see two fields and a few buttons, **Raw**, **cURL**, and **PowerShell**. These three buttons deal with advanced configurations and terminal operations. As for the chapter's purposes, there is no need to cover them. We only need to copy the **Push URL**. As the name suggests, this is a particular type of URL. It represents the necessary API link to allow Revit to send data from the model to our **Power BI workspace**.

If you accidentally closed this final window, don't worry. Just go back to the **My workspace** page from the Power BI web application and navigate the available reports and datasets to find the one you created before. Then, mouse over it to show the options icon. You can recognize it because it has three vertical dots. Click on the three-dots icon, as shown in the following screenshot, and select **API Info** to open up the page we were looking for:

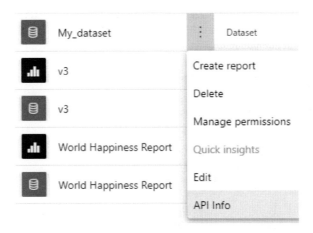

Figure 4.29 – Click on API Info to open the required page

Well done. We now want to copy the **Push URL** and paste it inside Visual Studio. Let's do that:

1. Open up Visual Studio 2019.

2. From the **Solution Explorer** panel, click on `Command4.cs`.

3. At line **9**, replace the provided URL with the **Push URL** that was just generated. Make sure not to delete the opening and closing quotation marks. Once you're done, you should see something like the following screenshot:

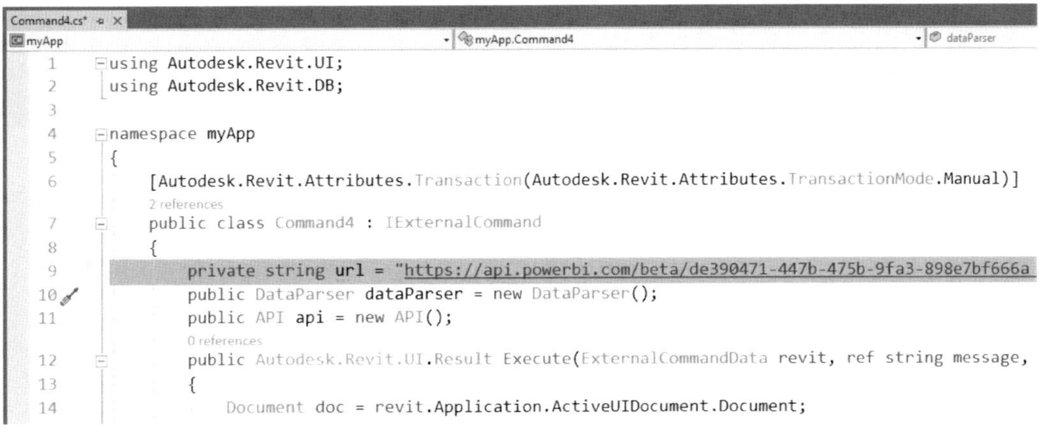

Figure 4.30 – Replace the default URL with the Push URL at line 9

Finally, we completed the link between our Revit plugin and the Power BI streaming dataset. By doing so, we ensured that Revit has the right keys to push data to Power BI. We are now on the right track to complete the real-time data exchange between the BIM authoring and the business intelligence tools.

In this section, we learned how to configure a streaming dataset using the Power BI web application. Also, we learned how to format the data correctly and, next, how to get and set the API key needed to allow communication from Revit to Power BI.

In the next section, we are going to build and visualize the Power BI report. Let's go.

Building the Power BI report

Our data stream connector is now ready. Furthermore, we have a working Revit plugin that pushes data from the model to our Power BI workspace. In this section, we will take advantage of the data bridge to build fantastic charts and share them with colleagues and peers. We want to create simple charts that are able to deliver some project insights using real-time data. We can monitor specific aspects of the project files, for example, and collect information from the users who work and interact with those models. We will explore all the required steps to finalize the connection between the Revit plugin and Power BI in the following sections.

Visualizing the data in Power BI

As for the Visual Studio project file, you'll find the Power BI file too. Just go back to the downloaded GitHub folder and open the `Revit to PowerBI.pbix` file. This time, we want to use the Power BI Desktop application. If you haven't downloaded Power BI Desktop yet, you can find the download link at the beginning of this chapter, in the *Technical requirements* section. Let's now follow these steps:

1. Open the file `PowerBI.pbix` included inside the GitHub folder previously downloaded.

2. At the start, you should see a warning message like the following:

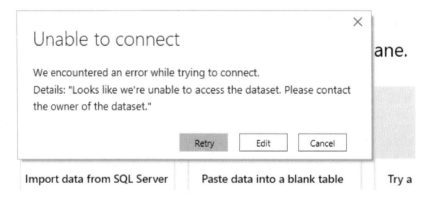

Figure 4.31 – Unable to connect warning message

Don't worry about that. It's showing up because we haven't pointed the file yet, to the dataset we created in the previous *Preparing Microsoft Power BI section*.

3. Now please click on **Edit** to open a new window where we can select our dataset.

4. You should now see a list of datasets, as shown in the following screenshot, including the one created in the previous *Preparing Microsoft Power BI section*. Please go ahead and select it and click on **Create**:

MTI 3 - Dashboard_v3	Ernesto Pellegrino	ernesto.pellegrino@lasia.it	a year ago
My_dataset	Ernesto Pellegrino	ernesto.pellegrino@lasia.it	28 days ag
v3	Ernesto Pellegrino	ernesto.pellegrino@lasia.it	a year ago
World Happiness Report	Ernesto Pellegrino	ernesto.pellegrino@lasia.it	6 months

Create

Figure 4.32 – Select your dataset (in my case, My_dataset) and click Create

5. At this point, we should be able to open the dataset correctly. In some cases, though, you could get two error messages related to the Power BI Desktop version. Please take a look at the following screenshot:

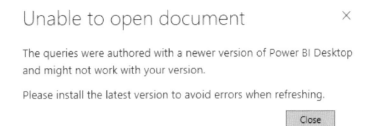

Figure 4.33 – Possible error message related to the version of Power BI Desktop

If you see the error message, you can click on **Close** as it is not necessary to update to the latest Power BI Desktop version. When you do that, you will see one more error message, but it's not mandatory to update Power BI. It's more of a recommendation. Click **Close** again if you see the second warning message.

6. Now the dashboard is showing up, but of course, it's empty, as shown in the following screenshot:

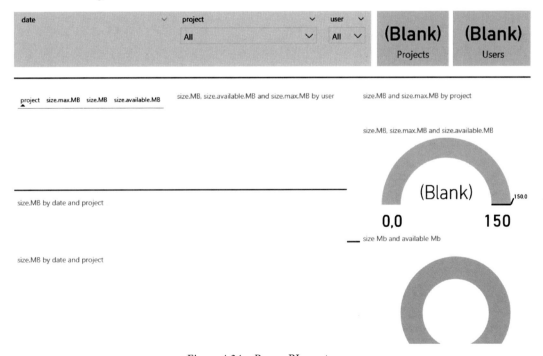

Figure 4.34 – Power BI empty page

The page is empty for two reasons. The first one is that we didn't save the file yet, and the second one, the most important, is that we didn't push any data from Revit. So, let's do that.

7. As the first thing to do, we need to save our file as shown in the following screenshot:

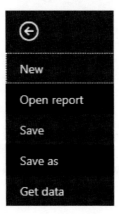

Figure 4.35 – We need to save the file first to show data in our dashboard

Please go ahead and click **File**, then **Save as**, and choose a destination folder to save the Power BI file.

8. Next, we want to push data from Revit, so let's open up Visual Studio to start up the solution. Make sure to select **Debug** from the top ribbon of Visual Studio as shown in the following screenshot:

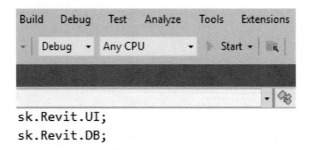

Figure 4.36 – Select Debug before starting the solution

When you select **Debug**, you can click **Start** to start up the solution. At this point, it may take a few seconds for Revit to show up.

9. When Revit shows up, you could get the **unsigned add-in** warning message like the one we discussed previously, in the *Exploring the toolbar section*. Just go ahead and click **Load Once**.

10. Now we're in the Revit startup window. Please go ahead and use the project you want to push data from the model to Power BI. *Keep in mind that after you choose a project, you need to enable the worksharing features if you haven't already.* This is fundamental because our Revit data will start its journey to Power BI every time we sync the model. Now, let's enable the worksharing features and save the file.

11. After saving the file, we are ready to push data to Power BI. We just need to synchronize the model. And by doing so, our plugin, at the same time, will send data to Power BI. Please sync the model as shown in the following screenshot:

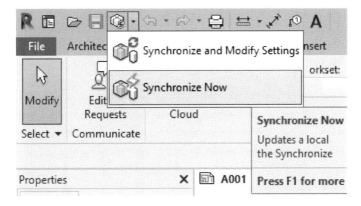

Figure 4.37 – Click on the Synchronize Now button

12. Don't go back to Power BI yet. Let's make a few more synchronization to show more data. Otherwise, the dashboard will look a bit empty, and we don't want that. So, let's create, for example, new floors, place a bunch of walls here and there, place other families too, or create new views and sheets. The goal is to increase our Revit model size. When you've done that, click **Synchronize now** again. Repeat this step a few times. Unleash your creativity by modeling something cool, and place families all over the Revit model. When you've clicked **Synchronize now** three or four times, we're ready to switch to Power BI. In my case, I've created new floors and placed a lot of walls and loadable families.

13. Back in Power BI, let's click **Refresh** from the top-center menu, as shown in the following screenshot:

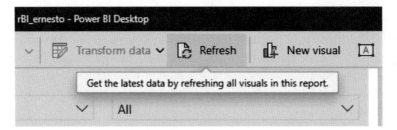

Figure 4.38 – Click the Refresh button in Power BI to get the latest data

When you click **Refresh**, the dashboard will get the latest data and update itself.

14. Although it may not contain lots of data yet, the newly updated dashboard starts to engage in size and users. When used with different central models for a few days of synchronization, our dashboard should look like the following screenshot:

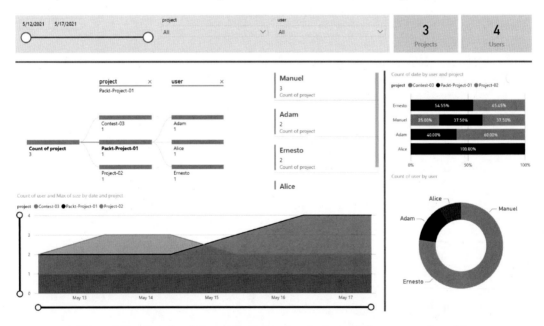

Figure 4.39 – Populated charts after using the plugin on different central models

The screenshot you're looking at shows data from the **user** page, which you can find at the bottom left of the Power BI user interface. We now start to have an overview of what's going on with our models – who is doing what, what models are being modeled by whom, and how many times each model has been synchronized.

Well done! At this point, you have correctly set up the Power BI file to allow it to receive data from Revit. Keep using the plugin on different models in the following days to populate the dashboards with more and more data. The more there is, the better!

Publishing and sharing your final report

With the last implementation, we completed designing the structure of our report. After saving our template, we can finally publish our work to Power BI web. All you need to do is click on the **Home** button, select **Publish** from the far right of the user interface, and select your dataset workspace. When the publishing process is complete, you should see a message like the one shown in the following screenshot:

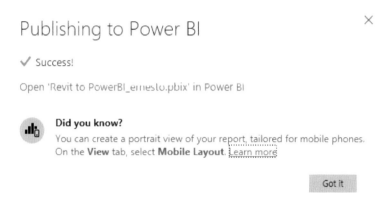

Figure 4.40 – Success message after publishing the Power BI report

When publishing the report, we must understand that we are not replacing the cloud dataset with the values visible from our desktop application. We are just updating the report structure used by Power BI cloud services to display our designed layouts.

Now we have dynamic reports available in the cloud. We can build new dashboards on top of them and share those assets with our company or specific colleagues. The cycle is complete. From now on, it is no longer necessary to add efforts to keep our **data flow** operational. As soon as our colleagues synchronize their work with central Revit files, our dataset will receive new information, and the published dashboards will show updated values in real time. Let's now see how we can share the report using the Power BI web application:

1. The first thing is to open up the Power BI web application using the following link:

    `https://app.powerbi.com/`

2. The second thing to do is to, of course, log in with our business account.

3. Now, from the menu bar at the left of the UI, please select **Workspaces**. Then click on the workspace in which you published the Power BI report. You should see a new page load up. Please scroll down to find the report, as shown in the following screenshot:

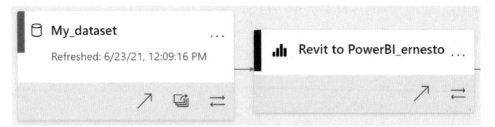

Figure 4.41 – Power BI report inside the personal workspace

4. Now click on the three dots at the side of the report rectangle, and click on the **Share** button.

5. It's important to know that the Power BI report sharing features are not included in the standard subscription plan. We should upgrade our account to a Pro license or activate a 60-day free trial to explore those features.

6. Whether we click **Try for 60 days** or **pay for the Pro license**, we get a new window to customize the sharing link options as shown in the following screenshot:

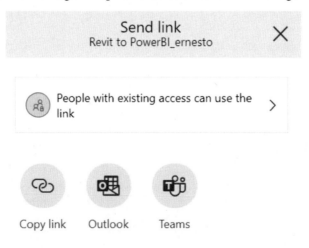

Figure 4.42 – Sharing options of the Power BI report

Perfect, we can now share the link of our report and send it to colleagues and peers to show them the incredible power of Microsoft Power BI!

We've covered a lot in this chapter. Although some of the topics covered are not for beginners, I wanted to show you that creating a Revit plugin in C# isn't that hard in the end. The power we gain when we monitor our models' data is incredible. We can have complete pictures of models, users, sizes, and all of the information we want to include in our plugin. Consider this as a starting point to become a developer in the BIM field. You'll do great things just by learning one of the many programming languages out there, C#, for example.

Summary

In this chapter, we learned how to set up Visual Studio and customize its environment to program our plugin. We understood how to configure the Revit API and how to start the plugin solution. Then we moved on to Power BI to finalize the streaming data connection from Revit, and next, how to visualize, publish, and share the report.

This chapter has set the flow to understand all the great plugins you will build on top of Revit. Software implementation is one of the gems in our field, helping us to set up workflows to save time and increase efficiency.

This chapter concludes our trip through the core of plugin development, helping us better understand how this application works.

Back to Ernesto

This chapter has been tremendous. Manuel, from what I recall, always leaned toward computer science applications and development. He is now a full-stack developer, and one of the most brilliant ones. I learned a lot here about plugin development, what the process is, and what is hidden behind the scenes. Although I didn't know about most of Manuel's topics that he explained to us, I now have the feeling I want to learn more about them. Becoming a full-stack developer would be a dream to me, but never say never. One day I'll create a plugin that even Manuel himself will recognize as something more remarkable than the plugins he usually creates—just joking! I am delighted Manuel participated in this project and worked on this chapter.

He wanted to share the message that today, working in our industry as a BIM developer is huge. It isn't something everybody can say about their work. By improving our computer science skills, we all will get there one day or another.

Now it's time to move on to the following chapters where we will not work with Visual Studio anymore, but instead, we will focus our energies on Dynamo and Revit. We will start with the next chapter, created by Luisa Cipriano Pieper, who will explain the basics of Autodesk Dynamo. I'll see you in the next chapter!

5
Getting Started with Autodesk Dynamo and Data Gathering

This chapter is written by Luisa Cypriano Pieper

Luisa is an architect, and works as a BIM manager in Spain for CES, a Belgian multinational company specializing in engineering and sustainable development. Luisa is an industry expert, and to me, it has been a pleasure working with her. She will lead the way in understanding the data-gathering part of the workflow to visualize data inside Power BI. She will teach us the fundamentals of visual programming using Autodesk Dynamo BIM.

This chapter is divided into two parts, both explained in a very visual and simple way, so you will realize that learning Dynamo is not rocket science.

In the first part, we will understand what **VPL (Visual Programming Language)** is, what Dynamo is, and how they can help us automate and qualify data management. We will also learn the basics of how Dynamo's interface and nodes work, what the basic data types are, and how to manage them.

Then, in the second part, we will get down to business and create two Dynamo scripts: one to export parameter values from Revit to Excel, and another one to update the parameters back in Revit by importing the data. The goal is to create a complete workflow starting from the Revit model's data, export it, update the data, and import it back into the model!

Take a look at the following diagram, which shows the entire workflow we are going to build together:

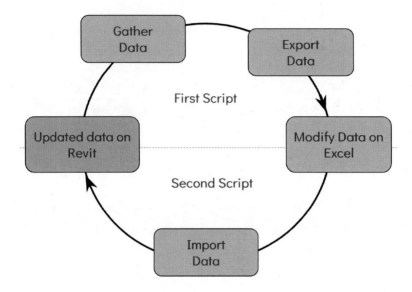

Figure 5.1 – Our planned workflow

In this chapter, we will cover the following topics:

- Understanding visual programming
- Introducing Autodesk Dynamo BIM for Revit
- Understanding the Dynamo UI and its basic components
- Creating the data-exporting script
- Creating the data-importing script
- Final thoughts and resources for self-learning

By the end of this chapter, you will have learned how to use Autodesk Dynamo by creating, saving, and executing your own scripts. You will also understand how to export and import data from and to the Revit model, using Dynamo and MS Excel. Let's get started!

Technical requirements

For this chapter, we require the following software:

- **Excel**: We will need to have it properly installed and licensed. Any version of Excel will do.

- **Revit**: We will also need Revit properly installed and licensed. You can download any of the versions available on the Autodesk website here: `https://www.autodesk.com/`

- You need to log in first. If you don't have an Autodesk account, go ahead and create one. Once ready and logged in, you should click on your profile in the top-right corner, select **Products and Services**, and finally navigate to Revit to download it.

- The entire script here has been developed using Dynamo version 2.4. I recommend that you use this build of Autodesk Dynamo, but, if you have a future version installed, you should not have any problems following the exercises. Earlier versions, on the other hand, will probably not be compatible with the chapter's exercises.

- To check what version of Dynamo you're currently using, just open up Revit, go to the **Manage** tab, and click on the Autodesk Dynamo icon on the far right of the Revit's ribbon. Now, click on the **Help** button from the top menu and select **About**. A new window will pop up; just check the version number on the left of this window, right next to Dynamo Revit.

If you have an older version of Dynamo installed on your computer, please install the new version using this link: `https://dynamobuilds.com`. Download the version ending in `.exe` as it runs directly within Revit and execute it as Administrator to install it.

> **Pro Tip!**
> Versions starting with **DynamoCoreRuntime** only allow the use of standalone/minimal setup versions of Dynamo, which is primarily used just for providing feedback on new features. The forced installation of these versions within Revit is not recommended.

The files for this chapter can be found here: `https://github.com/PacktPublishing/Managing-and-Visualizing-Your-BIM-Data/tree/main/Chapter05`

Understanding visual programming

The goal of this section is to familiarize you with visual programming general concepts. This is key if you want to become an Autodesk Dynamo super user!

The use of images and language to carry instructions over time goes back to the history of human civilizations. We have needed to find ways to communicate instructions so that we always arrive at the same result when forging metal, building bridges, or … cooking omelets. Yes, written recipes date back to the 4th Century AD even for very simple things, such as cooking omelets. The written instruction for an omelet recipe nowadays, for example, would probably look something like this:

- **INPUT:** Eggs, salt, and pepper
- **Processing actions**:

    a) MIX the eggs, salt, and pepper in a small bowl until blended.

    b) PLACE the mixture in a frying pan with melted butter.

    c) PUSH the cooked portions from the edges toward the center with an inverted turner so that uncooked eggs can touch the hot pan's surface.

    d) SERVE when folded.

- **OUTPUT**: Meal (omelet) for two people

Or, if we wanted to explain the same processes graphically, it would look like this:

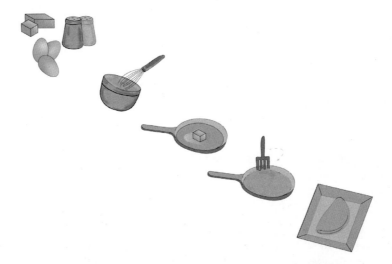

Figure 5.2 – Graphical representation of making an omelet

Programming is not much different. We need to pass certain "recipes," which are called algorithms, to delegate the execution of tasks to computers. There is a large variety of programming languages, with different pros and cons, that allow us to take advantage of what computers do best: repeatedly accomplish any set of tasks, without delay and devoid of human error.

Just like human natural language, programming languages also serve to pass information from one entity to another, having their own syntax and dialects and being represented in either a textual or graphical way.

The programming language that lets users create and manipulate algorithms graphically rather than by specifying them textually is called a **Visual Programming Language** (**VPL**). Although no scientific studies can prove that visual languages are inherently easier than written languages, it is impossible to deny that VPLs are very popular among people with a well-developed right side of the brain, which is responsible for spatiality.

One of the earliest examples of VPL in history is Sketchpad. Considered an ancestor of **Computer-aided design** (**CAD**) and object-oriented programming, it allowed the drawing of groups of lines and identified these groups of lines as objects, recognizing a "master drawing" from which "instance drawings" would be created. Once the master drawing was changed, all instances would be changed in the same way. Although there are many other examples of the use of VPL, probably the most well-known one is called Scratch, a computer game created by Media Lab in 2002 to introduce children to programming. The Scratch **User Interface** (**UI**) looks like the following screenshot:

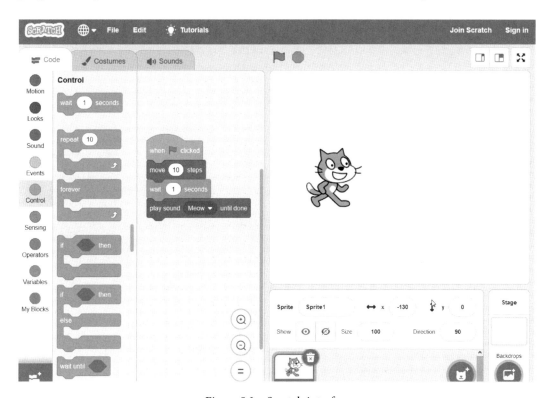

Figure 5.3 – Scratch interface

As you can see in the preceding screenshot, this colorful and straightforward UI is easy to understand. It provides an excellent introduction to logic and programming to kids who are curious about the subject.

Once you understand and use it in your day-to-day life, it will enable you to get rid of repetitive tasks related to your computer models, providing an inclusive visual programming environment.

At this point, we've learned what visual programming is and how it started. This introduction to VPL is fundamental to understanding my favorite VPL software – Autodesk Dynamo. Indeed, Dynamo has become one of the most reliable and efficient pieces of VPL software in our industry. In the next section, we will deep dive into Dynamo BIM for Revit by explaining how it works and why it is so important in our day-to-day tasks.

Introducing Autodesk Dynamo BIM for Revit

To compete with it's natural competitor, Grasshopper, from which it takes partial inspiration, Dynamo was first released in 2013. It is a program backed by Autodesk that essentially lets you interact with any program that contains an **API** (**Application Programming Interface**). Since Revit 2017, Dynamo has also become an inherent part of Revit, being accessible through the **Manage** tab, with no separate installation required.

If you are puzzled by the term *API*, take a look at the following diagram to understand the context:

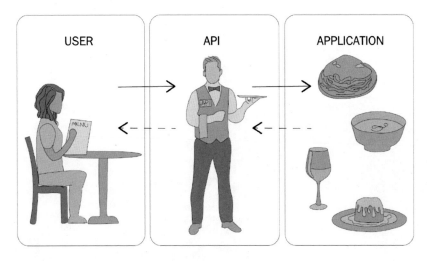

Figure 5.4 – The waiter (API) is responsible for communication between the user and the application

Although this is not a chapter on programming and computer science, I want to explain a little more the API/waiter example. Imagine you're sitting at a fancy restaurant table and you have a menu of choices that you can order. When you order something, you know there is an "engine" (the kitchen) to understand your order and prepare the food. So, we have a person who orders a dish and an engine responsible for the dish preparation. We need one more thing to make it work – an API (the waiter). The waiter indeed will be responsible for accepting your order and communicating it to the kitchen. This is precisely what an API does. The API is responsible for taking "inputs" and sending them to the backend (the engine) of an application. When the task is completed, the API will come back to you with a response.

If you're curious, I suggest that you do some more research into APIs because today, every software or application we use communicates using APIs. But for now, let's come back to Dynamo and see what it can do!

From the very definition of Autodesk, the company that created and owns the software, Dynamo is "what you make it." Given its characteristic of allowing operational effectiveness, data management, or design support, thought interaction with essentially anything that has an API – meaning it can interact with Office and Autodesk software, Windows, or even WhatsApp – this makes it an attractive investment. When used in combination with Revit, there are two main streams in terms of its target objectives:

- Geometries
- Data

Dynamo, indeed, can create, modify, and remove geometries from both the design environment and the family environment, although it is not particularly virtuosic at processing geometries. The following example shows the creation of a complex geometry using Autodesk Dynamo:

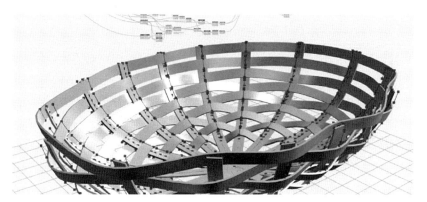

Figure 5.5 – Organic forms created through Dynamo

If you want to know more, you can navigate to the following link and explore some exercises provided by the Autodesk Dynamo team to help us understand this awesome tool: https://dynamobim.org/.

While Dynamo does help create unthinkable shapes, *Dynamo's typical and convenient use is data management* within the model. As we know, **BIM** stands for **Building information modeling**, and with Dynamo, it's the "I" that can be exported or imported, handled, or automated even between different software.

The following diagram illustrates the two focuses that Dynamo can have, their intersection, and a few examples of scripts within these contexts that can be useful:

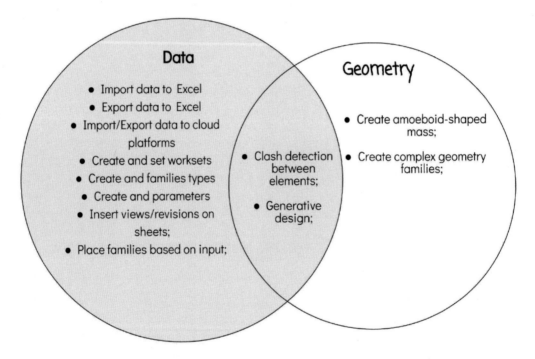

Figure 5.6 – Graphical scheme with some possibilities that Dynamo brings

As you can see from the preceding diagram, Dynamo's main use involves data manipulation on one side, and geometry manipulation on the other. In this chapter, we will focus on the data manipulation area; in particular, we will learn how to create two scripts for exporting and importing data from and to the Revit model.

Knowing the possibilities of this tool is key to planning and developing our scripts. In the next section, we will start opening Dynamo and exploring its UI.

Understanding the Dynamo UI and its basic components

In this section, we are going to learn the basics of the Dynamo user interface and features. When we start creating our scripts, it is necessary to know the Dynamo UI. Let's start by opening Autodesk Dynamo first.

To access Dynamo, we can open up Revit, navigate to the **Manage** tab, and then, on the far right of the screen, at the **Visual Programming** section, we can click on the **Dynamo** icon. If you have more than one version installed, a tab will appear to let you choose which version you want to use as default. The following screenshot shows where to find the Dynamo icon inside Revit:

Figure 5.7 – Dynamo icon under the Manage tab, on the far right

Clicking on the Dynamo icon will start the program. Now, let's learn about its basic options by commenting on the following diagram:

Figure 5.8 – Dynamo start up interface

So, the start up interface is pretty straightforward. We have two main areas at the center of the screen. The first one is on the left, and its scope is to help us create new files, create custom nodes, open up saved files, or scroll through the recent ones. The second area is on the right, and its scope is to help users be involved in the Dynamo community and provide instructional content. Now, let's create a new script to explore the Dynamo script environment.

You can use the shortcut *Ctrl + N* to create a new script, or you can simply click on **New**. You should see something like the following screenshot:

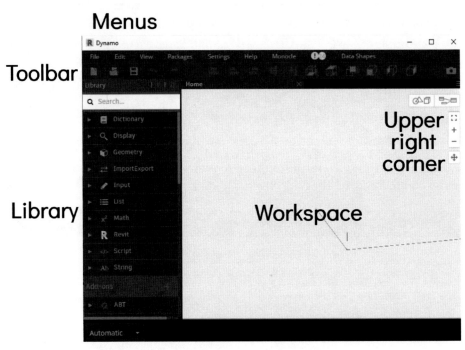

Figure 5.9 – Dynamo script environment

Here we have four major areas. Starting from the top, we have **MENUS**, which is self-explanatory. From the menus, we can open up the program's settings, and we can download packages. We have **TOOLBAR** below the menus, which shows a few icons for opening a saved script or saving the one we're currently working on. On the left side, we have **LIBRARY**, which we use to navigate through the nodes we want to place inside our workspace. Below the library, we can see a couple of buttons. This area is called **EXECUTION BAR**, and we interact with it every time we run the script.

At the very center of the screen, we have **WORKSPACE**. The larger area at the center is indeed where we place our nodes and write our code to test things out and make things work. Also, last but not least, we have the upper-right corner, an area we use to switch from the node placement mode to the 3D viewer mode. Other than that, we also have a couple of buttons for navigation. Now, let's deep dive into each one of them!

Menus

The menus dropdown is the place where you will find many basic settings and functionalities of the Dynamo application. The following screenshot shows the top menu:

Figure 5.10 – Dynamo menu

The main things to understand here are the **File**, **Packages**, and **Settings** menus.

The **File** menu is essential because it allows us to perform basic tasks such as opening, saving, and exporting our script. Let's say we have issues executing our script, and we want to ask for help on the Dynamo BIM forum. Click on **File** and then **Export workspace as an image**. This will help the power users on the forum to better understand what's going on, so they can help us to solve our problem. Of course, we can't ask for help with every little thing we can't solve on our own while developing our scripts, but, if you demonstrate that you tried to solve it with different solutions, yet the problem is still occurring, you'll be welcomed and helped on the forum. There are many great people out there who will try to help us. Give it a try!

Then we have the **Packages** menu, which allows us to manage and download external libraries or packages. From there, you can download, for example, a package called **Data-Shapes**. Data Shapes can help us understand and guide us on how to come up with more elaborative ways of inputs by using a UI. Not everybody wants to use Dynamo, and even fewer people want to learn it! The solution may be the use of the **Data-Shapes** package. To give you a super-simple example, let's say we want to automate the Revit project's setup. We could develop a script that, when executed, will do the following:

- Fill in the project's information
- Import some families
- Create levels
- Save the file inside a specific directory path

We could develop this script in two ways. The usual way would be opening Dynamo, customizing the variable we need, and then click **Run**. If we have a script that imports some families, we may want to specify what kind of family we will import. To do so in the usual way, it is necessary to open up Dynamo, change the family type of the lamp we intend to place, and then click **Run**.

On the other hand, we could use the **Data-Shapes** package to create a simple UI window for our colleagues who don't know how to manage a Dynamo graph. This window will pop up when we start our script without even opening Dynamo BIM for Revit. That's awesome!

Now back to the interface of Dynamo, last but not least, we have the **Settings** menu. Here, we can set how many decimals we want on numbers, how much memory the software should use to render our geometries, or manage the folder where we place our Dynamo packages.

Those menus – **File**, **Package**, and **Settings** – are the ones you should know by heart. Every time you develop a new Dynamo script, you will probably need to set up something, so my advice is to explore those menus each time you have the chance!

The upper-right corner

Then, we have the one and only **upper-right** corner. I couldn't find a better name for classifying this area of buttons, but let's give it this name for the sake of simplicity. Here, we will see mainly tools for navigation through the workspace.

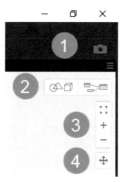

Figure 5.11 – Dynamo upper-right corner menu

Starting from number 1 at the top, these areas are used for the following:

1. Exporting the whole workspace as an image

2. Switching between graph view and 3D navigation

3. Providing zoom commands (the first one from the top is **Zoom to fit**, followed by **Zoom in** and **Zoom out**)

4. Panning, which is the same as for Revit; just click the mouse wheel to move around the graph

As you can see from the preceding screenshot, we can use the *upper-right corner* buttons to navigate our workspace. *The workspace itself is divided into two layers.* The first one is for placing and connecting nodes, while the second one is for navigating the 3D environment. We often use the 3D environment when we deal with geometries. Instead, when working with data import, export, or any other data-related operations, we don't need to use the 3D environment at all. But it's there, and we can use it when creating surfaces, meshes, and geometries in general.

Library

The Dynamo library is where we can see all the loaded nodes, both the default nodes that come with the software installation, also called **OOTB** (**out of the box**), and any custom package nodes, which can be installed from **Package Manager**. To place a node inside the workspace, search for it by using the Library's search bar and click on its name to place it. The following screenshot shows a few details on the Dynamo library:

Figure 5.12 – Dynamo library

As you can see from the preceding screenshot, the library is composed of the following:

1. The **search bar**, used to search a specific node we want to use.

2. **Categories** and sub-categories are included in single sets of libraries, such as the **Dictionary** library, the **Display** library, or the **Geometry** one.

3. When you open a library, you'll see a series of categories, including **Color**.

4. Each category contains a set of **nodes**, divided into sub-categories. In the preceding screenshot, you can see three different symbols on the left. Those symbols are there to help us understand what activity those nodes will perform. There are three symbols:

    •   **Create**, with the symbol of a cross. The nodes grouped under the **Create** sub-category will create something inside the workspace. It could be a new geometry, or a new list of data, for example.

    •   **Action**, with the symbol of a lightning bolt. These nodes usually perform a task that does not create something, but *changes* one element into another. For example, you can have a list of information, and you can split this list into two, three, or as many lists as you may need.

    •   **Query**, with a symbol of a question mark. The nodes grouped under this sub-category will query information from other nodes. You may want to know the category of certain family instances placed inside the Revit model. The node you're looking for, **Element.GetCategory**, for example, will be grouped under the **Query** type of nodes.

For now, you don't need to worry about the library. It's pretty straightforward, and we will use it later on when developing our scripts. I want you to understand what is in the Dynamo UI so that you can navigate and use its features effortlessly.

> **Important Note**
> The library search engine is quite sensitive and often does not show the searched nodes when the exact name is not typed. On the other hand, Autodesk is working on different Dynamo improvements, and the search bar is one of them. So, we should get an improved search bar very soon.

Up to this point, we have learned where to go to search for a specific node, and how to recognize what the node will do, by looking at its sub-category icon. Next, we will take a look at the execution bar.

Execution bar

The execution bar is the area where we execute our scripts. You will find it at the bottom-left of the Dynamo user interface. There aren't many options to choose from, but the main point here is that you can set the execution of the script in **Manual** mode or **Automatic** mode.

Manual mode is the best one in my opinion, especially if you are new to Dynamo. This mode means that every time you want to execute your script, you have to click on the **Run** button, as shown in the following screenshot:

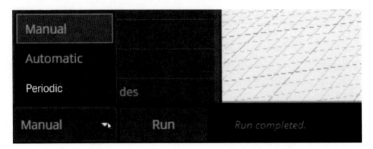

Figure 5.13 – Execution bar library

After a while, for a simple script, you could switch it to **Automatic** mode. However, keep in mind that each time you change a variable or connect a new node to the graph, Dynamo will automatically execute the script for us. If you're developing a super-complex script that will place doors and windows on each floor of the model, you may want to leave it to **Manual**. Once the script execution is complete, you'll get some information about the success or not of the operation. In the preceding screenshot, for example, you can read **Run completed** to the right of the **Run** button.

Nodes

Here we are, the bricks of our scripts. Nodes are the objects that perform the operations inside Dynamo. Making an analogy with our omelet recipe, nodes are the ones we would use to perform operations, create and hold data, perform a function on it, or visualize it. Nodes need to be connected to define the flow and the order in which they should be processed. You can also group your nodes to organize them by functions. I always do that because it will create a visual differentiation of what is going on, and in the event of issues, you'll be able to separate the problematic nodes from the rest of your script and solve the problem more quickly. The following diagram shows some additional information on what nodes and groups are:

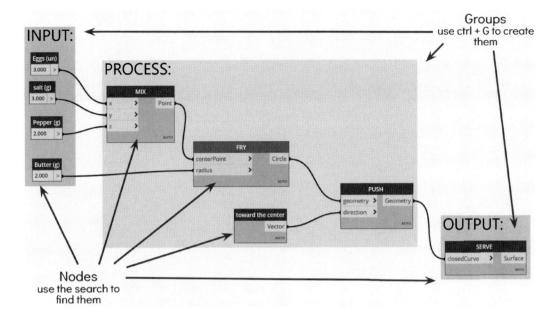

Figure 5.14 – Graphical explanation of nodes and groups

As we said, a good practice for organizing nodes with the same intent is to use groups. Groups allow you to separate functionally distinct parts of a script, letting you quickly identify and move them around. To create a group, select the desired nodes and click *Ctrl + G*, or instead, right-click on the workspace environment and then choose **Create Group**. You can create a template to define the functions of each color grouping. This is useful when, within your organization, multiple users need to manage, create, and update Dynamo scripts. As shown in the preceding diagram, I've used a light blue for inputs, light green for nodes processing information, and dark green for the data output.

You can also add a new node to an existing group. To do so, select the existing group and the nodes to be added, and then right-click on one of the nodes and select **Add to group** or use *Ctrl + G*. Alternatively, if we want to remove a node from a group, we need to click on **Remove from group**.

Alongside the node's group organization, it's also common to place a bunch of notes when needed. Notes are just a few lines of text inside a rectangle. They do nothing to the script. But we can use them to tell the user what is going on in that area of the script, or we can use them as a manual or guide for future users who want to customize the script. You can create notes by using *Ctrl + W* or opening the **Edit** menu and clicking on **Create Note**. Now, let's learn about node states!

Node states

When we develop our scripts, we will inevitably notice that the nodes change in colors or display a little message above them. By learning to identify color patterns, we will quickly understand the state of the node we are watching. There aren't many states, but understanding and associating color patterns with the type of message is a huge help in terms of speeding up our development and problem-solving skills. Following is a list of descriptions and images for each state:

- **Active**: Nodes whose minimum required inputs have all been successfully connected.

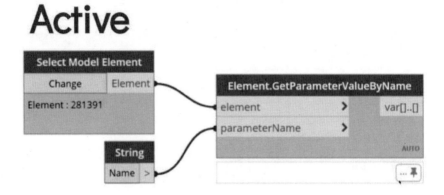

Figure 5.15 – Active state

- **Inactive**: Nodes whose minimum required inputs have not all been connected yet.

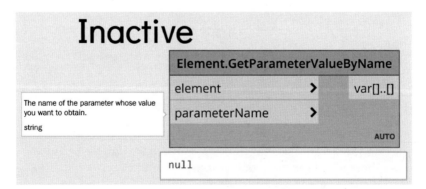

Figure 5.16 – Inactive state

- **Error State**: Nodes in red indicate an error state. Those types of errors mainly refer to missing package libraries.

Figure 5.17 – Error state

- **Frozen**: Frozen nodes have their execution suspended. Sometimes, you don't want the script to write to Excel every time you're testing things out. You want to execute a smaller part of it. You can do that by clicking on the particular node you don't want to execute, right-clicking, and selecting **Freeze**.

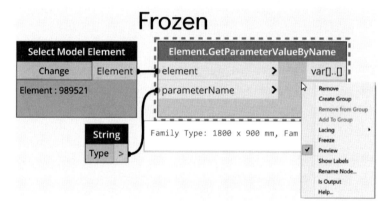

Figure 5.18 – Frozen state

- **Selected**: Nodes currently selected are outlined in blue.

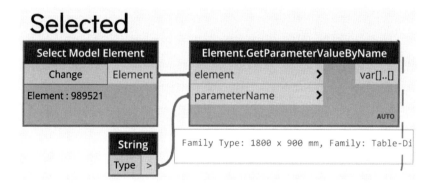

Figure 5.19 – Selected state

- **Warning**: Nodes in yellow are in an alert state, meaning they may deal with incorrect data types.

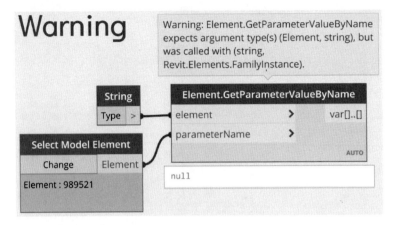

Figure 5.20 – Warning state

As you can see, states are easily identifiable. They can help us quickly identify at least the category of an issue, in the case of yellow nodes, which means a warning, and most of the time, the inputs provided are of the wrong data type. For example, if you need to get the value from an element's parameter, like the one shown in the preceding screenshot, you can't utilize the Boolean node as input. Instead, you should use the name of the parameter as a string of text.

> **Pro Tip!**
> If the visual program has warnings or errors, Dynamo will provide additional information about the problem in a tooltip above the node. Hover your mouse over the tooltip to expand it.

So far, we have learned a lot about the Dynamo UI. We understood where to go to search for a node, how to take a high-quality screenshot of our script from the top-right corner area, and how to recognize the state of nodes by learning the color codes associated with the warning messages. Next, we will learn the Dynamo data types.

Types of data

There are four essential data types that I would like to introduce to you. Those data types, in computer science, are often called **Primitives** or **Primitive data types**. The following screenshot shows **String**, **Integer**, **Booleans**, and **Double** data types:

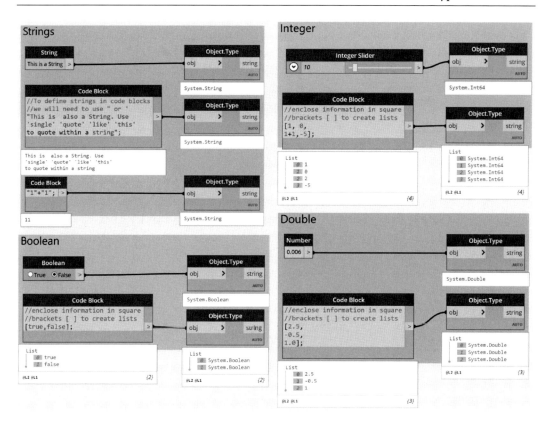

Figure 5.21 – Different primitive types of data

Strings literally represent text data. As you can see in the top left of the previous image, strings can contain numbers, but unlike integers or doubles, the numbers are read as characters. You can identify strings by the opening and closing quotes at the beginning and the end of them. For example, **"1" + "1"** will be equal to **"11"**, and not **2**, as you may expect. Using the plus symbol between strings means concatenating this string with the next one, not summing their values, even if those strings include numbers such as **"2"** or **"554"**. For computers, they are strings, not numbers, so if we sum **"1" + "1"**, the computer interprets them as strings and shows us **"11"** as a result, and not **2**. This concept, if you have never learned the basics of computer science, might seem weird at first. But in no time, you'll learn how to recognize data types and provide nodes with the correct data type input. This is crucial when learning any programming language.

Integers are much simpler to understand. *Integer* stands for integer numbers, including negative numbers and zero. So, an integer could be *44*, or *6.509,* or *-250*. An integer is simply a number recognized by computers as a number this time that doesn't have a decimal place. That's all.

This leads us to **Doubles**. This data type represents a number, but that number has decimal places. So, *16.45* or *4006.569* are both considered doubles. Next, we will start setting up our environment by saving an Excel file that we will use later on for the data import/export. Also, we will use a Revit schedule to monitor how our data changes.

The last data type I want you to understand is the **Boolean**. A Boolean is a data type that represents one of two possible states – true or false. Sometimes, you can read about Booleans such as one or zero, or on or off. The concepts are the same. To give you a practical example, we could query the Revit model to see whether there are windows larger than one meter. Dynamo will output true if it finds at least one window larger than one meter, or false if all windows aren't larger than one meter. Booleans are useful for querying information and allowing the Dynamo script to do this or that in case of True/False statements. For example, we could create a script that collects all information from doors inside our model. Then we could query whether each door has a handle, and at that point of the script, we could create two separate branches of the graph. The first one will deal with the doors WITH the handle, while the second one will deal with doors WITHOUT handles. Maybe we could develop the script in this way:

- In the case of True, meaning that the door has a handle, we could tell Dynamo to do nothing.

- In the case of False, meaning that the door doesn't have a handle, we could tell Dynamo to change the door type to one with a handle.

Up to this point, we have learned the basics of data types, which will be useful if you want to learn to program in the future. It will not matter what language you pick to start learning programming; those data types are common among all programming languages (which is why they are called primitives). Before we start our script, we need to do one last thing – set up our environment.

Setting up the environment

In this section, we will follow a few steps to set up the environment. The goal here is to prepare an Excel file and create a Revit schedule. We will use both of these to export our data and check their values:

1. The first thing to do is create an Excel file with the name and location of our choice. To do this, open Excel, select a new blank document, and save it. I suggest you name it `EXPORT_data to excel` on your desktop for didactic purposes.

2. Then we want to open the Revit sample project. To do this, in Revit's ribbon, we want to click on **File | Open | Sample Files**. We will open `rac_basic_ sample_project`, as shown in the following screenshot:

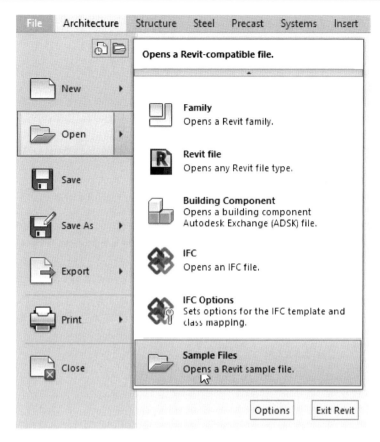

Figure 5.22 – Opening the rac_basic_sample_project in Revit

3. Create a door schedule with all of the parameters that will be changed. Change the following parameters for this exercise: **Description**, **Manufacturer**, and **Cost**. I assume you're already confident with creating Revit schedules. However, to summarize what needs to be done:

- Go to the **View** tab.

- Select the **Schedule** button from the **Create** group of buttons.

- Then, select **Schedule/Quantities** to create a new schedule.

- A new window will pop up. Select **Door** from the category list and click **OK**.

- Now, select the fields you want to include in the **Door** schedule. You may want to add at least **Family and Type**, **Description**, **Manufacturer**, and **Cost**.

4. Then, as we've seen before, click on the **Manage** tab on Revit's ribbon and then click on **Dynamo**.

5. The Dynamo interface will open on your screen. Click on **New** or type *Ctrl + N* to start a new script.

6. At the bottom of the UI, don't forget to switch from **Automatic** mode to **Manual** mode.

Now that we have completed those first steps, we are ready to start developing our script. In the next section, we will learn how to export data from Revit to Excel using our friendly tool, Dynamo!

Exporting data from Revit

For the first script, we want to export the values of some parameters: **Height**, **Width**, **Thickness**, **Description**, **Manufacturer**, and **Cost**. Those are parameters of each door type that have an instance in the project. From now on, I will present images of each part of the script so that we can create the script together. Follow me as I create the script by searching, placing, connecting, and clicking **Run** for each new node added. If you feel more comfortable, please download the entire completed script from the following link: `https://github.com/PacktPublishing/Managing-and-Visualizing-Your-BIM-Data/tree/main/Chapter05`.

In the first part of the script, what we want to do is collect all the door instances within our project and make a list of each of their types. We can do so by placing the nodes as shown in the following screenshot:

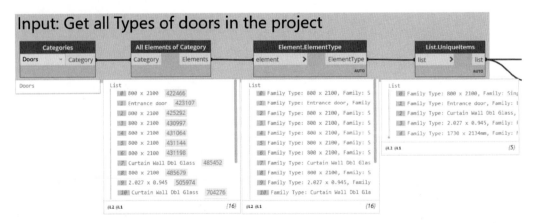

Figure 5.23 – Getting all door types that have at least one instance in the project

We start with a **Categories** node, which can be customized by selecting the category we need. In this case, I've chosen **Doors**. After that, we need to collect all element instances from the model, using the **All Elements of Category** OOTB node.

When we finally get element instances, we need to retrieve the family type. To get this information, we want to place the **Element.ElementType** node, and then we can filter the results with the **List.UniqueItems** node. This is pretty straightforward; nothing crazy is going on. We've just collected a little information on door families from the model. When you're done, click on **Run** and check whether your script looks like the previous screenshot. Also, you could expand the output preview window of each node by hovering on it and fixing it in position by clicking on the pin icon. If it is, you did well. However, it may well be the case that you missed something. But do not worry; go back and start from the beginning.

Then, we need to get the ID, which is the identification number, of each door type so that we can quickly identify them when we re-enter the data. Remember that **element id** is unique, so, for example, if a door has an ID such as **123456**, there will be no other doors with the same ID value in the same project. To get the element ID, we use the **Element.Id** node. On the other hand, we want to collect the values for a series of parameters from that element. We use **Element.GetParameterValueByName** as a function and apply it to each element in the list using a list map node. Also, please make sure that the **Code Block** node looks exactly like the following screenshot. If not, you may need to press *Enter/Return* a few times to align the strings as shown:

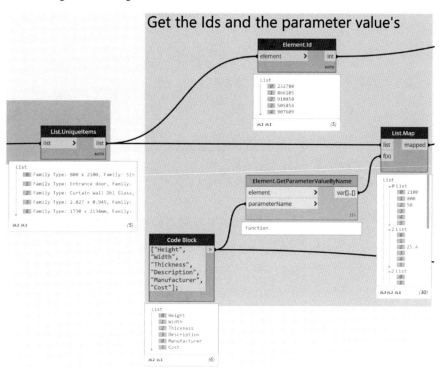

Figure 5.24 – Getting the IDs and parameter values

We want to have a list in which each sublist contains the ID of the door type and all the values of its parameters. To achieve this, we will use the **List.Transpose** node twice. In this way, we will group each ID with each door type and the parameter's values. Take a look at the following diagram, where the **List.Transpose** node has been placed before and after the **List.AddItemToFront** node:

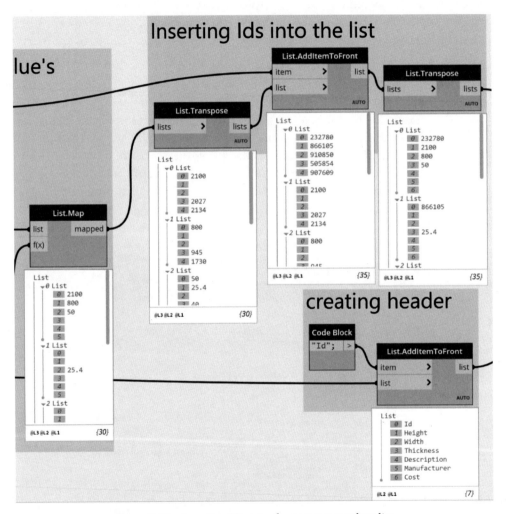

Figure 5.25 – Inserting IDs into the parameter values list

Then we want to have the ID as the first item of our parameter list, thus creating the header of our table. Indeed, the strings that you see in the following screenshot, right under the **List.AddItemToFront** node, are the column headers that we will find on our Excel sheet later on. Please note that if you're having problems connecting the inputs and outputs of the nodes, you may want to open up the completed script provided to have a better idea of what is going on.

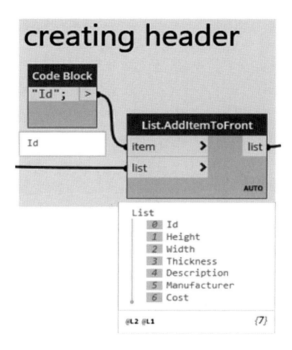

Figure 5.26 – Adding an ID to the parameter to create the header parameter group

To complete our task, we need to export the data to the previously saved Excel file. We browse the Excel file, create the code block by double-clicking on the workspace (or searching for the node in the library), and add the header as the first sublist in our data list.

Once you've completed the preceding steps correctly, click on **Run** one final time so that the **Data.ExportExcel** node sends the data to our Excel file. You'll see an Excel file opening when you run the script at this point. The final part of the script is as follows:

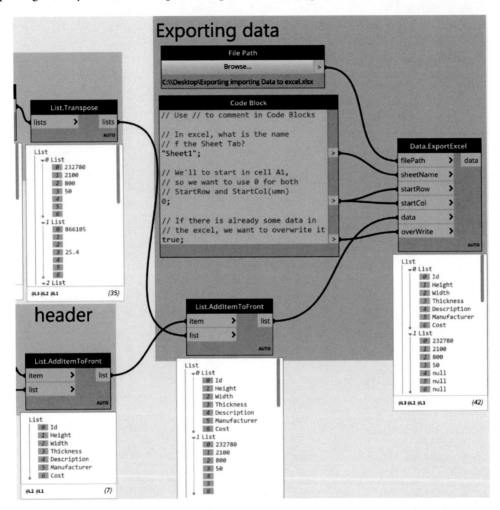

Figure 5.27 – Exporting data to Excel

Now, if you see the Excel file opening and the data being written inside it, congratulations! You've completed a Dynamo script that takes data from the Revit model, in this case from Doors, and exports that data to an external Excel file. *Remember that all of this has been done using Dynamo, Revit, and Office APIs!*

If you don't see the desired results, go back and try to find the issue. This is also good for improving your problem-solving skills. Unless you're a Dynamo ninja or a super experienced user, you will face problems all the time when developing your scripts. This is part of the game. It doesn't mean that you are not good at Dynamo. All of us need to face that kind of problem. The trick is how quickly you identify those issues and how quickly you are able to find a solution to that particular problem. Over time, you'll see that you need less and less time to find and solve issues inside the Dynamo workspace. *And that will definitely be a good sign of your skills improving!*

To wrap things up, here, we've learned how to write data from Revit to an Excel file. And once you master that, you'll be able to do so many things with Dynamo you wouldn't believe. I advise you to exercise yourself by testing other kinds of categories and different parameters as well. After a couple of exercises, you'll find yourself more and more confident! When this happens, you're ready to go on and learn a new step on the Dynamo skill ladder. You now know how to export data from Revit to Excel. But what about the opposite? What about importing data from Excel to Revit? Let's learn about that in the next section!

Updating data in Excel

As we have already mentioned, once we have completed our script to export data from Revit to Excel and clicked **Run**, an Excel tab will open, similar to the following screenshot:

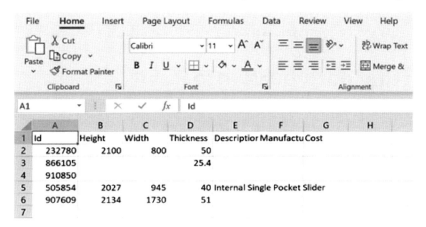

Figure 5.28 – Data exported to Excel

This data is coming from the door instances that Dynamo found inside the Revit model. We now want to update that data by making a couple of changes and then importing the updated data back to Revit. To accomplish this, we will modify a number of values as seen in the following screenshot:

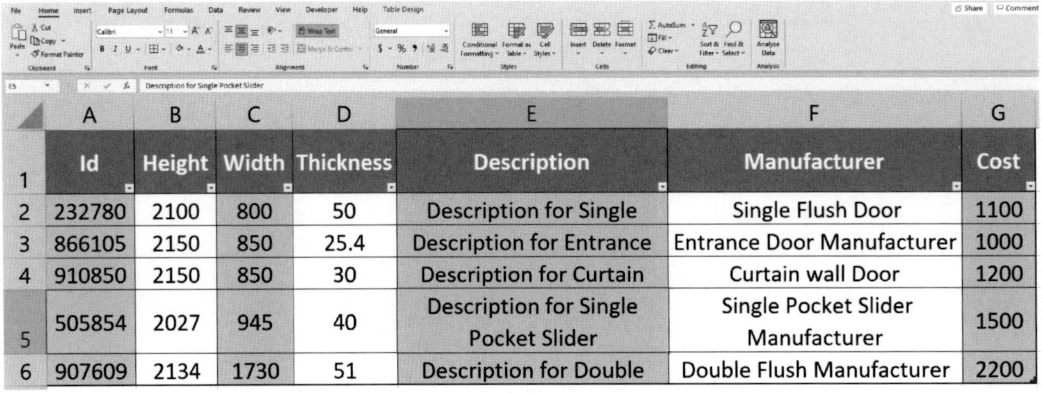

	A	B	C	D	E	F	G
1	Id	Height	Width	Thickness	Description	Manufacturer	Cost
2	232780	2100	800	50	Description for Single	Single Flush Door	1100
3	866105	2150	850	25.4	Description for Entrance	Entrance Door Manufacturer	1000
4	910850	2150	850	30	Description for Curtain	Curtain wall Door	1200
5	505854	2027	945	40	Description for Single Pocket Slider	Single Pocket Slider Manufacturer	1500
6	907609	2134	1730	51	Description for Double	Double Flush Manufacturer	2200

Figure 5.29 – Excel with value parameters modified

I've created an Excel table on that data. This will let us see the data a little bit more clearly. As we said previously, we want to update the description, manufacturer, and cost of those doors. Also, we can update geometric parameters including **Height**, **Width**, and **Thickness**. So, change those values as you want, and when you are satisfied with the changes, save the file and start the next section. We will use the updated values on the Excel file to update the doors' values inside the Revit model.

Importing data back into Revit

Now that we have modified all the values in the Excel file, let's adapt in Revit the values for the following **Door** parameters: **Description**, **Manufacturer**, and **Cost**. To follow this section using a completed version of the second script, please download it from here: `https://github.com/PacktPublishing/Managing-and-Visualizing-Your-BIM-Data/tree/main/Chapter05`.

We already know the first part of the script. It is the same as the one we created previously for exporting data to Excel. You can now choose to recreate this part of the script again, or follow those steps if you want to copy that first part from the previous script:

1. Open the first script, the one for exporting data from Revit.

2. Navigate to the first part of the script, the one entitled **Input: Get all types of doors in the project**.

3. Select the nodes shown in *Figure. 5.30* with the left mouse button.

4. Open **Edit** from the menu; you'll find it after **File** in the top-left corner of the interface.

5. Select **Copy**.

6. Now, close this file.

7. Create a new one by clicking on **File** and then **New**, and then select **Home workspace**.

8. Finally, click on the **Edit** menu and select **Paste**.

In this way, we will be collecting all the door types that have instances in the project, as we did before.

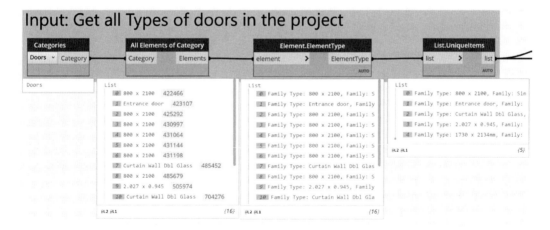

Figure 5.30 – Getting all door types that have at least one instance in the project

We will get the element ID of each of these elements, exactly like the previous script created in the *Exporting data from Revit* section. We need to use these to insert the data in the correct family type. When getting the ID, you will notice that the data type is an integer. Since the data we need to compare with data imported from Excel is a string, we need to convert the integers into a string. Notice that the lists look identical, but by connecting the **Object.Type** node, we can see that the data types are different.

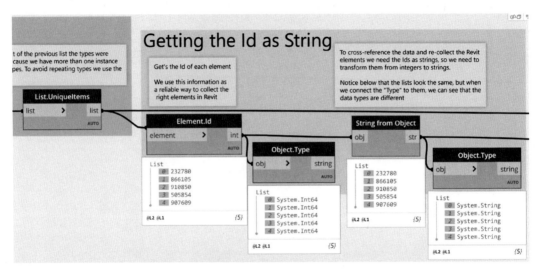

Figure 5.31 – Getting a list of IDs and converting them to strings

> **Pro Tip!**
> This workflow using the element ID is more reliable than using the family name, for example, because users cannot modify the IDs!

Besides, we need to import the data from Excel. If your Excel file is open, keep in mind that the data that Dynamo will import inside Revit is the data present in the current version of the Excel file. Dynamo will import the data present in the last saved version of it. To import data from Excel into Revit, we want to use the **Data.ImportExcel** node, as shown in the following screenshot:

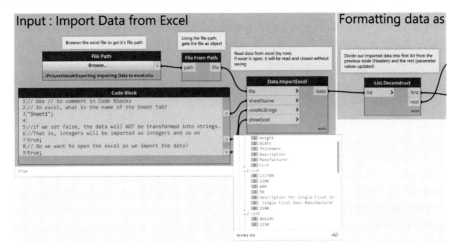

Figure 5.32 – Importing data from Excel

At this point, we've imported the data from the Excel file inside Dynamo. We now need to manage and manipulate that data to send the correct value to the right family type. The first thing to do is to format our data. We will use **List.Deconstruct** to separate the header from the data. Then we will transpose our data to have, in each sublist, all the values of the same parameter.

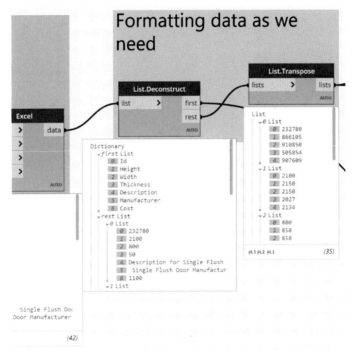

Figure 5.33 – Formatting data imported from Excel

Note that we can use many different approaches to split lists or to pick a specific item, as shown in the following screenshot:

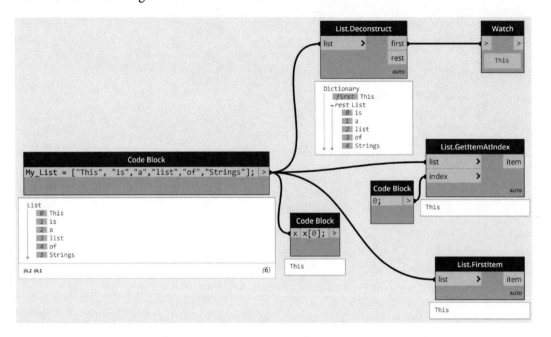

Figure 5.34 – Exploring ways to divide a list

As you can see, starting from the bottom left, we can place a code block and type x[0], where x is the variable, and 0, inside square brackets, represents the item's index. The item index is the address where that specific item can be found. In this case, *we're picking up item 0 from the list x.* Instead, we can use **List.FirstItem**, which is self-explanatory. Then we can use **List.GetItemAtIndex**, which takes two inputs. The first one is the list. The second one is the address or the index of the item we need to get. Basically, we can use this node to retrieve any item from any list. The last one is the **List.Deconstruct** node, which is quite helpful when dealing with imported data from Excel because it separates the headers from the rest of the data, as you can see in the node's output, on its right.

Next, we want to collect the doors in Revit in the same order as they appear in Excel. Here, there is a crucial element that needs to be taken into account: using **List.IndexOf**, we are searching the list of Revit elements for the IDs in the same order as they appear in Excel, and then collecting them with the **List.GetItemAtIndex** node. This is important because it will ensure that the data will always be inserted into the correct element, even if the order of the elements is changed or some types are created or deleted in the meantime between exporting and importing the data back into Revit. To summarize, we use **List. IndexOf** because we want to ask Revit *what are the addresses or indexes of those elements inside that list?* Revit will reply with a list of numbers representing each index of each object provided as input of the **List.IndexOf** node. The following screenshot shows how to place that node correctly:

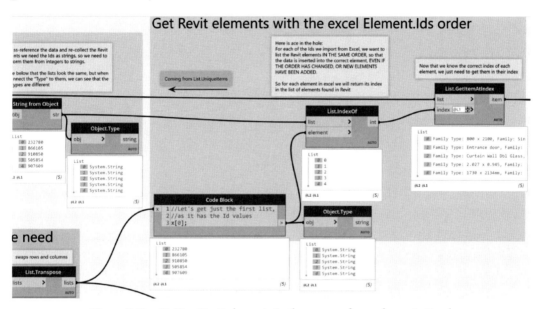

Figure 5.35 – Getting Revit elements in the same order as shown in Excel

Using the same strategy from the previous step, in the list of headers, we will query the index of the items we want to modify (**Description**, **Manufacturer**, **Cost**). Next, we will get the parameter values using **List.GetItemAtIndex**, which will allow us to get just the index of the sublists we need. At the end of this step, you will notice that we will have a list in which each sublist has all the door values for the same parameter.

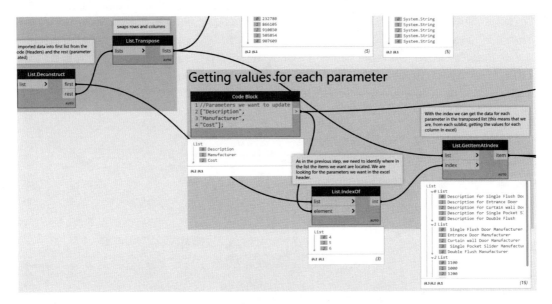

Figure 5.36 – Getting the values for each parameter

Among those parameters, **Manufacturer** and **Description** have a string object type, while **Cost** is stored as a double (a number with a decimal point), as seen previously. To check the storage type of a parameter, you need to place the **Object.Type** node and connect its input to the element you want to analyze. The parameters that we want to check the data type with are shown in the following table:

DOOR BUILT IN PARAMETERS	PARAMETER NAME
MANUFACTURER	STRING
COST	DOUBLE
DESCRIPTION	STRING

Figure 5.37 – Parameter storage types

Since the cost parameter has a data type of double, we will transform items with just numbers into numbers, applying **String.ToNumber** to each item through **List.Map**. This causes us a temporary problem: Items that contain any character other than a number will return null. To replace the null values with the write string values we already had, we will use `object is null` as a function, so every null item will be replaced by the value in the original list. Take a look at the following diagram:

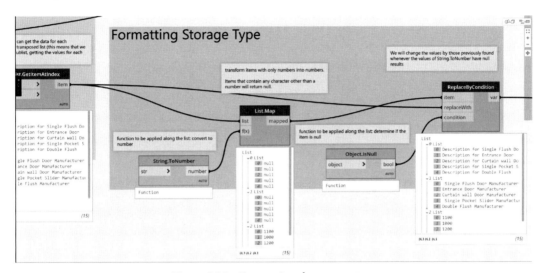

Figure 5.38 – Formatting the storage type

As you can see, to replace every null produced inside the **List.Map** node, we used the **ReplaceByCondition** node, which helped us to do exactly that. The **ReplaceByCondition** node, indeed, has been provided with three inputs:

- **item**: This is the list of data that needs to be replaced.

- **replaceWith**: This is the input where we provide data that we want to use as the replacement.

- **condition**: Here, we specify the logic of the replacement. In this case, we provided an **Object.IsNull** node. By doing so, Dynamo will check whether there are any **Null** elements in the list. If the answer is **True**, Dynamo will replace those elements using the list provided in the **item** input. If the element is not a **Null** one, Dynamo simply skips it.

> **Important Notes**
>
> Note that when we apply a function on a list with the **List Map** node, no errors will be reported when the function has not been applied successfully, for example, when trying to transform a string containing letters into a number.
>
> Note also that we could have manually selected the sublist to be converted, but this approach would have been a bit more limited since it assumes that the order of the lists will never be changed and that the same script will never be updated to use some other parameters.

We are almost done. The final step to complete inside Dynamo will be to set the values in the elements we have already collected correctly. The type of data structure we need to pass in this last node is a list in which each sublist refers to a single door type, thus enumerating the parameters/parameter values to be modified for a single type. To get this data structure, check the following diagram. Now you can run the script one last time. In the next step, we will check the updates.

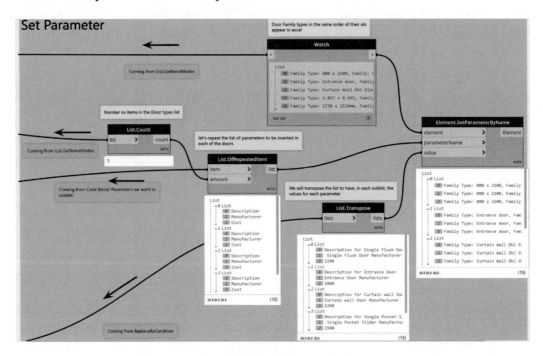

Figure 5.39 – Setting parameters at the door types

As you can see, we provided the **Element.SetParameterByName** node with three inputs. The first one is a list of our elements, in this case, our door types, that the node will target when updating the values of the **Description**, **Manufacturer**, and **Cost** parameters. The second input is the parameter name. Here, we provided a repeated list of those three parameters we've just mentioned. That is because we want to update those parameters for each family type. And because of that, we want to provide each family type with the parameter's names to update. The final input is the value input. Here, we want to provide the updated values for **Description**, **Manufacturer**, and **Cost**.

As a final step, we will check that Dynamo has correctly updated all of the data inside the schedule created previously.

<Door Schedule>

A	B	C	D
Family and Type	Description	Manufacturer	Cost
Curtain Wall Dbl Glass: Curtain Wall Dbl Glass	Description for Curtain wall Door	Curtain wall Door Manufacturer	1200.00
Entrance door: Entrance door	Description for Entrance Door	Entrance Door Manufacturer	1000.00
M_Double-Flush: 1730 x 2134mm	Description for Double Flush	Double Flush Manufacturer	2200.00
Pocket_Slider_Door_5851: 2.027 x 0.945	Description for Single Pocket Slider	Single Pocket Slider Manufacturer	1500.00
Single-Flush: 800 x 2100	Description for Single Flush Door	Single Flush Door Manufacturer	1100.00

Figure 5.40 – Checking results at the schedule

Well done! Now you've unlocked a new Dynamo superpower. You are now able to export data *from Revit to Excel* and import data *from Excel to Revit*. This is huge! You will soon see the potential of that workflow by practicing yourself and trying to solve problems that your company may encounter.

Summary

We have reached the end of this brief introduction on how to get started with Dynamo. In this chapter, we explored what a VPL is, what Dynamo is, and how and why companies and professionals are using it as a way to automate and manage models. We also learned in a very visual way the basics pertaining to the interface, the nodes, and the data types so that we are ready to take our first confident steps with this powerful software. Lastly, we got down to business and created our first two scripts, which will allow us to export parameter values from families to Excel and re-import them by changing all the values accordingly. *As we have learned in previous chapters, companies are moving toward an increasingly data-driven business model. This means that the demand for professionals who understand programming logic will be growing in the AEC industry. As a result of this chapter and this book, you will be better prepared for the challenges that will come next.*

Back to Ernesto

Luisa has given us an excellent introduction to Dynamo for Revit. By learning these two steps alone, importing and exporting data from and to Revit, you'll cover most of the office requirements in terms of automating tasks and updating information. We see power users on LinkedIn posting super-duper complex shapes, bridges, and related stuff. Those are super cool scripts to work with, but, as Luisa said previously, the average user just needs to manage data correctly. That's all. But that doesn't mean we can't create a script representing a futuristic and extraordinary shape.

I want to point out that the everyday use of Dynamo is focused on manipulating data. And that's why we're here, right? We want to manage data and take advantage of it by turning raw data into useful information. We can achieve that by using a data visualization tool, such as Power BI or Tableau. But what if, other than the data itself, we would like to include a Revit floor plan inside the data visualization tool that interacts with our charts? Wouldn't that be super amazing?! We can find the answer to that question in the next chapter. Gavin Crump, an experienced design technology professional and founder of BIM-Guru, will show us a unique workflow for importing data inside Power BI, including a Revit floor plan that interacts with the Power BI charts. That sounds crazy to me! See you in the next chapter!

Further reading

If you want to continue enhancing your knowledge of this software, I suggest the following links as free and reliable resources for self-learning:

- `https://forum.dynamobim.com`
- `https://primer.dynamobim.org`
- `https://dynamopythonprimer.gitbook.io/dynamo-python-primer`

6

Importing Revit Plans in Power BI Using Shape Files

This chapter is written by Gavin Crump

Gavin is an architect too and is the founder of a BIM consultancy company working in Australia. Gavin is very active on social media, and thanks to him, I've often learned new ways of doing "things." His level of expertise in design technologies is very high, and I am happy to have worked with him to develop this chapter. Gavin will show us a fantastic workflow on importing Revit plans inside Power BI and making them interactive with the rest of the charts. Enjoy reading!

The overall goal of this chapter is to expose you to the importance of processing Revit elements into a more workable format and how Dynamo is a powerful interoperability tool to facilitate these types of workflows. Shape files are some of the most common vector-based file types used in software and on the web in the present day, and their use will only increase in the future.

In this chapter, you will learn about the following:

- Setting up Dynamo
- What are Shape files?
- Writing our data sources for Power BI
- Setting up Power BI with Synoptic Panel
- Visualizing our data in Power BI

Technical requirements

To undertake this workflow, you will need the following tools:

- A **Revit** model that contains rooms and floor plans (we suggest the Autodesk Advanced Sample Project, which comes with each installed version of Revit).
- **Dynamo** for Revit (we suggest version 2.3.0 for the best results).
- The **Illustrator**, **Data Shapes**, and **Monocle** custom packages for Dynamo, which can be installed under the **Manage** tab in Dynamo itself.
- The **Dynamo script** available in the shared folder.
- **Power BI** (in this chapter, the **Desktop** version is used specifically).
- The **Synoptic Panel** custom visual, produced by OKVIZ.
- You can download everything you need to follow this chapter from the following link: `https://github.com/PacktPublishing/Managing-and-Visualizing-Your-BIM-Data/tree/main/Chapter06`.

In the next section, we will learn how to set up the Dynamo environment to execute the script correctly. During this chapter, if you feel you don't fully understand one or more steps, no worries. You can always go back to *Chapter 5, Getting Started with Autodesk Dynamo and Data Gathering,* by Luisa Pieper, as she covered more details about getting started with Autodesk Dynamo.

Setting up Dynamo

In this section, we are going to overview the packages needed to build the Dynamo script.

For this chapter, the report has been produced using **Revit 2020**, currently at build **2.3.0** at the time of this publication. Dynamo is available with this version of Revit by default and can be found in Revit under the **Manage** tab.

The script may be reproducible in lower builds of Dynamo, but it is likely some changes will be required depending on the features available to that respective build. The following image indicates the custom packages used to produce this script and achieve the required outputs:

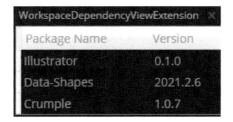

Figure 6.1 – Dynamo custom packages

Here we can see one of the packages, Crumple, in the Dynamo script:

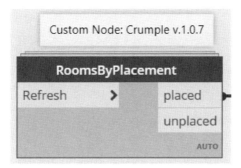

Figure 6.2 – Crumple in the Dynamo script

Later builds of these packages should work also, but for the best results, these builds will be most suitable to use. Now it is the time to download the required packages:

- Open up Dynamo, click on **Packages** from the top menu, then select **Search for a Package**.

- A new window will pop up. Wait a few seconds then type all of the required packages names as follows. At this point, please go ahead and download these packages:

- Illustrator 0.1.0

- Data-Shapes 2021.2.6

- Crumple 1.0.7

Now let's quickly see what each package is about. **Illustrator** is a small package for Dynamo that allows the production of shape files from the input of polygons in Dynamo. We will be taking advantage of this package to bridge our Revit data to Power BI successfully. The **Data Shapes** package will be used to construct a simple **User Interface (UI)** that helps users less familiar with Dynamo to comfortably run the script. **Crumple** is a package built and maintained by myself, which I have used for a few efficiency nodes to simplify the overall script.

These nodes are all written in the Python programming language and can be viewed by right-clicking the custom node, then by selecting **Edit Custom Node**. From here, you'll see a new window open in the workspace. This new window is the custom node editing environment. You will also see the background color change to a yellow one. Although this is an advanced environment to start with, you'll be ready to explore this environment in no time once you complete the book. It is beneficial to speed up the development of your Dynamo scripts.

Inside this environment, you can right-click on the node called **Python script**, then select **Edit**. Now you will see the editor for Python scripting. If you don't have any programming language skills, no worries. I want you to know that you can access the Python editor from here. In the future, you might learn this programming language to create scripts more efficiently.

Custom nodes are easily identified by the stacked graphic behind their header and have been annotated in the script for your convenience using the **Monocle** package for Dynamo.

Now that we have explored the packages that we will use to create our Dynamo script, we need to learn what shape files are. In the next section, we are going to cover precisely that and more.

What are shape files?

Power BI, at its core, is a program designed to enable us to visualize our data. When capturing our Revit model in Power BI in a visual manner, a suitable architectural diagram to use is a **floor plan** (a top-down representation of a building level). While we could export a static image of our documentation plans, a far more effective technique is introducing a responsive diagram that visually interacts with the data we capture in Power BI itself.

The most suitable file format to achieve such a workflow in Power BI is .SVG (**Scalable Vector Graphics**, or simply **Shape file**).

Shape files are used extensively in **Geographical Information Systems (GIS)**. This type of file helps us to store the shape, location, and attributes of geographical features.

Shape files can store polygons in the form of a list of vertices with attached metadata such as the shape's related name, captured in the same row of data. The following screenshot shows a typical shape file, opened in the Notepad++ application:

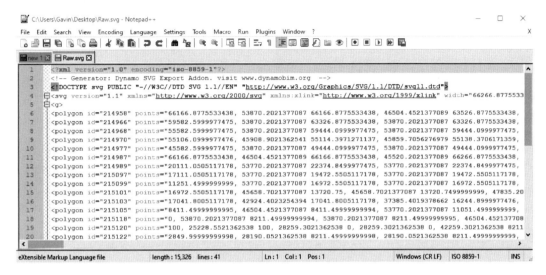

Figure 6.3 – A typical shape file opened in Notepad++

Don't worry! We are not going to write all of those rows with the keyboard. Instead, we will take advantage of the Autodesk Dynamo superpowers and create such a file.

We can see that the shape file begins with the specific versioning data of the file itself, which we usually refer to as a **Header**. Once we surpass this area of the file, we can begin specifying polygons that the file contains (beyond line 5, where we see <g>). Polygons are declared using <polygon, followed by any metadata associated with that shape – in this case, we can see each polygon in the previous file contains an ID in the form of a number. From here, the remaining content is declared as points in the form of XY coordinates, which guide the polygon's path.

Regional File Formatting

A common error that may occur in this workflow is due to the way in which Windows handles data separators in different regions. Many European nations use a comma (,) to represent a decimal place, whilst other regions typically use a full stop (.).

Should you find that your shape file is entering Power BI in a truncated (messy) format, you may need to update your computer's regional settings before generating shape files using Dynamo. It is important to review shape files before loading them into Power BI – we suggest using an advanced text editor such as Notepad++.

Overall, our goal will be to use Dynamo to produce a shape file similar to the one above, which we can import into Power BI and connect visually to our Revit room data.

In this section, we covered some basic shape file subjects, but as you can see, shape files are more than that. Next, we are going to prepare our data for Power BI.

Writing our data sources for Power BI

At this point, we will get our hands dirty!

We need to create our first piece of the script to let us visualize floor plans in Power BI. The first piece of the script usually involves the Data-Shapes package; this is because the package's scope is to create a small user interface to help inexperienced users. Many architects and engineers around the world may only need to interact with a Dynamo script just a little bit. They don't know (and often they don't want to know) how to customize a script in the Dynamo environment, and Data-Shapes is exactly what is needed. It interprets user inputs by using text bars, buttons, and other UI elements we are all used to, and then it transfers those inputs to the Dynamo engine to complete the script execution.

From this point onwards, it is strongly suggested that you have the Dynamo script provided in the shared folder open; this is so you can check Dynamo throughout the development of the script and to help you understand each point more clearly. Remember, you can find the link to the folder in the *Technical requirements* section.

In the case of this chapter, the **Autodesk Advanced Sample Project** has been used, which contains three main levels: level 1, 2, and 3. The script will be run three times, to generate three sets of shape files and their corresponding Excel data.

The Dynamo script that we are using to generate our shape file is broken down into a few key areas, we will cover them one by one throughout the chapter.

We will explore each step in more detail, but in summary, the tasks of each section are as follows:

- Understanding the script UI window using the Data-Shapes package
- Collecting and filtering all the Revit rooms
- Exporting room data to Excel
- Processing room boundary geometry
- Generating a shape file
- Manipulating the shape file to include metadata

Let's take a look at each one now. As said before, the first one involves the development of a UI window, using Data-Shapes. So, let's get started!

Understanding the script UI window using the Data-Shapes package

When building Dynamo scripts, it is important to consider who will use your scripts, taking into consideration their skill level and confidence in using visual coding. Most users would typically prefer not to open Dynamo itself if possible and instead run the script from **Dynamo Player**. The **Data-Shapes** package, as anticipated previously, is intended to provide scripters with the ability to add user interfaces to their scripts to achieve exactly this outcome. The next image shows our node layout used to generate the user interface for the script. The UI window that will pop up when the script is executed should be like the following screenshot:

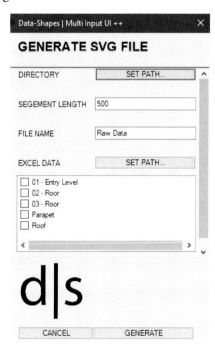

Figure 6.4 – User interface window generated using the Data-Shapes package

To generate this type of UI window, you have to use a few nodes from the DS package. Although this chapter won't cover creating a UI with the DS package, I want to show you an overall image of the used nodes. It isn't necessary to use the DS package, but I want you to understand that this may be a powerful tool to help colleagues and peers with less experience. Even if you don't know how to create a UI with this package, you should try it because it is pretty intuitive and easy to master. The UI shown previously was created with these DS nodes:

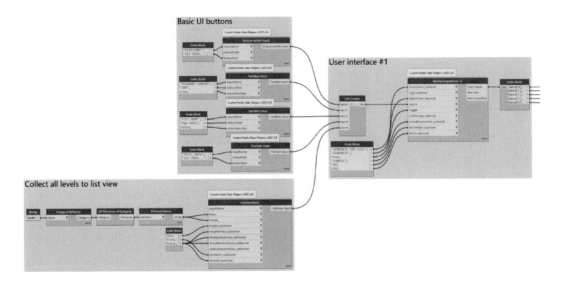

Figure 6.5 – The script section that generates the user interface

It may look complex to a basic user of Dynamo, but the logic behind constructing a Data-Shapes user interface is straightforward once explained. Each portion of the interface is scripted using dedicated nodes from the Data-Shapes package, for example, the directory path where the shape file will be written to – this will be one of the buttons of the interface itself that the user can interact with. The buttons are then collected as a list and provided to the main node, which generates and processes the actual interface displayed (the **MultipleInputForm++** node).

Upon running the script, the interface will be displayed to the user, and the script will be in a paused state until the user nominates their inputs and selects the **GENERATE** button. The inputs will then be passed through the main interface node to a code block in our script, where the inputs are split into separate rows from their current list structure. From here, these inputs are fed through the script to support the remainder of the workflow.

Again, I want you to understand the power of creating a UI using the DS package. If you try to build something with it, you'll create a fantastic UI window in no time. However, if you can't complete a UI with Dynamo, there is nothing to worry about. This chapter aims to write room data to an SVG file and then use it inside Power BI. Let's see, in the next section, how to collect Revit room data.

Collecting and filtering all the Revit rooms

The shape file that is generated will comprise all rooms that belong to a particular level of the model. The user interface requires that at least one Revit level is nominated to collect these rooms from. It is suggested that you do not nominate any levels with rooms sitting on top of one another (for example, a mezzanine floor). We use the following nodes to collect our room boundaries by level:

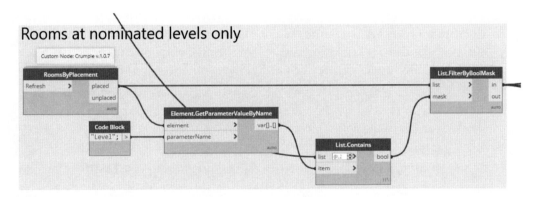

Figure 6.6 – Rooms are collected and filtered by their level

As you can see, in the first part of the script used to collect room boundaries, I've used my own **RoomsByPlacement** node. Then we use the **out-of-the-box (OOTB)** node **List. FilterByBoolMask** to filter them by level. Next, we want to create surface areas and sort them. The following screenshot shows the second part of the room boundary nodes:

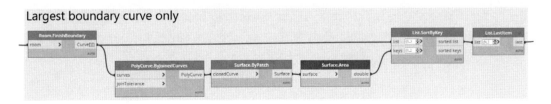

Figure 6.7 – The second part of the room boundary nodes

This part of the script starts with the **Room.FinishBoundary** OOTB node, and from here, we pass the curves to a new node responsible for creating polycurves from curves. Then we place a **Surface.ByPatch** node, which accepts the newly created poly curves as input. Finally, we use the **Surface.Area** OOTB node to sort the curves.

These portions of the script work as follows:

1. Collect all rooms in our model using **RoomsByPlacement**.

2. Using **Element.GetParameterValueByName**, check their **Level** names, and using the **ListContains**, filter the ones created by users.

3. Filter our rooms by matching level names using **List.FilterByBoolMask**. At this point, the rooms we want to review are now in the in output.

4. Obtain the room finish boundaries using **Room.FinishBoundary**. Note that these are returned as curves, so we can then join them using **PolyCurve.ByJoinedCurves**.

5. Some rooms may contain more than one boundary (for example, one with a hole inside it). To find the largest one, which must be the outer boundary, turn the boundary into surfaces using **Surface.ByPatch** and **Surface.Area**.

6. Use these areas to sort each room's related poly curves. We can do this using **List. SortByKey**, where our keys are the areas, and our lists are our curves. Note we are working across each sublist here, at level 2 (@L2).

7. We now have our curves, sorted from the smallest area to the largest for each related room. From each list, take the last item (largest area) using **List.LastItem**. Again, we are working across each sublist, at level 2 (@L2). Note that most rooms will only have one boundary, but this will still be the last item in this case.

With those instructions, you should have a great overview of what we did and why. In this section, we learned how to collect room data and use it to create the poly curves that we will export later on. In the next section, we are going to export that data to Microsoft Excel.

Exporting room data to Excel

The Power BI data source in this case will be provided in Excel format, primarily as it is a simple and workable data format both within and outside Power BI. You can adjust, add, or rearrange any data in the output with ease prior to connecting it to Power BI. A .csv file could also be generated but is more difficult to manipulate between the two programs.

In the following figure, you will see the data layout we are targeting in our `.xlsx` file, as well as the nodes we are using to construct this file:

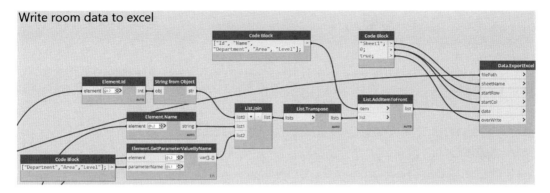

Figure 6.8 – Revit data is collected, processed, and sent to an Excel file

This portion of the script works as follows:

1. From our previously filtered rooms, collect their unique **Element Id**, **Name**, **Department**, **Area**, and **Level**. We do this using three pathways, which involve the **Element.Id**, **Element.Name**, and **Element.GetParameterValueByName** nodes. In each case, we are working across our list of rooms at level 2 (`@L2`).

2. Combine this data using the **List.Join** node.

3. Currently, our data is listed by column, but we need it to be arranged into rows. We use the **List.Transpose** node to "flip" our list structure to this format.

4. Insert a row of data to the front of the list using **List.AddItemToFront**, as well as a manually written list of headers.

5. Now that our data is in a desirable layout, we can export it to the Excel format using the **Data.ExportExcel** node. Note that we are collecting the file path originally nominated in the user interface previously.

This section was pretty straightforward. We needed to get a few attributes from the previously filtered rooms, and we combined and transposed that data.

> **Important Note**
> In case you didn't know, **transpose** means converting rows into columns and columns into rows.

We need that OOTB node to organize the data correctly for Excel. After that, we just need to provide a few things to the **Data.ExportExcel** node: a file path, a sheet name, the coordinates of the data entry point, and the data itself. The coordinates are generally 0 for both **startRow** and **startColumn** because they correspond to the top-left cell inside the Excel spreadsheet.

In the next section, we are going to do a little bit of geometry data manipulation! Let's get started.

Processing room boundary geometry

The main challenge in our workflow is that we are aiming to construct a single polygon for each related room. A polygon must be comprised of straight sides only, so we must apply an algorithm to facet all arc/curved segments of our room boundary. In the following diagrams, we can see the intended result of applying this algorithm.

The first diagram shows the segmentation algorithm set to 200:

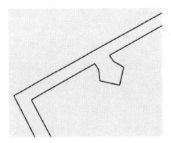

Figure 6.9 – The segmentation algorithm set to 200

The second diagram shows the segmentation algorithm set to 50:

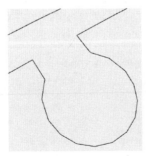

Figure 6.10 – The segmentation algorithm set to 50

The diagrams clearly show the results that can be achieved by using different values for the segmentation process. You may want to adapt this value to your needs. If you need more precise lines, you should reduce the segmentation value. On the contrary, if your output needs to be less detailed, you want to increase this value.

The following figure shows what's going on behind the scenes, inside our favorite VPL software, Autodesk Dynamo. It isn't intended for you to read each and every node, but only to show you the shape of this group of nodes, so you can find them inside the Dynamo environment using the provided script:

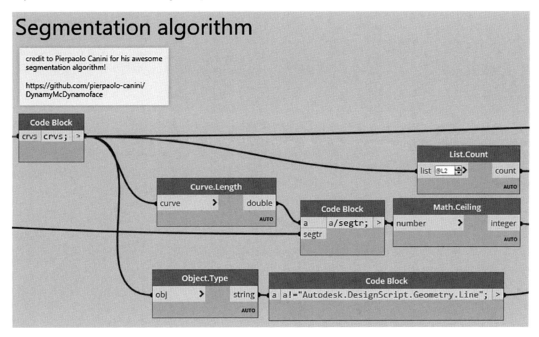

Figure 6.11 – The group of nodes that make the segmentation algorithm work

The algorithm that facets our curves is quite complex, so it is best to inspect the nodes and process in Dynamo itself. Annotations have been included in the script to summarize what is happening at each step.

To summarize, we are isolating all non-line-based edges of each room's boundary, dividing them into linear segments, and recombining the resultant segment points with the original linear edges. It is important that the order of these edges is maintained for each room in the list so a valid polygon can be created afterward.

A more precise segmentation value can be provided via the user interface to divide the curved edges more precisely. A figure between 50 and 200 is recommended as the original input for this value, as lower values may lead to a large shape file.

Once we have generated polygons from each room boundary, the polygons are mirrored across the Y plane as the shape file is read in Power BI from the bottom rather than the top, as we would typically read our floor plan in Revit.

In the next section, we will focus on the shape file part of the script. We will describe what we achieved and complete our last step to create the final version of the shape file.

Generating the Shape file

The **Illustrator** custom package makes producing a shape file quite straightforward. We have previously specified the directory for export and the filename. Unlike an Excel file, Dynamo can create a new shape file without writing data to a premade file:

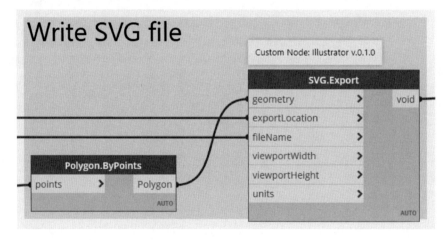

Figure 6.12 – Writing the shape file in Dynamo

The figure shows the last node, **SVG.Export**, used to write the actual shape file. It's the same thing as the node we used previously to write the Excel file. But this time, we don't need to specify the sheet name, starting row, or columns, as those are Excel's attributes. The following screenshot shows the shape file opened in Notepad++:

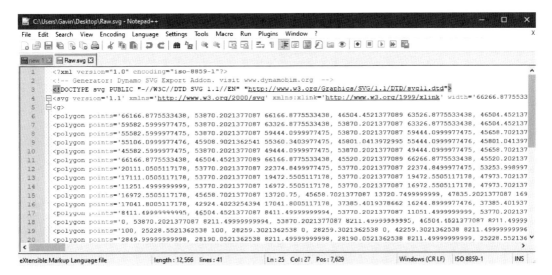

Figure 6.13 – The resulting shape file opened in Notepad++

When you finally export the shape file, you should achieve something like what is shown in the previous screenshot. As discussed previously, the shape file is just a text file containing geometry information and metadata, row by row.

In the previous section, we generated a shape file that is able to be loaded into Power BI. However, a problem in the current file is that each polygon contains points but has no associated metadata. Without something to match our Excel data to, we are unable to dynamically relate these polygons to data in Power BI, so we must introduce additional data to each polygon's row. In our next section, we will cover how to manipulate this shape file into a valid form to use in Power BI.

Manipulating the shape file to include metadata

The key piece of data we need to add to each polygon is the element ID of the room from Revit it is to represent, which we collected previously using the **Element.Id** node. We can use this to align our data between the shape file and the Excel data in Power BI.

The following figure shows a Python script we will use to insert this data into our Polygon data in the shape files:

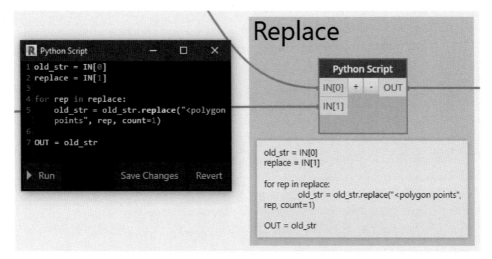

Figure 6.14 – Replacing each polygon row header using Python scripting

As you can see, we only need a couple of Python rows, literally, to make it work! To give you a bit more context, we do the same thing inside Excel, or Word, for example, when we want to find a particular text inside lots of cells, and we want to replace that text altogether. The difference is that this time, we are doing the same thing on a shape file, using simple Python code.

This Python script works as follows:

1. Collect our shape file data (as a whole string, not just by row), and store it in the first input, `IN[0]`, assigning it to the variable `old_str`.

2. Collect our replacement data (collected earlier in the script), and store it in the second input, `IN[1]`, assigning it to the variable `replace`. Note that this is in the form of a list of strings.

3. Using a `for` loop, we go through `old_str` one replacement at a time. Because we are transforming the `old_str` variable each time, it will find each occurrence of the string we are searching for to replace, `"<polygon points"`.

4. Finish by returning our output, `OUT` as the final version of `old_str`.

5. The output now represents the corrected shape file contents to be rewritten and this is done using the **FileSystem.WriteText** node. Our script now effectively writes our shape file, modifies its contents, and updates the shape file itself.

In this section, we covered the last part of the shape file creation. Using just a few code lines, we can now replace information inside the shape file itself, as we could do in an Excel or a Word file.

Overall, we went through many steps, starting with gathering data on rooms, filtering that data, generating poly curves, and then organizing everything for the shape file to be written. To summarize, you now are able to do the following:

- Collect room data.
- Filter and manipulate room data to extract poly curves.
- Organize and export this information to Excel.
- Export and replace data inside the shape file using a few lines of code.

Next, we are going to open up Power BI and learn how to use our shape file information to create a floor plan that interacts with other charts! We went through a lot of things here, so take your time and allow all that information to sink in. When you're ready, meet me in the next section!

Setting up Power BI with the Synoptic Panel

To display our shape files in Power BI, we will take advantage of the **Synoptic Panel** custom visual, shown in the following screenshot.

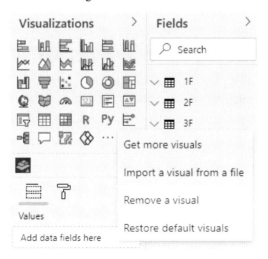

Figure 6.15 – Synoptic Panel

Like Autodesk Dynamo with packages, Microsoft Power BI can include more chart types than just the default ones. Inside Dynamo, we use the package manager to download and install different package versions. With Power BI, instead of using a package manager, we need to download new chart types using the internet browser.

In this example, we are going to download the Synoptic Panel chart, which will be responsible for processing the shape file and "drawing" the floor plan we exported from the Revit model.

To access this custom visual, follow these steps:

1. From the **OKVIZ** website, download the Synoptic Panel custom visual. This can be found at `https://okviz.com/synoptic-panel/`.
2. Open Power BI.
3. On the right side of the screen, in the bottom-right corner of the **Visualizations** panel, click on the three dots (**...**) to open up the **Options** menu.
4. Select **Import a visual from a file**.
5. Navigate to the Synoptic Panel custom visual file you previously downloaded and select it for importing to Power BI.
6. You should now see the custom visual on the **Visualizations panel**.

Our Dynamo-based workflow avoids the need for the use of the external web-based Synoptic Designer for Power BI (which can be found at `https://synoptic.design/`). By using the **Synoptic Panel** custom visual as well as our Dynamo workflow, the need for this website-based method is bypassed as we can use the panel internally inside Power BI.

Visualizing our data in Power BI

Once the script has been run for each relevant level in the model, you should have the following files for each level:

*   An Excel file, which you must load as a **Data Source** in Power BI.
*   A shape file, which you must nominate as the source for the **Synoptic Panel**.

Here are the steps to set up your **Synoptic Panel** custom visual in the report:

1. Click the custom visual button under the **Visualizations** tab.
2. Select the visual on the Power BI report canvas that has been placed as a result of the previous step.

3. Click on the **Change** button that appears at the top left, and navigate to your shape file for the building level you are reporting for. You should now see your floor plan as a collection of 2D shapes in Power BI.

4. In the **Category** and **Measure** fields of the visual, assign the `Id` field from your Excel data source. The shapes in your visual should now be connected to your data source.

A possible layout for a Power BI report is shown in the following screenshot:

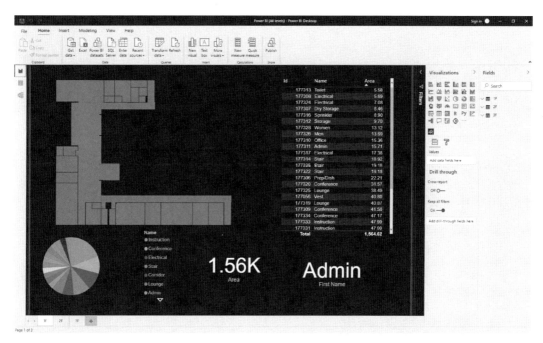

Figure 6.16 – The sample report, which contains both the data and the shape file

This report has been constructed from the following Power BI visuals:

- **Synoptic Panel** (for the shape file).
- A **Table** containing the **Id**, **Area**, and **Name** of each room from the Excel data source.
- **Cards** indicating the first name and total area (sum) of filtered rooms.
- A **pie chart** broken down by room name count.

By clicking on elements in Synoptic Panel or the data visuals, you can filter the data shown in the Power BI report. Polygons in the shape file will be dimmed or highlighted depending on whether they are in the data currently being filtered, and other visuals should likewise adjust. The following screenshot shows a report where data has been filtered by selecting a specific room name from the pie chart visual:

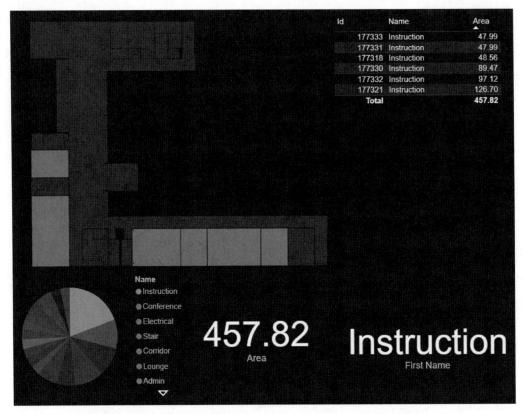

Figure 6.17 – The Synoptic Panel visual interacting with data filtering

Specifically, we have nominated the name **Instruction** from the previous pie chart. This filters the table, tallies the total area, displays the first name (in this case, the only name), and dims unselected rooms in the Synoptic Panel visual.

Should your data require updating, you can generate and overwrite your data sources (shape file, Excel) using Dynamo. From here, reload the shape file into the Synoptic Panel visual and/or refresh your data source. If your Excel data sources change name or location, you can update their path under the **Queries** tab on the **Home** panel using the **Transform data** tools.

We have now completed a workflow that successfully visualizes our Revit model in both a graphical and data-related format, tied together in a Power BI report! I find this workflow very useful because it helps us to visualize both the floor plans and their data. In this way, we have a bigger overview of what is going on with our models.

Summary

You should now understand how to create shape files from Revit elements using Dynamo scripting, generate a Synoptic Panel/shape file visual in Power BI, and combine both data and visual elements in a Power BI report.

Throughout this whole chapter, we have reinforced the need to deeply understand the data structure of files (such as shape files), as well as the fact you will often be required to manipulate them into more workable files before introducing them to programs such as Power BI.

Should you feel comfortable doing so, it is suggested to try exporting different room data in your Excel export and try different report layouts in your Power BI report. This will help you master the Synoptic Panel and cross-report data, and process Revit data from Dynamo to external data sources – essential skills for a datasmith in the AEC industry!

> **Back to Ernesto**
>
> I thank Gavin for his work and for sharing with us his fantastic workflow. He showed us an advanced way of analyzing the Revit model's data inside Power BI by importing floor plans. To accomplish that, it is necessary to create a script that converts floor plan data into a shape file. Thanks again, Gavin! I also advise you to get in touch with him on socials because he posts many exciting things that may help grow or sharpen your skills.
>
> In the next chapter, we will learn many other things through the development of a Revit issue tracker dashboard. My mind just blew up, thinking of such a dashboard! Architect Dounia Touil, from NWS Arkitektur, has written the next chapter. She is an extraordinary woman and professional working in AEC. Like the architect Gavin Crump, she'll be teaching us many things on how to take data analysis to the next level! See you later.

7

Creating a Revit Model-Check Dashboard Using Dynamo and Power BI

This chapter is written by Dounia Touil

Sadly, this is the last chapter of the experts' section. But with this chapter, written by Dounia, we will ride off into the sunset! Dounia is an architect working at NSW Arkitektur. She leverages BIM and design technology to provide professionals with methods and practices to improve project outcomes. Dounia will teach us a tremendous workflow on creating a Revit model check dashboard. And to do that, she uses, of course, our friend Dynamo and our best friend Power BI! Enjoy the reading!

An important part of the **Building Information Modeling (BIM)** process is the evaluation and auditing of 3D models to avoid production performance issues through design and construction. This has traditionally been a tedious task of running through model elements that warrant special attention for the BIM, the VDC, or the model manager.

Implementing an automated workflow for model auditing that can be run on multiple projects is crucial to ensuring quality, reducing errors, speeding up work, guiding the management to better target staff training needs, and informing the project teams on best practices to be followed.

In this chapter, we will go through the main steps to create a **Revit model check dashboard**, also referred to as a **model health check** or **model audit**. These steps include the following:

1. Identifying what data to track in **Revit**
2. Collecting and exporting data using **Dynamo**
3. Building a dashboard using **Power BI**

The key learning outcomes from this chapter can be summarized as follows:

- Learn how to identify what data to track for conducting a Revit model check.
- Learn how to collect, organize, and export relevant data from a Revit model to Microsoft Excel using Dynamo as a visual programming tool.
- Learn how to use the exported data to build a dashboard with an easy-to-consume graphical format using Power BI.

By the end of the chapter, you will be able to create your own Dynamo script to collect data from the Revit model, export that data into Excel, and use it to develop a Power BI dashboard. By using these simple-to-leverage tools, you will be able to audit, track issues, and interactively visualize your model's data.

Technical requirements

To follow along, these programs will be required:

- Autodesk Revit v.2020.2.5, Dynamo v.2.3.1, and the Dynamo packages listed in the following screenshot:

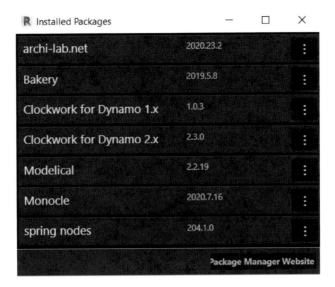

Figure 7.1 – Dynamo packages – technical requirements

- Microsoft Excel and Microsoft Power BI Desktop
- Synoptic Panel by OKVIZ: `https://okviz.com/synoptic-panel/`
- Synoptic Designer: `https://synoptic.design`
- A Revit sample file or a project file of your choosing

All the Dynamo scripts shown in this chapter can be found here: `https://github.com/PacktPublishing/Managing-and-Visualizing-Your-BIM-Data/tree/main/Chapter07`.

> **Important Note**
> Since Dynamo and Packages are frequently updated, changes compared with the screenshots and diagrams presented in this chapter can be expected. Any program version outside of what is listed in the *Technical requirements* section would need to be tested by the reader.

Identifying what data to track in Revit

In this section, we are going to explore both the criteria and a list of data categories we will be targeting later inside our Dynamo script. Before we create our dashboards, we need to identify what data to gather and, more importantly, why we need to gather it. To help us identify what to track, the data needs to fulfill certain criteria.

Criteria

Before building the Revit model check dashboard, we first need to identify what data to track, and what data will later be visualized. "There are five important criteria to think about when deciding what to track" (*Kunkel, J. (2019). Revit Dashboards the Cheap and Easy Way, Autodesk University*):

- **Quantifiable**: The data is countable.
- **Trackable**: The data is within the Revit model.
- **Changes over time**: The data is changeable over the different project phases.
- **Impact on model performance**: The data affects the model's integrity or "health." This criterion is particularly important for model auditing as, over time, the accumulation of certain elements in a Revit model could result in poor model performance, slow opening and synchronization times, incorrect data scheduling, or even file corruption.
- **Worthwhile beyond the project**: The data can provide project teams with new insights about the project.

Some of the data that satisfies those criteria includes, for example, the project information, the file information, or the in-place family information. We want to track the project information because it represents the model's "business card." The project information contains data pertaining to the organization, the project address, and the delivery date, for example. We want to track the file information data as it can help us, for example, with monitoring the Revit file size over the different project phases. We want to track the in-place family information within the model to detect any over usage or accumulation that can cause a decline in model performance.

We will now explore other categories of information we will be gathering in the following section.

Potential data to track

To perform a Revit model check, we will follow the previously mentioned criteria to select what could potentially be tracked. This list does not include all possible items, but it does represent the most important ones that comply with the criteria:

- **Project Information**
- **File Information**
- **Model and Detail Groups**
- **In-Place Families and Generic Models**
- **Links and Imports**
- **Purgeable Elements**
- **Views**
- **Placed Elements**
- **Warnings**

> **Note**
>
> In this chapter, we will focus on a collection of the data mentioned in the list of "potential data to track." However, you can customize the list and target other categories of information to suit your company's or project's needs.

In this section, we started the path for collecting our model's data. We explored the criteria that our data must satisfy to help identify what to track, and we learned some of the most important data categories to collect for model auditing. Next, we are going to learn how to collect and export information from Revit to Microsoft Excel using Dynamo.

Collecting and exporting data using Dynamo

In this section, we are going to learn what the Dynamo script is made of. We want to start developing our Dynamo script that will collect data and save it to an external Excel file. This section is divided into smaller subsections. Each one is useful for completing a specific task of the whole workflow. In the next subsections, we will not go too much into the technical details, assuming you are now more confident with Dynamo, and you know what an **Out Of The Box (OOTB)** node is, what a **Python Script** node is, and how to ask for help on the Dynamo BIM forum, as has been explained by Luisa Pieper in *Chapter 5, Getting Started with Autodesk Dynamo and Data Gathering*.

Collecting data

To access and process Revit data, we will use Dynamo. The main advantages of using Dynamo in this step are its flexibility in terms of how to filter the information and structure the data, as well as its ability to export data into different platforms.

After identifying the data to track to perform the Revit model check, we will build a Dynamo script to collect the data we are interested in.

Dynamo script

To collect the data necessary for conducting a Revit model check, a single Dynamo script has been used. It combines different groups that perform data collection for our previously mentioned list of potential data to track. The script functions using a combination of **Out Of The Box Nodes (OOTB)** nodes as well as **custom** nodes. The latter have been annotated using the **Monocle** package (**Monocle** > **package usage** > **package usage doge** > **Annotate Custom Nodes**). The final Dynamo script should look like the one shown in the following diagram, where each set of nodes is organized under its respective group:

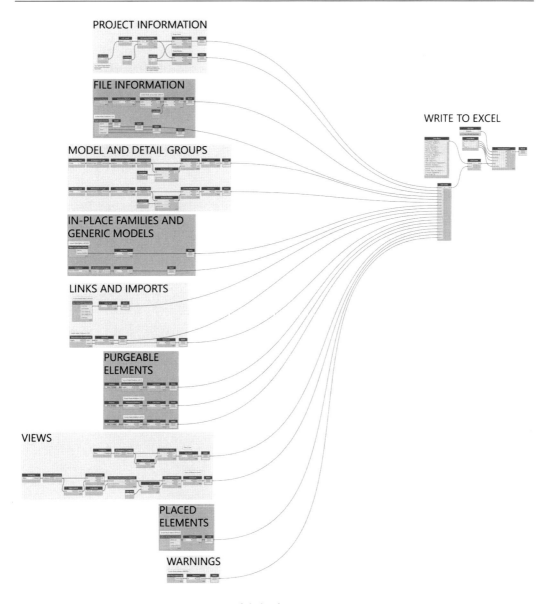

Figure 7.2 – Revit model check – Dynamo script overview

It is neither a big nor a complicated script. The most important part when developing a Dynamo script is not the node placement, but rather the logical flow of information. Where does the information come from? Where do we need to collect it? Where does it go and how? These are the complex parts of developing a script, the thinking process, not the script itself.

> **Note**
>
> As it is difficult to visualize the totality of the script and its content in a single image (*Figure 7.2*), we will break it down in the next subsections into its different groups for ease of understanding and follow-up. Each group title of the overview diagram corresponds to the title of each subsection.

We will now create the different parts of the script shown in the overview diagram. First, we want to collect the project information from the Revit model.

Project Information

Project information parameters such as the project name and number will be retrieved from the Revit file and used on the model check dashboard.

We will use a **Python Script** node in Dynamo to retrieve the project information parameters quickly and easily. To start with the project information data gathering, place a Python Script node, double-click the node to open the Python Script editor, and enter the code as follows (don't forget to click on **Save Changes**):

```python
import clr


clr.AddReference("RevitNodes")
import Revit
clr.ImportExtensions(Revit.Elements)


clr.AddReference("RevitServices")
import RevitServices
from RevitServices.Persistence import DocumentManager
doc = DocumentManager.Instance.CurrentDBDocument


clr.AddReference("RevitAPI")
import Autodesk
from Autodesk.Revit.DB import *


doc = DocumentManager.Instance.CurrentDBDocument
```

```
project_info = FilteredElementCollector(doc).
OfCategory(BuiltInCategory.OST_ProjectInformation).
ToElements()[0]
```
```
project_info_parameters = project_info.Parameters
```
```
output_list = []
```
```
for parameter in project_info_parameters:
        output_list.append([parameter.Definition.Name,
            parameter.AsString()])
```
```
OUT = output_list
```

The first few lines of code are boilerplate, while the rest will help us to retrieve the `ProjectInfo` object using `FilteredElementCollector`, and iterate through each parameter, outputting its name and value. With these few lines of code, we retrieved the project information object, and from that we collected its parameters. Next, we iterated through the project parameters with a `for` loop and printed the results in an output list.

The preceding Python script outputs all the project information parameters at once; therefore, we need to take what we want to track precisely from the outputted list by getting the desired items such as **Project Name** and **Project Number** using the **List. GetItemAtIndex** OOTB node, as shown in the following diagram:

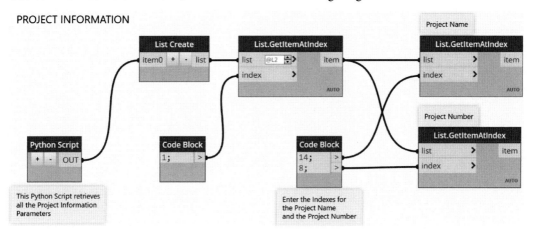

Figure 7.3 – Project information – Dynamo script

This example is the only one using textual programming. Next, we will rely solely on visual programming to collect data, starting with file information data.

File Information

File information is data related to the Revit model file, such as the file size and the file version. The file size is a metric to keep track of for a good overall performance and stability. The following diagram shows the Dynamo script used to collect the file size information and the file version information:

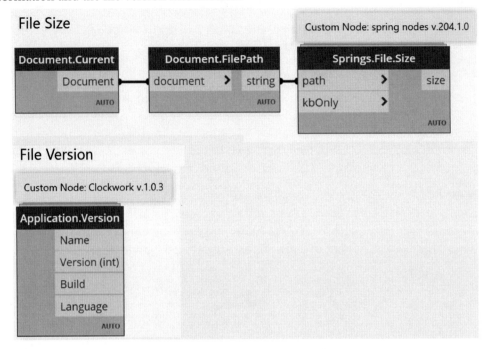

Figure 7.4 – File information – Dynamo script

The script quickly gets the file size of the current document using the **Springs.File.Size** custom node from the **Spring nodes** package as well as the Revit version using the **Application.Version** custom node from the **Clockwork** package.

Note

The Dynamo script used for the collection of the file information data (*Figure 7.4*) contains custom nodes. However, there are alternatives, often longer ones, for getting tasks done using only OOTB nodes inside Dynamo. Getting the file version information, for example, can be completed using only OOTB nodes as shown in one of the many "concepts" by Marcello Sgambelluri in his latest book (*Sgambelluri M. (2020). Dynamo and Grasshopper for Revit Cheat Sheet Reference Manual*).

Once the project and the file information have been collected, we can now look into gathering data related to Revit elements that are placed within the 3D model.

Model and Detail Groups

In Revit, model or detail elements can be grouped together and then placed in the project to help in maintaining consistency among repeated elements. However, there are certain behaviors to avoid when working with groups, such as "putting datum objects in groups, nesting groups, grouping hosted elements and their hosts together, using attached relationships in groups and mirroring groups" (*Vandezande, J. and Krygiel, E. (2016). Mastering Autodesk Revit Architecture 2016*). All these rules make it hard for novice Revit users to master groups. Knowing how many groups are within the model can help detect any abuse of the use of this tool. If there are too many groups in the model, perhaps this can be regarded as an opportunity for training or a quick refresher on best practices to follow?

The following two diagrams show the Dynamo script used to collect information related to model and detail groups:

Model Groups

Detail Groups

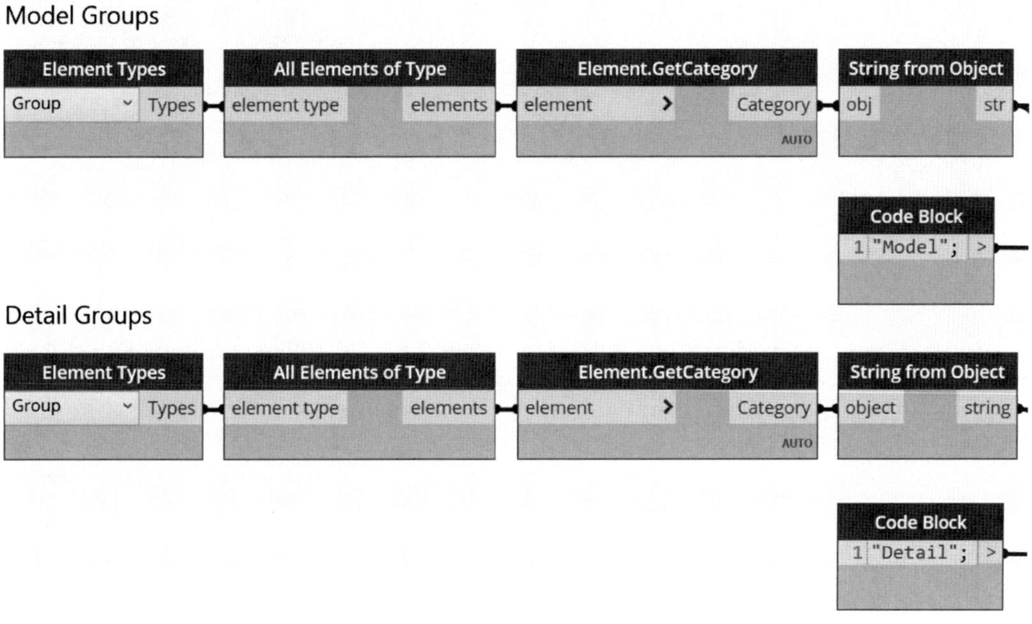

Figure 7.5 – Model and detail groups – Dynamo script (part 1)

Figure 7.5 shows the first part of the script, which consists of getting all the groups within the model using **Element Types**, followed by **All Elements of Type** OOTB nodes, and then getting their category by using an **Element.GetCategory** OOTB node. *Figure 7.6* shows the second part of the script:

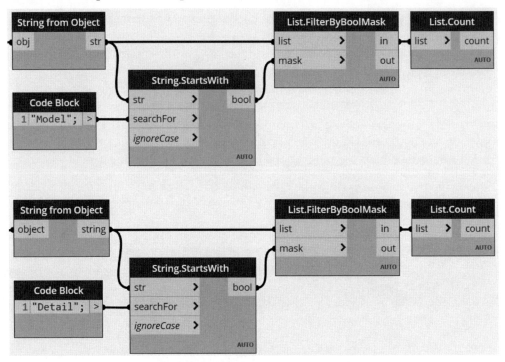

Figure 7.6 – Model and detail groups – Dynamo script (part 2)

Using the **String.StartsWith** OOTB node and, searching for `"Model"` in the element's category name, we get the model group count. Following the same logic, we also get the detail group count by searching for `"Detail"` in the element's category name.

We will now collect information regarding other Revit elements, namely, in-place families, and generic models.

In-place families and generic models

In-place families can be created in the context of the Revit model. Unlike loadable families, they are only available in the project in which we create them. Although in-place families are easy to use, it is recommended to narrow their number down as they affect the model's performance, especially if they are being copied multiple times in the project.

The Dynamo script shown in the following diagram quickly gets the number of generic models and in-place families in the Revit model using OOTB nodes and the **Report on Inplace Families** custom node from the **Bakery** package:

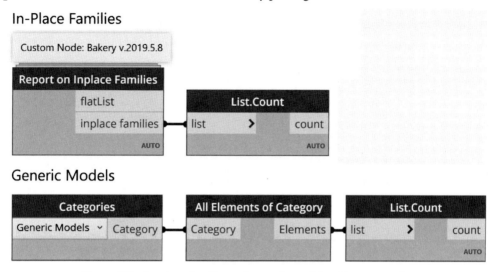

Figure 7.7 – In-place families and generic models – Dynamo script

If a project continuously encounters a high number of in-place families and generic models, maybe this can be regarded as an opportunity to review educational training for the design teams?

Next on our data collection list are links and imports. Whether it is CAD or Revit files, we will see how we can get their count in Dynamo.

Links and Imports

Opening a Revit model that hosts multiple links can take a long time to load. Keeping an eye on both linked Revit files and linked CAD files is necessary to prevent slow opening and synchronization times as well as other performance issues.

The following diagram shows the Dynamo script, which detects all the links and imports in the current project file:

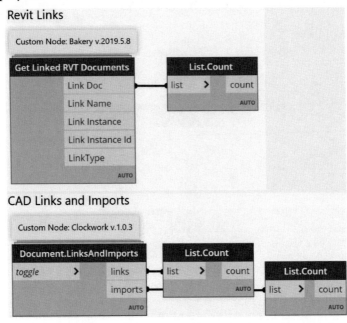

Figure 7.8 – Links and imports – Dynamo script

We get all the linked Revit files using the **Get Linked RVT Documents** custom node from the **Bakery** package along with the imported and linked CAD files using the **Document. LinksAndImports** custom node from the **Clockwork** package.

> **Note**
>
> Importing CAD files should be used carefully and thoughtfully. Instead, use the CAD link (**Insert > Link CAD**). The reason is that imported CAD files can be difficult to find in the model, can slow down the model's performance, and novice users can explode them, which then results in an undesirable list of imported line patterns. In the next subsection, we will learn how we can report on, and eventually delete, unused line patterns.

After collecting the links and imports, we can now look into unused objects within the model: purgeable elements that require cleaning up on a regular basis.

Purgeable Elements

After working on a Revit model for a while, purging unused elements is a good routine to follow. Revit offers the possibility to purge unused views, families, and text styles using the **Purge Unused** command (**Manage** > **Purge Unused**). However, it does not offer the possibility to purge other elements, such as unused view templates, filters, and line patterns, which forces the model manager to clean up these elements manually or by using third-party add-ins.

The following diagram shows the Dynamo script used to collect purgeable elements:

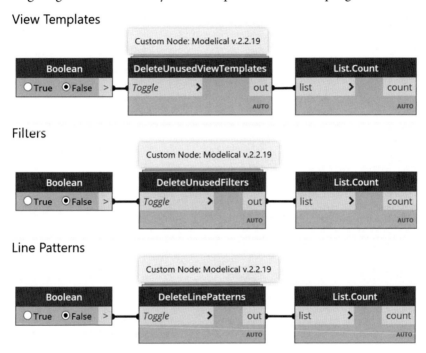

Figure 7.9 – Purgeable elements – Dynamo script

Using custom nodes from the **Modelical** package, we get unused view templates, filters, and line patterns. We can either delete them by setting the **Boolean** to **True** or keep them for reporting purposes by setting the **Boolean** to **False**.

> **Note**
>
> There is another longer method for collecting and deleting unused view filters by using only OOTB nodes (*De Filippi, D. (2021). Dynamo Shorts – Ep 8 – Delete Unused View Filters, YouTube video*), and another one for collecting and deleting line patterns also by using OOTB nodes (*Sobon, K. (2014). Delete Imported Line Patterns Using Dynamo, archi-lab.net*). As mentioned previously, there are multiple methods for completing a task using Dynamo, which might or might not rely on custom nodes. Some companies prefer to rely solely on package-free scripts as they are easier to deploy across project teams. Others prefer to take advantage of the available packages and ensure solid management of dependencies using tools such as the **Orkestra** cloud-based platform (`https://www.orkestra.online`).

Next on our data collection list is views in the project browser.

Views

With many people working in a Revit model at once, it is challenging to keep the number of views to a minimum, which results in longer times required to navigate between views. Having an overview of the number of views in a Revit model is a good way to monitor the status of the project browser and reduce the model file size.

The following two diagrams show the Dynamo script used to get the views count as well as a report on views not placed on sheets:

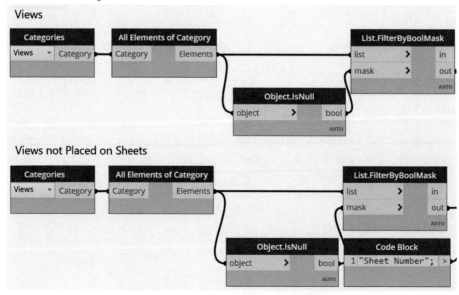

Figure 7.10 – Views – Dynamo script (part 1)

The first part of the script (*Figure 7.10*) consists of getting all the views within the model using **Categories**, followed by **All Elements of Category** OOTB nodes. This way, we get the total number of views in the model. The second part of the script filters out the views that are not placed on a sheet.

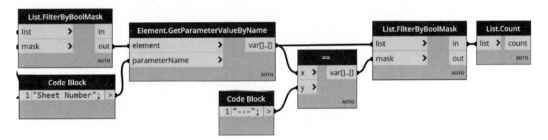

Figure 7.11 – Views – Dynamo script (part 2)

We want to focus on the number of views not placed on sheets, as their number tends to extend what is really needed and these views are usually not part of the deliverables. We can do that by looking for a sheet parameter such as: **"Sheet Number"** and filter our list using a **List.FilterByBoolMask** node, as shown in *Figure 7.11*. The **in** outputted list represents the views not placed on sheets, whereas the **out** outputted list represents the views placed on sheets. The total count of these views combined should naturally equal the views count.

At this point, we have now collected data related to specific Revit elements, but what if we want to get information related to every single element placed in the 3D model? We will now see how we can do that.

Placed Elements

For model auditing, it is useful to get every single element in a Revit model with its corresponding category.

The following two diagrams show the Dynamo script used to collect all the elements in the model:

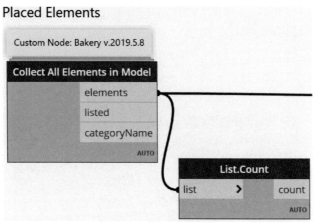

Figure 7.12 – Placed elements – Dynamo script (part 1)

Using the **Collect All Elements in Model** custom node from the **Bakery** package, we get the elements count (*Figure 7.12*). We can also get the count by category, as shown in *Figure 7.13*, and later narrow the list down to filter specific categories:

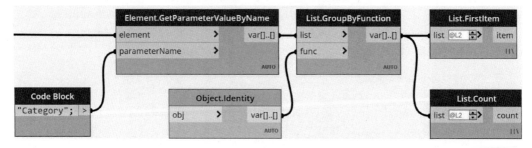

Figure 7.13 – Placed elements – Dynamo script (part 2)

We do that by using the **Element.GetParameterValueByName** node and searching for the parameter name **"Category"** and then the **List.GroupByFunction** node. However, if the model contains too many elements, this second part of the script may take some time to run or even crash, which represents the downside of it and why we have been creating specific graphs for each data category we want to track.

The last data we want to look at in our data collection list is the warnings.

Warnings

Warnings affect the model's performance as well as the file size. The higher the number of warnings, the higher the file size will be. It is therefore advised to solve warnings regularly. However, warnings can be challenging to solve as Revit's **Review Warnings** dialog box (**Manage** > **Review Warnings**) does not offer a severity score for these warnings nor any classification system, and you would quickly become discouraged when dealing with hundreds or even thousands of them.

To perform a quick check of the number of warnings, we can use the following graph:

Figure 7.14 – Warnings – Dynamo script

Using the **Warning.GetWarnings** custom node from the **archi-lab.net** package, we get a count of the warnings. This small graph represents the last part of the Dynamo script for the Revit model check (*Figure 7.2*).

We will now create another Dynamo script that goes further into parsing Revit warnings and later into building the Power BI dashboard for warnings.

Working on large projects in Revit often means that team members are responsible for specific areas of the project or entire floor plans. It then becomes useful to structure the warnings according to their level, to be able to assign the task of resolving them to the team members in charge. The following Dynamo script will allow us to assign a severity rating to the warnings, organize the warnings according to their associated level in Revit, and more:

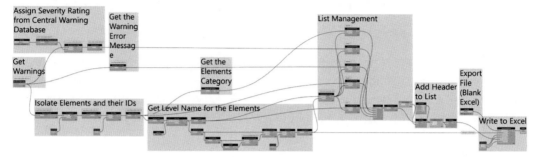

Figure 7.15 – Warnings – Dynamo script overview

Using several custom nodes from the **archi-lab.net** package, which handles warning parsing, and other custom nodes from the **Clockwork** and **spring nodes** packages, this Dynamo script offers the possibility to achieve the following:

1.   Get warnings and assign a severity rating to them, as shown in the following diagram:

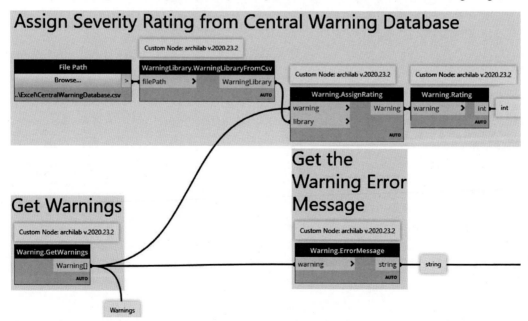

Figure 7.16 – Warnings – Dynamo script step 1

The severity rating ranges from 1 to 3 (1. ignorable, 2. moderate, and 3. severe) using a **central warning database** (*Sobon, K. (2017). Digging through Revit warnings to find meaning, archi-lab.net*).

> **Important Note**
>
> The central warning database is a `.csv` file that gathers the Revit warning error messages and the severity score assigned to them. This file can rarely regroup all the Revit warnings, but it will rather be a selection of warnings according to the team's preferences on what type of error message to prioritize. The selection of warnings as well as the severity score is set within the company's standards. If the warning error message is not within the central warning database, the rating will return a 0 value, which means that there is no severity rating assigned to that specific error message.

2. Isolate the elements causing the warnings, as shown in the following screenshot:

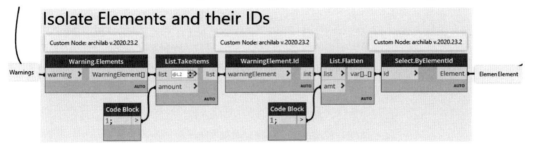

Figure 7.17 – Warnings – Dynamo script step 2

Using the **WarningElement.Id** custom node from the **archi-lab.net** package, the script retrieves the element's unique ID.

3.   Get the level names, which will later be the sheet's name in Excel, as shown in the following two diagrams:

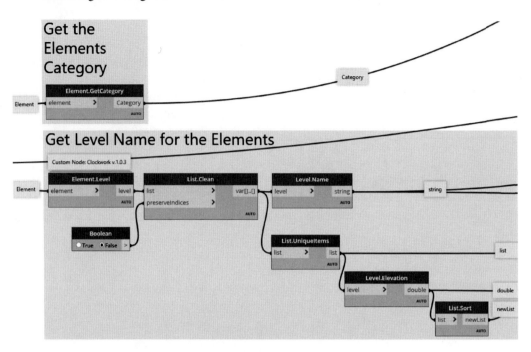

Figure 7.18 – Warnings – Dynamo script step 3 (part 1)

The first part (*Figure 7.18*) consists of using the **Element.GetCategory** OOTB node to get the element's category and the **Element.Level** custom node from the **Clockwork** package to locate the element's level. The second part (*Figure 7.19*) consists of list management techniques:

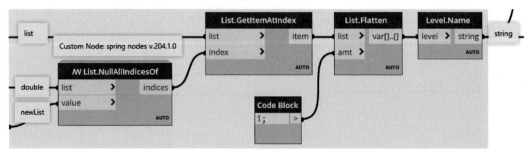

Figure 7.19 – Warnings – Dynamo script step 3 (part 2)

By using several list management nodes, we get a sorted list of the project's level names.

4. Organize the collected data, as shown in the following two diagrams:

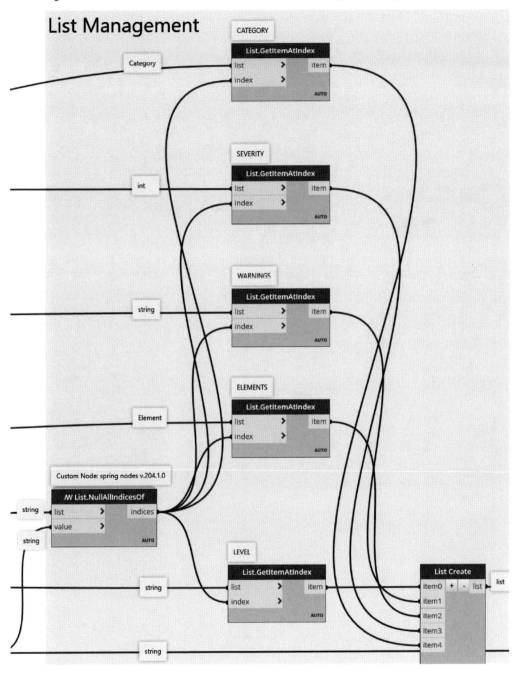

Figure 7.20 – Warnings – Dynamo script step 4 (part 1)

We can now organize the warning's script data, namely, **Level**, **Warnings**, **Elements**, **Severity**, and **Category**, into their respective lists using the **List Create** node. Next, we add a header to each list, as shown in the following diagram:

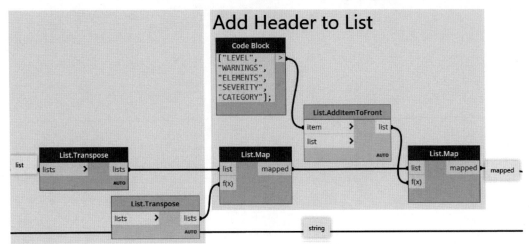

Figure 7.21 – Warnings – Dynamo script step 4 (part 2)

The headers are inserted using a **Code Block** node to specify the title and a **List. AddItemToFront** node.

5. Export the organized data to a blank Excel file, as shown in the following diagram:

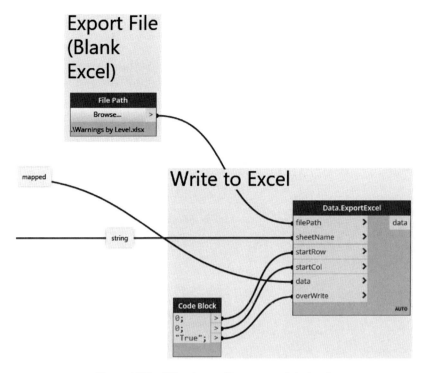

Figure 7.22 – Warnings – Dynamo script step 5

Using the **Data.ExportExcel** node, we can export all our organized data regarding warnings into a blank Excel file. The resulting Excel document will have multiple sheets reflecting the project's levels. Opening the Excel document will quickly reveal which floors accumulate more warnings, meaning that team members responsible for those floors can be advised on dealing with their warnings without interrupting the rest of the team working on floors that may not have many warnings.

We are now finally done with data collection. In this section, we learned how to use both OOTB nodes and custom nodes to create Dynamo scripts that collect the most important data for Revit model checks, namely, **Project Information, File Information, Model and Detail Groups, In-Place Families and Generic Models, Links and Imports, Purgeable Elements, Views, Placed Elements,** and **Warnings**. We also learned how to create a more advanced Dynamo script to parse warnings and restructure them according to their associated level in Revit.

We will now export the collected data to an Excel file.

Exporting data

Dynamo allows us to export data to different platforms such as **Microsoft Excel**, **Microsoft Access**, **Microsoft SQL Server**, **MySQL**, and **SQLite**. Many data serialization formats, such as **XML**, **JSON**, and **HTML**, are supported. In our case, we will use Excel due to its simplicity of use and popularity among AEC professionals.

The following diagram shows the last section from the Revit model check Dynamo script shown in the overview diagram (*Figure 7.2*):

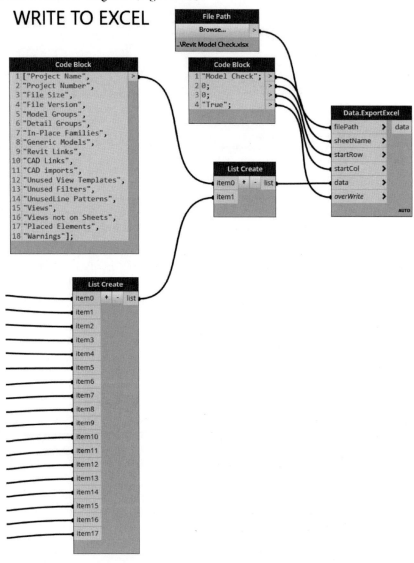

Figure 7.23 – Write to Excel – Dynamo script

Using a **Code Block** node inside Dynamo, we can specify a title for each type of data we have gathered previously, and which will later be the header of our Excel document. From there, we can export our data into a blank Excel file, using the **Data.ExportExcel** OOTB node.

Figure 7.24 shows what the resulting Excel document from the **Revit model check Dynamo script** seen in *Figure 7.2* should look like:

	A	B	C	D	E	F	G	H	I
1	Project Name	Project Number	File Size	File Version	Model Groups	Detail Groups	In-Place Families	Generic Models	Revit Links
2	DRAMMEN	201528	292 MB	2020	474	354	305	202	15

	J	K	L	M	N	O	P	Q	R
1	CAD Links	CAD imports	Unused ViewTemp	Unused Filters	Unused LinePatter	Views	Views not on Sheets	Placed Elements	Warnings
2	121	76	1	5	1	1130	432	132696	1633

Figure 7.24 – Revit model check spreadsheet – Excel

The resulting Excel document will consist of a table with two rows. The first is the title for each type of data and the second is the data itself, which is mainly numerical information coming from the script's parts we have seen in the previous subsections. The columns represent each type of data gathered previously and defined earlier in this chapter as our list of "potential data to track."

Figure 7.25 shows what the resulting Excel document from the **Warnings Dynamo script** seen in *Figure 7.15* should look like:

	A	B	C	D	E
1	LEVEL	WARNINGS	ELEMENTS	SEVERITY	CATEGORY
2	Plan U1	A wall and a room separation line overlap. One of them may be ignored wher	Wall	2	Walls
3	Plan U1	A wall and a room separation line overlap. One of them may be ignored wher	Wall	2	Walls
4	Plan U1	A wall and a room separation line overlap. One of them may be ignored wher	Wall	2	Walls
5	Plan U1	A wall and a room separation line overlap. One of them may be ignored wher	Wall	2	Walls
6	Plan U1	A wall and a room separation line overlap. One of them may be ignored wher	ModelCurve	2	Lines - <Room Separation>
7	Plan U1	A wall and a room separation line overlap. One of them may be ignored wher	ModelCurve	2	Lines - <Room Separation>
8	Plan U1	Highlighted walls overlap. One of them may be ignored when Revit finds roon	Wall	3	Walls
9	Plan U1	A wall and a room separation line overlap. One of them may be ignored wher	Wall	2	Walls
10	Plan U1	A wall and a room separation line overlap. One of them may be ignored wher	Wall	2	Walls
11	Plan U1	Highlighted walls overlap. One of them may be ignored when Revit finds roon	Wall	3	Walls
12	Plan U1	A wall and a room separation line overlap. One of them may be ignored wher	Wall	2	Walls
13	Plan U1	A wall and a room separation line overlap. One of them may be ignored wher	Wall	2	Walls
14	Plan U1	Highlighted walls overlap. One of them may be ignored when Revit finds roon	Wall	3	Walls
15	Plan U1	Highlighted room separation lines overlap. One of them may be ignored wher	ModelCurve	2	Lines - <Room Separation>
16	Plan U1	Highlighted walls overlap. One of them may be ignored when Revit finds roon	Wall	3	Walls
17	Plan U1	A wall and a room separation line overlap. One of them may be ignored wher	Wall	2	Walls
18	Plan U1	Highlighted walls overlap. One of them may be ignored when Revit finds roon	Wall	3	Walls
19	Plan U1	Room Tag is outside of its Room. Enable Leader or move Room Tag within its	RoomTag	1	Room Tags

Figure 7.25 – Revit warnings spreadsheet – Excel

The document consists of multiple Excel sheets reflecting the project's levels. Each sheet has five columns, representing the warning's script data, namely, **Level**, **Warnings**, **Elements**, **Severity**, and **Category**.

> **Important Note**
>
> The reason for creating two Excel documents is to be able to create two pages on the Revit model check report. The first page is for **Revit model check overview**, which combines useful information for BIM managers and model managers to monitor the overall "health" of models. The second page is for **Warnings**, which resumes warnings by level and severity, and is often useful for team members working on the model, so as to evenly distribute the responsibility for dealing with warnings.

We have now learned how to achieve two of the three main steps to create a Revit model check dashboard. In the first step, we learned how to identify what data to track in Revit using five criteria: **quantifiable**, **trackable**, **changes over time**, **impact on model performance**, and **worthwhile beyond the project**.

In the second step, we learned how to create Dynamo scripts to collect the data we are interested in. In our case, we gathered data from the Revit model regarding **Project Information**, **File Information**, **Model and Detail Groups**, **In-Place Families and Generic Models**, **Links and Imports**, **Purgeable Elements**, **Views**, **Placed Elements**, and **Warnings**. We also learned how to export that data from Dynamo to Excel.

Next, in the third and final step, we will explore ways to create a Power BI dashboard using the collected data and how to easily perform updates.

Building the Power BI dashboard

Power BI is a Microsoft software for data visualization, allowing the conversion of data from different sources to build interactive dashboards. In our example, we will use the free version, **Power BI Desktop**, to create a visual report based on the Excel document created in the previous section. Once the data is imported into Power BI, the software allows a multitude of customization and filtering of the information.

> **Note**
>
> For this step, you will use your own created Excel document. Whether you have been using a Revit sample file or a project file of your choice, you can follow the instructions in this section to achieve similar results.

The Revit model check report will consist of two pages; the first page is an **overview** dashboard, which resumes the data we have previously gathered using the Revit model check Dynamo script (*Figure 7.2*) and exported to the Excel document shown in *Figure 7.24*. The following diagram shows the overview dashboard:

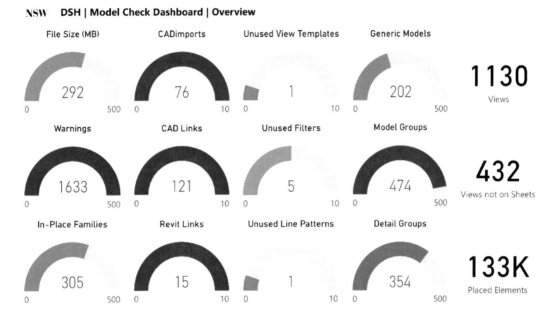

Figure 7.26 – Overview – Report page

The data is visualized using the **Gauge** visual in Power BI. Maximum and minimum values have been set for each type of data in the **Gauge** axis, along with conditional formatting to automatically generate the color according to predefined values. These configurations allow us to highlight which element requires more attention from the project team as well as get an instant overview of the overall health of the model.

The second page of the report will consist of the **Warnings** dashboard, as shown in the following diagram:

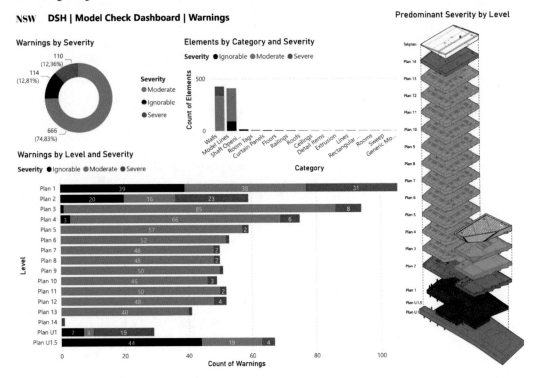

Figure 7.27 – Warnings – Report page

The warnings dashboard is composed of different interrelated and dynamic visuals highlighting the warning's data. We will now focus on how to build this dashboard using the Excel document created previously and shown in *Figure 7.25*.

We start building our dashboard by opening a blank Power BI document and inserting a project title using **Insert** > **Text box**, and a company logo using **Insert** > **Image**. Next, we will import the Excel data and start creating the visuals.

We will now explore how we can import the Excel data gathered previously.

Importing Excel data

In Power BI, Excel data can be imported through the following steps:

1. Select **Home** and click on the icon to import data from an Excel workbook.

Figure 7.28 – Importing Excel data into Power BI – Step 1

2. From the open window, select the Excel document to import and then select **Open**.

Figure 7.29 – Importing Excel data into Power BI – Step 2

3. From the navigator dialog box that appears, choose the data to import and then select **Load**.

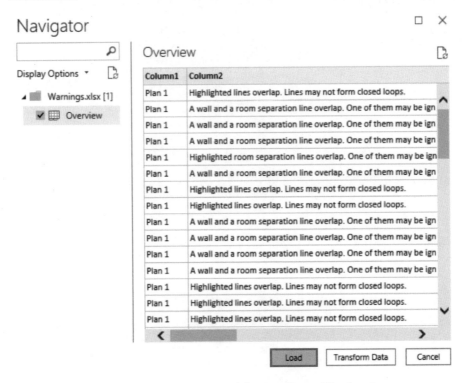

Figure 7.30 – Importing Excel data into Power BI – Step 3

> **Important Note**
>
> In this example, all Excel sheets shown in *Figure 7.25* representing the project levels have been merged into a single overview sheet. This can be achieved by using the **Power Query Editor** when importing data into Power BI, or beforehand in Dynamo by flattening the list of data and exporting it as one single sheet. In the dataset's 09_Warnings.dyn file, you will be offered the option to export the warning data into different Excel sheets and/or as a single overview sheet. The latter will come in handy for building the warnings report page, while the former is useful for quickly navigating warning data per project level without having to create a visual report.

4. Once loaded, the data is now available on the **Fields** pane. Column1 has been renamed to **Level**, Column2 to **Warnings**, Column3 to **Elements**, Column4 to **Severity**, and Column5 to **Category**.

Figure 7.31 – Importing Excel data into Power BI – Step 4

Once the data is imported into Power BI, we can start the fun part of creating the visuals using the **Visualizations** pane.

Creating visuals

In Power BI, the **Visualizations** pane allows a wide range of visuals to be inserted, depending on the type of data we want to visualize. To create a visual, we simply click on the type of visual we are interested in and then we drag the column's data from the **Fields** pane to the **Visualizations** pane.

In our example, we will use the following:

- The **donut chart** to visualize warnings by severity. Drag the **Warnings** column to **Values**, and the **Severity** column to **Legend**.

- The **line and stacked column chart** to visualize elements by category and severity. Drag the **Elements** column to **Column values**, the **Category** column to **Shared axis**, and the **Severity** column to **Column series**.

- The **stacked bar chart** to visualize warnings by level and severity. Drag the **Warnings** column to **Values**, the **Level** column to **Axis**, and the **Severity** column to **Legend**.

We have now learned how to import Excel data into Power BI, as well as how to create visuals using Power BI's **Visualizations** pane. Next, we are going to learn how to use a custom visual to insert a project illustration into the dashboard and link it to the data.

Inserting a project illustration

To insert a project illustration (plan, section, or 3D), we need to download **Synoptic Panel** from the Power BI custom visuals library (`https://okviz.com/synoptic-panel/`). After the download, we import Synoptic Panel into our Power BI dashboard by performing the following steps:

1. Select the ellipsis icon from the **Visualizations** pane, as shown in the following diagram:

Figure 7.32 – Importing Synoptic Panel into Power BI – Step 1

2. Select **Import a visual from a file** from the menu, as shown in the following diagram:

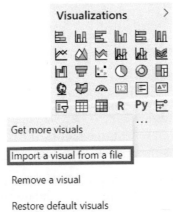

Figure 7.33 – Importing Synoptic Panel into Power BI – Step 2

3. Select the custom visual file in the folder you downloaded it to and then select **Open**, as shown in the following diagram:

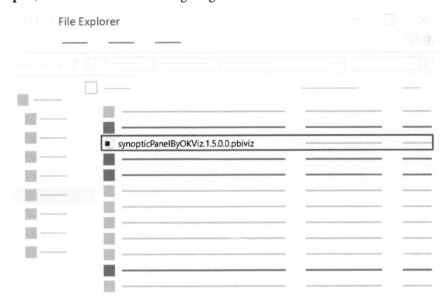

Figure 7.34 – Importing Synoptic Panel into Power BI – Step 3

4. The visual will appear as a new icon in the **Visualizations** pane, as shown in the following diagram:

Figure 7.35 – Importing Synoptic Panel into Power BI – Step 4

Once **Synoptic Panel** is imported, we can use **Synoptic Designer** to create our project illustration. Synoptic Designer (`https://synoptic.design/`) is an online tool that connects areas in an image with attributes in the data model, filling each area with a color related to a value in the data model.

The following diagram shows a project illustration example:

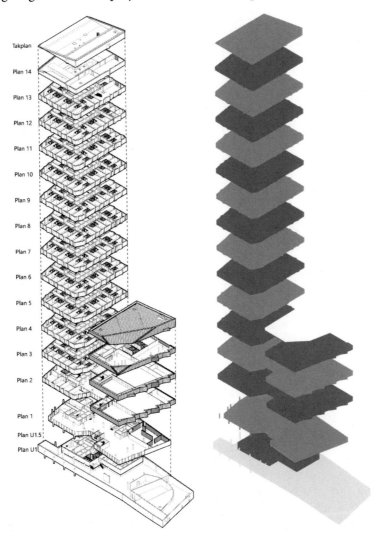

Figure 7.36 – Project illustration (Left: Underlay – Right: Shaded regions)

The image on the left represents the underlay illustration, which is a 3D exploded axonometric taken from Revit (**File** > **Export** > **Images and Animations** > **Image**), while the image on the right represents the shaded regions illustration created in **Adobe Illustrator** reflecting the different project levels. These shaded regions will come in handy inside Synoptic Designer to quickly pick the areas.

> **Note**
>
> In this example, the shaded regions illustration was quick and easy to make using an Adobe program. However, doing it for plans can be tedious and time-consuming. Follow Gavin Crump's method explained in *Chapter 6, Importing Revit Plans in Power BI Using Shape Files*, to automate the creation of Revit plans in Power BI using shape files (*Crump, G. (2021). Importing Revit plans in Power BI using shape files*).

To apply a color scheme to the project illustration and send it to Power BI, use a 3D illustration of your project (similar to the shaded regions illustration shown in *Figure 7.36*) and follow these instructions:

1. Drag the illustration on `https://synoptic.design/`.

2. Define the areas representing the different project levels by using **Automagically discover bitmaps areas** and enter the area name, in this case, the level names of your project (it's important to make sure the names match exactly the values in your data otherwise Power BI will not be able to match it).

3. Click on **Change image** and then choose the underlay illustration (similar to the underlay illustration shown in *Figure 7.36*).

4. Click on **Export to Power BI** and then right-click on the image and choose **Save Image as** > **SVG document (*.svg)**.

5. Click on the Synoptic Panel icon in the **Visualizations** pane in Power BI, and drag in the data from the **Fields** pane to the **Visualizations** pane. Drag the **Level** column to **Category**, and the **(Count of) Warnings** column to **Measure**.

6. Load the SVG document created using **Local maps** and begin to customize!

We now have our dashboard ready to be shared with the project team!

Exporting and sharing the dashboard

The final step consists of exporting the report to share it with our collaborators or the design team or for a simple work routine.

We can share our report by doing the following:

- **Creating a PDF**: In Power BI desktop, you can create a static PDF by clicking on **File** > **Export** > **Export to PDF**.

- **Publishing to the Web**: In the Pro version of Power BI, you can publish your interactive report to the web by clicking on **File** > **Publish** > **Publish to Power BI**.

- **Taking a screenshot**: The simplest, quickest, and easiest way to share the report is by taking a screenshot using the snipping tool to create a static image of the dashboard.

Updating the dashboard

Once we have created and reviewed the Power BI dashboard, there is going to be specific occasions for performing updates, for example, before a coordination meeting with the project team, for the BIM or model manager's own work routine, or before an important delivery, to make sure the 3D model is properly organized and free from any undesirable elements.

The good news is that once we have gone through and learned how to complete the three steps of this chapter, namely, identifying what data to track in **Revit**, collecting and exporting data using **Dynamo**, and building a dashboard using **Power BI**, it will be a straightforward process to update the created dashboard. To do that, there are two additional steps to include:

1. Running the Dynamo script via **Dynamo Player**
2. Updating the **Excel** document inside Power BI

In the first step, we can run the Dynamo script for **Revit model check** (*Figure 7.2*) as well as the Dynamo script for **Warnings** (*Figure 7.15*) using Dynamo Player, as shown in the following screenshot:

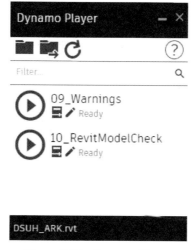

Figure 7.37 – Dynamo Player

These two scripts are compatible with Dynamo Player (all the inputs and outputs were specified for the scripts to properly function with Dynamo Player). Revit users, or another person performing the model audit, will not have to open the Dynamo script and run it, but simply run it from the Revit environment. This will update the Excel documents.

Running the 09_Warnings script will update the Excel document we created earlier in this chapter (*Figure 7.25*), and running the 10_RevitModelCheck Dynamo script will update the Excel document shown in *Figure 7.24*.

In the second step, we update the dashboard inside Power BI by right-clicking on the data source, which is available on the **Fields** pane, and choosing **Refresh data**, as shown in the following screenshot:

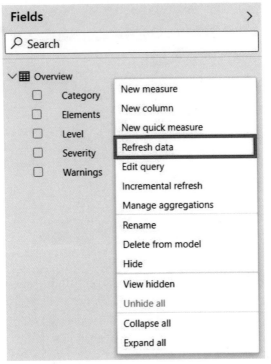

Figure 7.38 – Power BI – Updating the Excel file

Voilà! The dashboard is now updated with the latest data!

We have reached the end of this section dedicated to Power BI. We first learned how to import Excel data, and then we learned how to add an interactive illustration using a custom visual. Finally, we explored ways of sharing the created dashboard with the project team and how to update the dashboard with the latest model data.

Summary

Creating a model check dashboard is a powerful utility for the BIM, VDC, or model manager to help track trends, monitor the overall "health" of a Revit model, try to solve issues throughout the life of a project, and educate teams to be more efficient. The methods currently used to collect data are often manual and time-consuming or require third-party add-ins. In addition, reviewing this data can be difficult if the reviewer has little knowledge of the collected information or no time to go through it all.

With the method we explored in this chapter and with easy-to-leverage tools, such as Dynamo and Power BI, developing a workflow to automate the collection and visualization of data can be easy to replicate.

We learned how to identify what data to track using measurable indicators that impact the model's performance, and we also learned how to collect, organize, and export relevant information from the model. Finally, we learned how to use the exported data to build a dashboard for easy understanding and consumption.

In the next chapter, *Ernesto Pellegrino* will take us for a deep dive into Dynamo datatypes, where we will learn about primitive datatypes as well as more complex ones. The following chapter will give us a good basis to start creating more advanced scripts using Dynamo.

Back to Ernesto

Wow! Thanks Dounia, for helping me on this book project and for sharing your knowledge. As with all the other industry experts, I probably sent hundreds of emails to Dounia related to the work to do on the chapter. Every time, she and the others replied kindly and professionally. This could be obvious to you, but it isn't. A few more people wanted to join this project, but I picked Manuel, Luisa, Gavin, and Dounia because of their professionalism and competence. Thank you all for being part of this adventure!

Now, back to the book, the next chapter was challenging for me to write. It is not easy to come after the last four chapters, but I'll try to write good content just like the industry experts did. Indeed, the next chapter will focus on Autodesk Dynamo by deep diving into lists, indexes, string manipulation, regex, and more! We will need all of that in our everyday Dynamo tasks. You don't know how much of a life-saver regex is. Let's find out!

Section 3: Deep Dive into Autodesk Dynamo

Section 3 is the final part of the book and will be a completely hands-on section where you will get your hands dirty with the various exciting workflows available in Dynamo. I will guide you in setting up the tools, while teaching you more advanced data science skills. Along the way, we will create both Dynamo scripts and Power BI dashboards, exploring more and more features and software customizations. Indeed, this section will include a deep dive into Dynamo data types with a view to understanding more advanced workflows. Next, we will use our skills to create a script that places families inside the Revit model. Before the end, we will learn how to gather data from multiple Revit models at once and visualize that data inside Power BI. The last chapter will focus on Power BI, showcasing a workflow that collects information using a Google form and creating a live connection to our dashboards. You will have a lot of fun!

This section comprises the following chapters:

- *Chapter 8, Deep Dive into Dynamo Data Types*
- *Chapter 9, Using Dynamo to Place Family Instances*
- *Chapter 10, Gathering a Revit Model's Data from Multiple Models at Once*
- *Chapter 11, Visualizing Data from Multiple Models in Power BI*
- *Chapter 12, Having Fun with Power BI*

8

Deep Dive into Dynamo Data Types

In *Chapter 5*, *Getting Started with Autodesk Dynamo and Data Gathering*, Luisa did an excellent introduction to primitives such as strings, Booleans, and integers. In this chapter, we are going to deep dive a little more into Dynamo data types. We will need to learn how to perform more complex operations on strings, lists of strings, lists of lists, and so on because they are essential in our day-to-day script development. So, for example, we will answer questions such as the following:

- If I have a list of lists, how can I precisely select one item or a list of items?

- In a list of strings, if there is part of each string I want to update, how do I tell Dynamo to do that?

- If I want to split a list into two groups, should I use `if` statements?

- Also, if I want to perform naming rules validation, how can I do that?

Besides that, we will also focus on lists, indexes, how they work, and how to manage them. We will also introduce regular expressions, sequences of characters for building search patterns. At first glance, regular expressions look like geoglyphs, and in a sense, they are. If you haven't seen one before, a regular expression looks like this:

```
(? =,*?\d)(?=,*?[a-zA-Z])[a-zA-Z\d]+
```

It's weird, isn't it?! Those regular expressions, also known as **regEx**, will speed up replacing, splitting, and finding strings, especially when we deal with extensive data lists. Also, there are regEx versions for almost any programming language out there. That means that we have regEx for our Dynamo as well. However, not to worry; more on that later.

After this first part, we will discuss what variables and conditional statements are. Keep in mind that those computer science concepts are more or less the same for any programming language if you decide to study one later on. And I hope you do so, as we learned about hybrid jobs in *Chapter 1, Introducing Units of Digital Information*, and how they are essential in our digital economy.

To wrap things up, in this chapter, you will cover the following topics:

- What lists and indexes are, and how to manage them
- How variables and conditional statements work
- How to manage and work with strings
- What regular expressions are, and how they work

So, in the first section of this chapter, we will deal with some more complex operations on primitives. Let's do it!

Figure 8.1 – How to RegEx

Technical requirements

There is no need to download a full script, as I want you to develop it alongside this chapter. To follow along with the instructions in this chapter, you need to have Autodesk Revit and Dynamo installed. Any version of Revit will work as long as it is later than 2019. With Dynamo, you should be good to go with any version after 2.4. To make sure you have the correct software version, open up Dynamo, click on the question mark symbol from the top menu, and select **About**. The version number can be found right next to **Dynamo Revit**.

In case you missed it, in *Chapter 5, Getting Started with Autodesk Dynamo and Data Gathering*, Luisa told us how to download any Dynamo version. No worries; there is no need to go back. The link for that is here: `https://dynamobuilds.com/`.

OK. Now we're ready to start the chapter. Enjoy your reading!

Introducing lists and indexes

In this section, we are going to learn *everything about lists and indexes*. And to do that, we are going to use my favorite snack – chips! So, let's start by implementing a practical example. Let's say that we have a Revit model containing 100 chairs, and those chairs are placed on different levels. Now, let's compare that to chips.

Imagine we take a chip bag and grab one chip. We can do the same with Dynamo, *but instead of grabbing, we are selecting one element*, a chair, in this case, from the 100 available. Take a look at the following diagram:

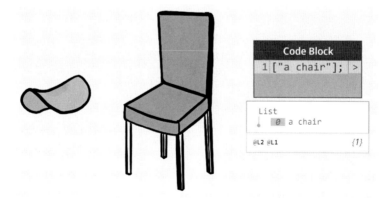

Figure 8.2 – Comparison between Dynamo and chips for selecting one element

As you can see, when we select one chair from the Revit model, we end up with a list containing exactly one element.

Next, instead of selecting only one element, we could select a bunch of them, let's say 20 chairs. The following diagram shows the comparison with chips:

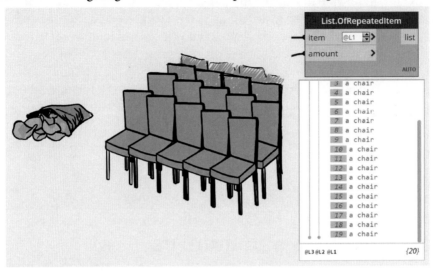

Figure 8.3 – Comparison between Dynamo and chips for selecting multiple elements

As shown in the preceding diagram, when we select those 20 chairs from the Revit model, we end up with a list containing the 20 elements, the same as the bag of chips.

Next, we might want to select chairs and group them by their position, for example, using floors. That means we will end up with a list containing several lists, each containing multiple elements. Take a look at the following diagram:

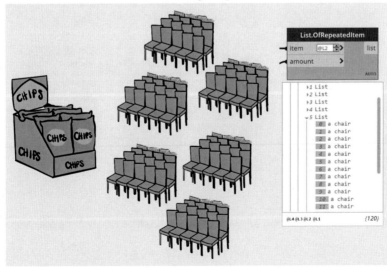

Figure 8.4 – Comparison between Dynamo and chips for selecting and grouping elements by floor

Starting from the left of the diagram, we have the multipack of bags of chips, where the multipack represents the main list, with each bag representing a sub-list, and the chips inside each bag representing single items. At the center of the diagram, we have the same organization, but with chairs inside Revit. All groups are on the main list. Each sub-group represents a sub-list and so on with the single chairs. To the right of the diagram, we have a code block indicating what we just said in relation to chips and chairs.

Of course, we can continue by saying that we can have a truck full of multipacks, and those are full of bags of chips, and so on. The same can be said of Dynamo, having a list with lists containing other sub-lists, and so on. We could go on forever, but let's keep it simple here! There is no need for overcomplicated examples. Now, I hope I didn't make you hungry. If so, grab a bag of chips or possibly something healthier and come back. We are now going to switch to Dynamo.

If you want, you can do the same things on your computer, but this isn't mandatory. For example, you could read first and exercise later. You choose.

Anyway, inside Dynamo, we can create the same example we were talking about before. I've used **Code Blocks** for that, which is an **OOTB node**. OOTB nodes mean out-of-the-box nodes, the ones that come as default Dynamo nodes. Now, take a look at the following diagrams:

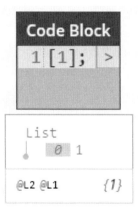

Figure 8.5 – Code block with one element

The preceding diagram shows one element inside one list. The total number of the elements can be found at the bottom-right of the code block output preview (the white rectangle), inside curly brackets. In this case, we have a total of one element. At the top of the output preview, you can read the word **List**, and right below that, there is a gray rectangle with the number 0 inside it. This number 0 is the index of the element in that list. The index of an element is its position inside a specific list. Think about it like the address of someone or something. In this previous example, *the address of element number 1 is 0*. By the way, you can activate the output preview by doing a mouse-over twice at the bottom of the node. I know that's tricky, but this is how Dynamo works right now. When you do that, you'll see a white rectangle, and when it appears, do another mouse-over on it to show the full output preview. From here, you can click on the pin icon to fix the output preview in position. I always do that as it annoys me doing a double mouse-over every time I need to check outputs! Take a look at the following screenshot. It shows the two mouse-overs and the click on the pin to fix in position. I hope it helps.

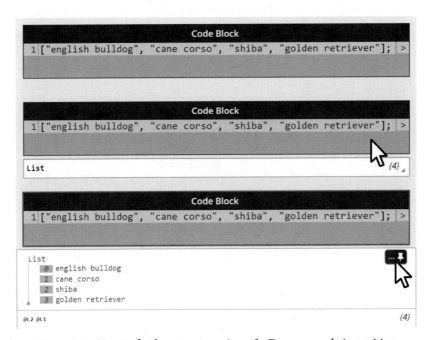

Figure 8.6 – How to fix the output preview of a Dynamo node in position

All you have to do is to hover twice and then click on the pin symbol. After a few attempts, you should get used to it. Moving on, let me now take another example. Let's say we have a list of strings like the one shown in the following screenshot:

```
Code Block
1 ["english bulldog", "cane corso", "shiba", "golden retriever"];  >
```

```
List
    0  english bulldog
    1  cane corso
    2  shiba
    3  golden retriever
@L2 @L1                                                              {4}
```

Figure 8.7 – List of strings using dog races

As you can see in the preceding screenshot, there are four strings inside that list. Each element or item of that list, in this case, displays a breed of dog. *If somebody were to ask you, what's the index of the golden retriever?*, as you can see from the gray rectangle to the left of the string, the answer is 3. This could be counterintuitive, but it isn't. As we wrote four strings, we were expecting that the position of the last item in the list has to be 4. But the answer is 3. Why is that? The truth is that computers start counting from 0 and not 1, as we do. This is important. Although we wrote four strings using four dog breeds, *the last element index is always the total number of the elements minus one.* For this reason, the index of the last element is 3 and not 4, and the index of the first element is 0, and not 1.

By the way, I forgot to say that this list with the four dog breeds is comparable with the bag of chips, where the bag is the list itself, and the chips are the dog breeds. The following example will be equivalent to the multipack containing many bags, each one containing many chips. Take a look at the following screenshot:

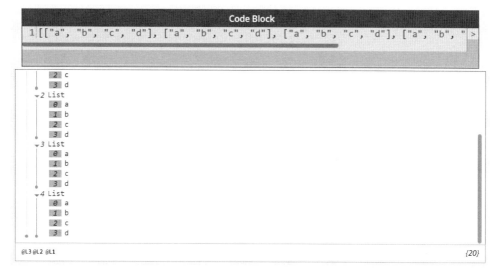

Figure 8.8 – List of lists, with each one containing a bunch of strings

Code Block shows the main list, containing a few other lists containing four strings. I want to ask you another question as the screenshot shows lists **2**, **3**, and **4**. *How many lists are there in total?* Remember that computers start counting at 0. Knowing this, we immediately also know that there must be, before list 2, a list 1, and a list 0. So how many lists are there? The answer is 5, and I am sure you got it correct too. If you take another look at the preceding screenshot, I am also sure you noticed the text in the bottom-left corner of the output preview window. You can see **L3**, **L2**, and **L1** preceded by an **@ symbol**, as shown in the following diagram:

Figure 8.9 – Levels of the list

The reason is that *lists inside Dynamo are organized in levels*. Those levels are more or less a way of grouping things. The previous example involved a list made by three levels, where the highest one is the main one. At the other end, the lowest one represents the level at which you can select every single item and not their list. Think about it this way: level three contains all of the lists at level two, and level two includes all of the lists at level one. I hope this is not too confusing. Previously, we said the index is the address of an item, but we also need to know its level to find it if there are many levels. The most accurate example I can think of right now is that *the level represents the street, while the index represents the house number!*

In this section, we learned what indexes and levels are, and how to manage them. I want you to learn those topics because they are essential in developing any script you will develop in the future. Next, we will focus on selecting elements using what we just learned – indexes and levels.

How to select elements

Let's now see how to select elements at different levels and lists. The first thing to do is to create a list containing some items. We will not deal with Revit families. For now, we will keep things relatively simple and generate the list with numbers this time, and we will use an OOTB node instead of hardcoding every single number. Later on, we will see how to do the same thing using code blocks. The OOTB node we are looking for is called **Sequence**, and to place one, you can right-click on the workspace environment and type *sequence*, or instead, use the library's search bar to the left of the Dynamo UI.

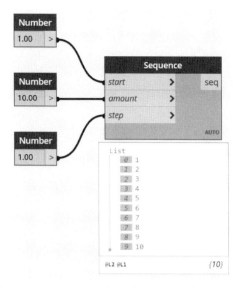

Figure 8.10 – Creating a sequence of numbers using the sequence OOTB node

The **Sequence** node wants three inputs – a **start** value, an **amount** value, and a **step** value. Use the **Number** OOTB node to achieve that. In this example, we ask the **Sequence** node to generate a list of numbers, starting from 1, creating 10 numbers, with a step of 1. Now let's say we want to select the number 5 from that list. You can use another OOTB node called **List.GetItemAtIndex**. Go ahead, place one in the workspace environment, and try to figure out on your own what inputs we need to provide to it.

Did you do it right? If the answer is yes, well done. If the answer is no, no worries, you'll be able to figure out those things on your own in no time. Just stick to the book's chapters without skipping anything!

The following diagram shows how to get the number 5 from the **Sequence** output:

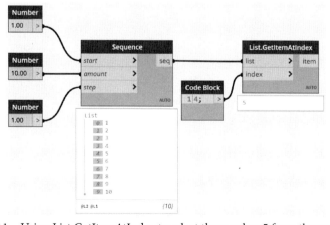

Figure 8.11 – Using List.GetItemAtIndex to select the number 5 from the sequence list

We can fairly say that this operation is quite simple to do, isn't it? Now, let's generate two sequences. Each sequence is in a separate list, and both of them are included in the main one. To do that, we must provide two lists of values to the **start** input of the **Sequence** node, so the node has to calculate the output two times. Take a look at the following diagram:

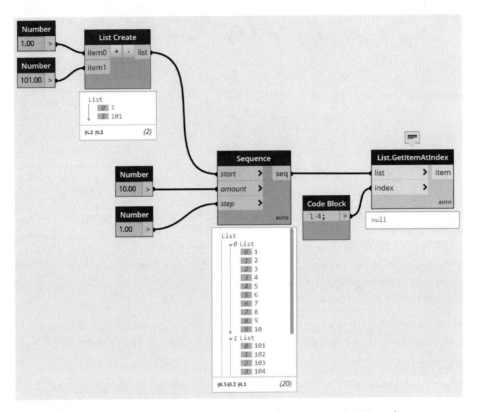

Figure 8.12 – Generating two lists using the sequence OOTB node

As you can see in the preceding diagram, we can add another node that you can place by searching **List.Create**. Once you place it, click on the plus icon at its center to create as many lists as you need. This time we will go with two. Connect everything and hit **Run**. You will immediately notice the **List.GetItemAtIndex** node turning yellow. As Luisa said in *Chapter 5, Getting Started with Autodesk Dynamo and Data Gathering*, yellow nodes mean that one or more inputs are probably wrong. Let's mouse over the yellow box on top of the node to read the warning message. The message says:

Warning: List.GetItemAtIndex operation failed. Index was out of range. Must be non-negative and less than the size of the collection. Parameter name: index

Here we go with some debugging again. Dynamo already told us everything we need to know. Indeed, I left the number 4 as the element's index from the previous example. This time, though, we have three list levels. So, to what list is number 4 being applied? If we do not specify the level of the list, by default, Dynamo will always look inside the list at the main level. Take a look at the output of the **Sequence** node:

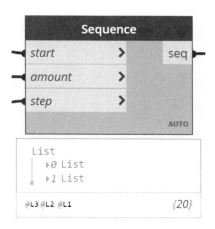

Figure 8.13 – Output of the Sequence node

I've just collapsed the lists for simplicity. Notice that at the top of **@L3**, there is a line. That means **L3** is the main list, containing all of the others. Next, we have level **@L2**, which includes the two lists, **List 0** and **List 1**. And in the end, we have level **@L1**, containing all of the items, in this case, a sequence of numbers. So, to get back to the previous warning message, we requested the **Sequence** output to get an item at index 4 without specifying the level. By doing so, Dynamo will use the highest level by default, and as you can see, there is no index 4 at level 3. The only indexes available at level 3 are index 0 and 1, and they correspond to the two number sequences. I hope this makes sense for you! Anyhow, let's create three more lists to create indexes 2, 3, and 4.

The thing to do is to click on the plus icon of the **List.Create** node and create three more lists. For simplicity, I made those lists starting from 101, 201, 301, and 401. Take a look at the following diagram:

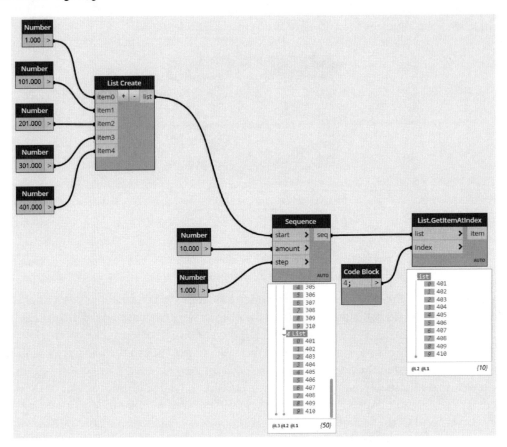

Figure 8.14 – The List.GetItemAtIndex node now works

The last node, **List.GetItemAtIndex** is now working because at level 3 and index 4, there is indeed a list. So we're now starting to understand how lists and indexes work and how to select elements using the OOTB node, **List.GetItemAtIndex**. But what if we want to specify the level to search for a specific item? That's an easy question to answer. Let's see how.

How to use levels to select elements

Let's start by saying that we want to select the number **307** from the **Sequence** output. The following diagram shows where that element is located:

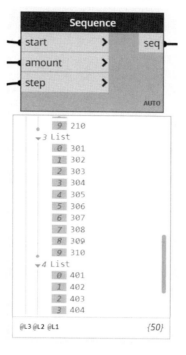

Figure 8.15 – Zoom in on list 3 to find the number 307

If you go to the **Sequence** node and activate the output preview, scroll down to **list 3** to find the number **307**, located at **index 6**. The level to use to get that item is **@L2**. At L2, there are all of the numbers of each list. So, if you need to select an entire list, you should go with L3, while if you want to select single elements from those lists, you need to go one level deeper, which is L2 in this example. Let's now take a look at the following diagram:

Figure 8.16 – How to specify the level on List.GetItemAtIndex

As you can see, I've already selected **@L2**. You can do the same by clicking on the black arrow to the right of the **list** input. When you do that, a new box will pop up. At the moment, just check **Use Levels** and don't mind the second checkbox. After checking **Use Levels**, you will see a new box appearing to the left of the black arrow. From there, you can use the up and down arrows to move through levels. Now, select **@L2**, and change the index input from **4** to **6**. Please pay attention that we are working here on the **List. GetItemAtIndex** node. When you're ready, hit **Run**. Almost immediately, you can check the output preview window. Did you notice that other than the number **307** that we were looking for, *there are also other numbers? Why is that?*

That's because we asked the **List.GetItemAtIndex** node to select whatever element was present, at level 2, index 6, from the input's list. If you scroll through the **Sequence** output preview again, you will see that at index 6, the number 307 isn't the only one. At index 6, L2, indeed, there are multiple elements. The following diagram shows the output:

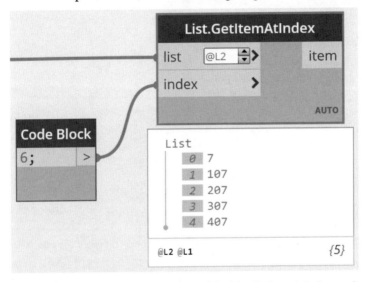

Figure 8.17 – Output preview window of the List.GetItemAtIndex node

Now that we have selected all of the elements at index 6, level 2, we can select the number **307** using another **List.GetItemAtIndex** node. All you have to do is place another **List. GetItemAtIndex** node, right after this last one, and connect them. But that's not exactly a good workflow.

Our algorithms must work so that every time we use them, no matter what objects are involved, they must work. Imagine that instead of the number 307, our script has to select a specific object with a particular set of parameters. We can't simply use **List.GetItemAtIndex** because the indexes of those elements can change. Imagine using this script on different Revit models. It won't be the case that the index of the element we're looking for is always the same. All I am saying is that we have to find a way to calculate the index first, and then, once we do that, we can provide the calculated index to the **List.GetItemAtIndex** node. To achieve that, we use **variables and conditional statements**. Have you ever heard about `if` statements? To give you an example with the last exercise, the question could be:

If, inside the list, there is an element with the number 307, give me its index.

And only after we have calculated the index can we complete the script. In this way, no matter where the number 307 is, we will find it! There is no way of escaping from our algorithm. Muahahaha! This was an evil laugh.

In this section, we learned how to use lists, levels, and indexes to find elements or lists of elements. We learned how to use some of the most common OOTB nodes to do exactly that. Remember that **List.GetItemAtIndex** is your best friend in those cases. As you start using Autodesk Dynamo every day, you will notice that mastering levels and indexes is fundamental. No scripts are made without using them. We use them because they allow us to move elements from one node to the next one, and the next one, and so on. *So, there is no way you can avoid using levels and indexes! You'd better learn them very well.*

However, now that we understand how levels and indexes work, we are ready to learn `if` statements and variables. I'll see you in the next section.

Figure 8.18 – The Dynamo script will work anytime meme

Learning IF statements and variables

In this section, we will learn more about `if` statements and variables. Before we re-open Dynamo, let's talk about those two things for a moment. Variables are the easiest to understand. In computer science, variables are data items that don't have a fixed value, as you may already know. Sometimes, variables are used because they make our life a bit easier. Especially when we are coding something, we can't use `var1`, `var2`, all the way to `var100`. It would be madness. Instead, we want to use variables to communicate their scope, not only to us, but also to colleagues and peers who may work on our scripts in the future. Let's say we need to develop a script that has to update the window's width. We want to calculate the width of the windows by using variables such as the following:

- `window_width_default`
- `window_width_calculated`

Those variable names aren't perfect, but they communicate their purpose pretty well to me. You want to avoid using variables such as the following:

- `w_width_1`
- `w_width_2`

I'm not a naming conventions expert, but those last variable names do not communicate their purpose and will cause problems in the future when you or your colleagues have to update or change the script. I know this subject may sound unimportant to you now, but believe me, naming variables, functions, and so on *is part of the development process, an important one.*

Enough with the introduction. Let's open up Dynamo and also talk about `if` statements.

I will use the window's widths in this example. Let's imagine we have 4 windows, and we got their width in a list, as usual. We want to calculate a new width only if the actual width is minor to 3 meters. So, like I always do whenever developing a script, I imagine asking questions to Dynamo. I know that's weird, but it works for me. It helps me to concatenate the logic of the algorithm. Anyway, the question I would ask Dynamo is:

Is the window width less than or equal to 3 meters? If yes, increase its value by 20%. If not, the width stays unchanged.

That question leads me to develop something like this:

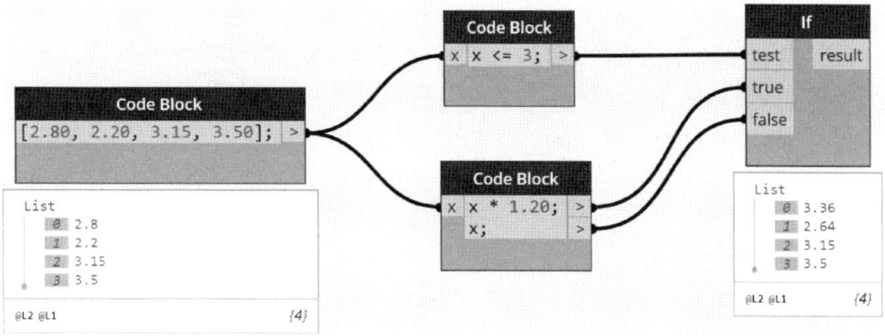

Figure 8.19 – Script to increase the window's width if it is less than 3 meters

At first, if you have never done something like that, it may look scary to you, but it really isn't. Let's take a look at each node. The first one, starting from the left, is just the initial list of window widths. I did that using a code block. Code blocks in Dynamo are general purpose nodes. You can use them to write variables, functions, and proper methods of the Revit API. The code blocks at the center of the diagram perform the checks and the calculations we wanted. The first one at the top checks whether each element in the input list is minor to 3.

To do that, I used this simple formula: x <= 3;.

> **Important Note**
>
> The closing semicolon is necessary at the end of every formula or function. Its purpose is to let Dynamo know that the formula or the function ends there. Otherwise, Dynamo will keep reading the remaining text, and it will consider it as part of the formula.

The next code block, the one at the bottom center, has two lines. The first one will perform the calculation by increasing the value of x by 20%. The second line just says x. Now let's pay attention to where those lines go:

- The formula x <= 3 goes to the **test** input of the **If statement** node. By the way, to place the **If** node, you already know to right-click on the environment and type the name of the node.

- The formula x * 1.20 goes to the **true** input of the **If** node.

- And the last line, the one with **variable x** only, goes to the false **input** of the **If statement** node.

Let's now explain how the **If statement** node works. Take a look at the following diagram:

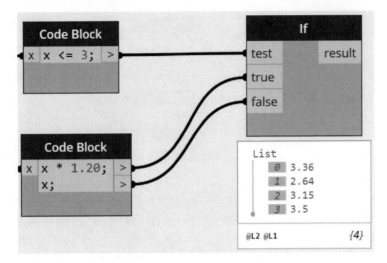

Figure 8.20 – Focusing on the If statement node

As we said previously, the **If** node has three inputs. The first one is the test, and as the word suggests, it tests something. In this case, we provided, as a test, the list with the results of the formula x <= 3. All that this formula does is that it checks for every element you provide as input if the formula is satisfied. So, when we hit **Run**, Dynamo does something like this:

As the first thing, Dynamo starts with the first node, which was the list of the following numbers:

- 2.8

- 2.2

- 3.15

- 3.5

Then it passes that list to the formula x <= 3, which applies to each input list item as it follows:

- Is 2.8 less than or equal to 3? **True**

- Is 2.2 less than or equal to 3? **True**

- Is 3.15 less than or equal to 3? **False**

- Is 3.5 less than or equal to 3? **False**

At the end of those calculations, Dynamo will produce two lists, one containing the results that are true, and another one containing the false ones. Finally, that list will be passed to the last node, the `if` statement one. This last node will read each item coming from the **test input** list as follows:

- The item **at index 0 is True**, so I will execute x * 1.20.

- The item **at index 1 is True**, so I will execute x * 1.20.

- The item **at index 2 is False**, so I will execute x.

- The item **at index 2 is False**, so I will execute x.

In the end, the output list coming from the **If statement** node represents the result of those operations. Are you starting to understand `if` statements? I am sure you are. Now, let's make another example using Revit families this time.

Let's start by opening Autodesk Revit, create a new file, and place on the floor plan four windows. I suggest you use the default window families provided by the Revit library, but this is not mandatory. Since I'm used to working with the metric system, I will create a new Revit project with the metric architectural template, but again, you can use the template you prefer.

To do that, follow these steps:

1. Create a wall on the floor plan. A length of 10 meters will suffice. The following screenshot shows the wall and its base and top constraints:

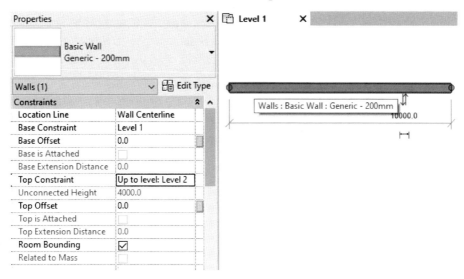

Figure 8.21 – Placing a wall with a length of 10 meters on the floor plan

2. Next, switch to the 3D view and place the four windows on the wall we just created, as shown in the following diagram:

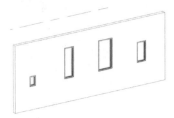

Figure 8.22 – Placing four default windows on the wall

I've used the family type **M_Fixed**, placed it four times, and then changed their types using the properties palette.

3. Now let's open up Dynamo and create a new script file.

4. Right-click on the workspace environment and type `Select Model Elements`. Then place that node into the environment. The node should look like the following:

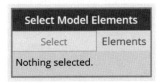

Figure 8.23 – Select Model Elements node

The node is in a warning state, but that's normal because we haven't selected anything yet. Let's do that right now by clicking on the **Select** button of the **Select Model Elements** node. When you click on **Select**, switch to Revit, and then select the windows previously placed. When you go back to Revit, you can use the default commands to select multiple families.

5. Position your mouse icon in the top-left corner (1) of those windows and press and hold the left mouse button. Then, move the cursor to the bottom-right corner (2) of the screen, making sure to include all four window families, as shown in the following diagram:

Figure 8.24 – Selecting all four windows using the Select button of the Select Model Elements node

6. Now come back to Dynamo. The **Select Model Elements** node should not be in a warning state now. If you do, repeat the selecting operation from the beginning.

7. If you did it correctly, you should see the node displaying the unique IDs of those elements.

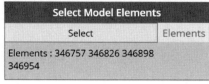

Figure 8.25 – The Select Model Elements node showing the four window's IDs

Now this means that Dynamo stored those four elements, and with those, we can do several types of operations. Our goal now is to do the same thing as we did previously with numbers. We want to check whether each window width is minor or equal to a specific value, and then, using the **If statement** node, we want to decide whether the window's width should be increased.

8. From now, the first thing to do is to get the value of each window width. We do this by using the **Element.GetParameterValueByName** node. I know this is a long name, but try to memorize it as it will be your best friend during, well, the development of all your future scripts. Now, proceed and search for and place that node.

    Before connecting everything, we need to place another new node onto the workspace environment. We will need to use **Element.ElementType**. As the dimension we are going to change, **Width**, is a type parameter and not an instance parameter, we need to extract the type first, and then we can work with its parameters. It is more or less like clicking on the **Edit Type** button in Revit. It would not be necessary if we were dealing with instance parameters instead. So, please search and place it.

At this point, we need to connect those nodes as shown in the following screenshot:

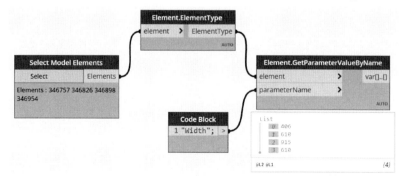

Figure 8.26 – How to connect the Element.ElementType node to get element type parameters

As you can see in the preceding screenshot, I've also placed the code block with the parameter name. Pay attention to the double quotes at the start and the end of the word **Width**. Those double quotes make sure that Dynamo understands those elements as a string and not other data types. Now hit **Run** and turn on the output preview window of the **Element.GetParameterValueByName** node.

Also, the values listed on the output preview window are in millimeters, as we work with those in Italy. If you come from a different country, I am pretty sure you may see values in other units, and that depends on your Revit's settings. If you prefer, you can update your Revit's settings as you wish and hit **Run** again to update the output preview window results.

Anyway, here, we just read those values. We now want to check whether they are minor or major to a specific number. Let's proceed by placing a code block and writing the following formula:

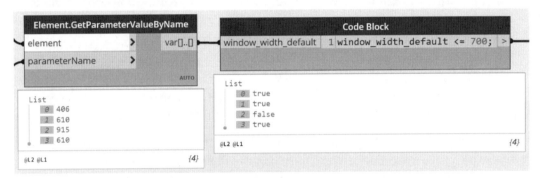

Figure 8.27 – Writing the formula inside the code block

This shouldn't be new to you. As you can see, we wrote the same formula before when we were working with the list of numbers, pretending that they were window widths. This time, though, we just changed x <= 3 to window_width_default <= 700. The only things that changed are the variable name, x, and the number 3. Of course, if you don't work with millimeters, you need to change the value 700 to something that works for your measurement system:

- Now, let's continue by placing the **If statement** node and the two condition actions, one if the result is true, and one if the result is false. When you do that, it should look like this:

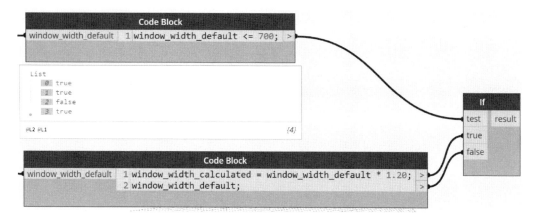

Figure 8.28 – Placing the true and false condition logic

Great! As you can see, I've used more human-readable names for those variables. The first one, the one that goes into the **true** input of the **If** node, is **window_width_calculated**, which is equal to the default one, times 1.20. That operation will increase the width by 20%. The second one, **window_width default**, which goes to the **false** input, stays the same as it will keep the width unchanged. Now, hit **Run** and turn on the output preview window of the **If statement** node.

The result should be as follows:

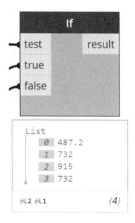

Figure 8.29 – Output preview window of the If statement node

Of course, your result should be the same only if you used windows with the same width values. Now that we have correctly calculated the new window widths, we have to insert those values back into their window element types.

As we previously used the **Get.ParameterValueByName** node to get the width, we will now use its opposite node – **Element.SetParameterByName**. This node, indeed, will take whatever value you have and insert it into whatever element you need. In this case, we want to use the calculated values from the **If** node and connect them to the value input of the **Element.SetParameterByName** node. Then we need to provide it with a parameter name, and as we already have a code block with it, we connect it to the **parameterName input** node. Last but not least, this node wants to know which elements need to be updated. To do that, connect the **Element Type** node we previously placed into the **element** input. When you're done, hit **Run** and check the results inside Revit:

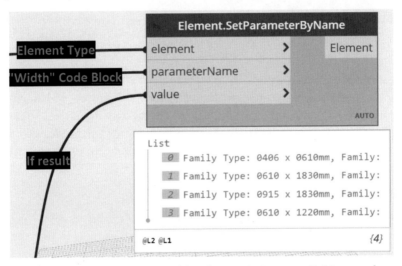

Figure 8.30 – Output preview of the Element.SetParameterByName node

Important Note

As you probably noticed, we updated the value of each window's width, but we didn't update the type name as well. From the output preview window of the preceding screenshot, you'll notice, for example, that the first item still shows a width of 406 millimeters instead of the calculated one. We won't update the names here; we will work with family names later on in this chapter, but I wanted to remind you that the parameter value is one thing, while its name is another. Keep that in mind when working with Dynamo. To update the name of the families, you need to work with strings, and do not worry, we will do that in the upcoming sections.

Well done. Did you notice that the windows inside the Revit model have changed their widths? Incredible, isn't it? And if you think about it, we're only using 1% of the Dynamo capabilities. *But what are all of Dynamo's powers anyway? How can I know what is possible and what is not?*

To reply to that question, I always repeat the following to my colleagues, peers, and students:

> *Pretty much all you can do with your mouse in Revit, you can do in Dynamo. Dynamo will help you only if you already know how to do things in Revit. Otherwise, it's pretty much useless on its own. But with a bit of Revit knowledge and the computational power of Dynamo, you can achieve many things.*

Figure 8.31 – That feeling working with if statements meme

I am happy to say that you have completed this section. Here, we learned what variables are and how to avoid mistakes when naming them. Then we learned how to work with `if` statements by performing simple yet straightforward operations using numbers and, later on, using Revit elements. *In the next section, we will cover one of my favorite topics – strings.* We will learn how to work with them and perform some of the most common operations, such as finding, splitting, concatenating, replacing, and organizing them in general. I can't wait for that. See you in the next section.

Concatenating strings

In this section, we will learn how to work with strings. Let's start by saying that strings are one of the most common data types used in every programming language, and Dynamo is no exception. Strings are sequences of one or more characters, including letters, numbers, and symbols. As a general standard in computer science, strings consist of whatever set of characters as long as they have single or double quotes at the start and end. Take a look at the following example:

- "This is a string."

- 'This is another string, a longer one.'

To computers, those two strings are the same thing. And by the same thing, I mean the same data type. They belong to the same category of objects. This means that with those, you can perform certain types of operations. To give you an example, let's say we have two numbers, **9** and **14**. If you write a simple formula like **9 + 14**, and execute it, the computer will output **23** because it recognizes them as number objects, and it knows it has to do a sum operation. If we do the same thing, but instead, we embrace those numbers in double quotes, we get **914**. **This is called the concatenation of strings**. And concatenating strings means attaching one to another. Even if the computer reads the number **9** and the number **14** inside the double quotes, it won't sum it because strings can't be summed; instead, they will concatenate.

To prove this, let's take a look at the following diagram:

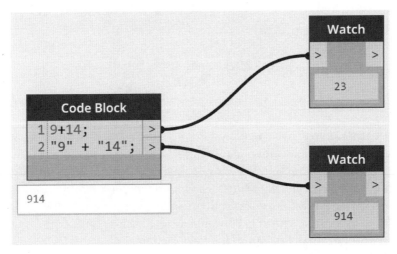

Figure 8.32 – Testing the difference between numbers and strings with a sum operation

As you can see, "**9**" + "**14**" results in a concatenation of the two numbers. And, of course, it will be the same for any string. They will always be concatenated if we sum them. Also, if you're wondering about other math operators, strings cannot be divided, subtracted, or multiplied, as shown in the following diagram:

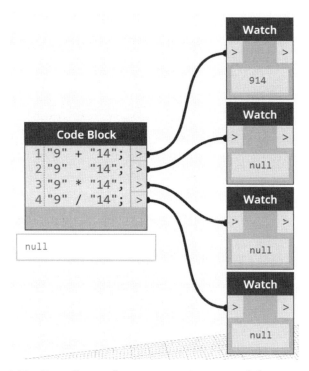

Figure 8.33 – Regarding math operators, strings can only be concatenated

As you can see from the preceding diagram, the result of those operations is **null**. *Null* objects appear when something does not execute appropriately. In this way, Dynamo informs us about the issue. A good thing to do is to place `if` statements here and there so that you can check whether something returns a `null` object. When there is a `null` object, do this. When there is none, do that. But for the moment, don't worry too much about them. OK, now let's do an exercise to allow the logic of concatenation to better sink in:

1. First, let's open up Dynamo and place a code block in the workspace environment.
2. Inside that code block, create three variables as follows:

    a) **myName**

    b) **myRole**

    c) **myCompany**

3. When you do that, you should see the three variable inputs on the left side of the code block, as shown in the following diagram:

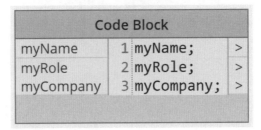

Figure 8.34 – Creating three variables using a code block

4. Now, place a new code block before that one. We will use it to connect strings to those variables.

5. Now, write the three strings as we did previously. Use the double or single quote to wrap the words and let Dynamo know that those values must be read as strings. Go ahead and type your name, role, and the name of the company you work for.

The following diagram shows the correct way of writing those strings:

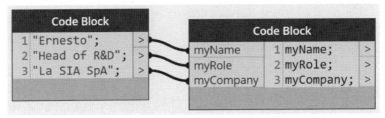

Figure 8.35 – Writing three strings as shown in the diagram

6. All we need to do now is to create a simple parametric formula that concatenates everything in a complete sentence. I want to write something along the lines of the following:

My name is **myName**, and I work as **myRole** at **myCompany**.

7. As we did previously with 9 and 14, try to create the parametric formula on your own before continuing with the exercise. Don't cheat by looking at the following diagram. To get started, place a new code block, begin writing the sentence as a string (using double or single quotes), close the double quotes, place a sum symbol, and start again with the rest of the strings. Try to do that on your own, and do not worry if you can't complete the exercise.

8. Now take a look at the following diagram. It shows the correct way to complete the exercise:

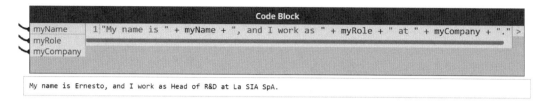

Figure 8.36 – Concatenating a string using variables

Do not worry if you didn't do it correctly on the first try. Working with strings, especially when concatenating long ones, can sometimes be challenging. You'll get used to working with strings in no time, I promise. Anyway, we just scratched the surface here.

Figure 8.37 – Becoming angry when you don't know how to concatenate strings

In this section, we learned how to concatenate strings, which is one of the most effortless operations in computer science. We know that in Dynamo, in order to concatenate strings, we need to sum them one after another, and by using variables, we can compose messages and customize them as we need. Next, we will learn more complex operations, such as searching and replacing. Let's go!

Working with strings (searching and replacing)

Now that we understand how to concatenate strings, let's see how to do more complex operations. First of all, open up Revit, and start a new project file using one of the samples provided by default. If you don't see any, do not worry. You can download the one you like from the following link:

Revit 2020 samples: `https://cutt.ly/rmxQloL`.

I've downloaded the `DACH_sample_project.rvt` file. But again, you can choose whatever you like. Once you download the model, open it inside Revit. If you're using Revit 2021, you need to wait a few minutes to upgrade the model. Then, of course, open Dynamo too. The goal here is to create a script that helps us rename family type names inside our model. And by doing so, we will learn how to split, join, and replace strings along the way.

Also, you may want to download, using the Package Manager, the following package:

- **Clockwork**

If you don't remember how to download a package, here is a refresher. Click and open the **Packages** menu from the top menu area. Then, select **Search for a Package**. Type `Clockwork` inside the search bar and install it.

Now, let's begin by following these steps:

1. As we need to retrieve family type information to manipulate them later on, and as families in Dynamo are also known as elements, search for the following OOTB nodes:

   a) **Element Types**

   b) **All Elements of Type**

2. Once you find them, go ahead and place them in the workspace environment.

3. Next, connect the **Element Types** output to the **All Elements of Type** input and hit **Run**, as shown in the following diagram:

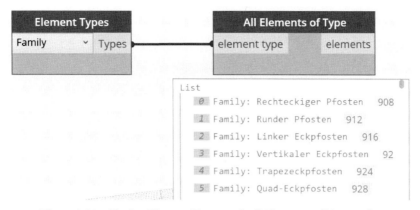

Figure 8.38 – Placing Element Types and All Elements of Type nodes

As you can see, you should get a list of all family types loaded into your Revit model. You should get similar results if you've downloaded the same model as I did.

Now that we have retrieved element types from the model, we want to search for a specific string and look for any matches. To do that, we need to convert those objects, which come from the **All Elements of Type** node output to strings.

4. First of all, search and place the **Object.Type** node to see what I mean. Of course, connect its input to the **All Elements of Type** output. When you hit **Run**, you should see that every element in that list is indeed a **Revit.Elements.Family** object type. Anyhow, Dynamo provides us with lots of OOTB nodes, and between them, there is one we want to use to convert objects into their string representation.

5. Go ahead and place the **String from Object** node, and then connect it to the **All Elements of Type** output. That node, **String from Object**, will convert any Dynamo object, such as integers, parameters, or elements, into their string representation, which means just text. And we need that text to perform string operations.

The first string operation we will use is **String.Contains**. That node allows us to search for "some string" inside a list of strings. Please search and place it.

That node has three inputs:

- **str**, which is the list of strings that it will use for the search

- **searchFor**, which is the string we want to search for

- **ignoreCase**, which is the setting to specify if we're going to use a case-sensitive or case-insensitive search

> **Important Note**
>
> For computers, the "Welcome" string and the "welcome" string, even though they have the same letters, are two different strings. If you want to search the exact match of a string, you may want to use a case-sensitive string, which is indeed sensitive to the capitalization of letters.

6. Let's now connect those node inputs. The first one, **str**, needs to be connected to the **String from Object** output. The second one, **searchFor**, needs to be connected to a code block, so place one by double-clicking on the workspace environment. And the last input, **ignoreCase**, needs to be connected to a **Boolean** node. Please search and connect it, too. The final configuration of those nodes should look like the following diagram:

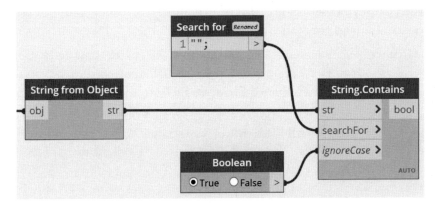

Figure 8.39 – How to connect the String.Contains inputs

7. As you can see, the code block I've connected to the **searchFor** input has been renamed. That is a good practice just to keep things clean and organized. To rename a node, you need to double-click on its title, which is the top darker area. Also, I've typed double-quotes symbols inside the renamed code block as a placeholder for the string we want to search. Now, all you have to do is scroll the **String from Object** node output preview and find some families with the same starting name.

Here is a diagram to show what I want to use for the replacement:

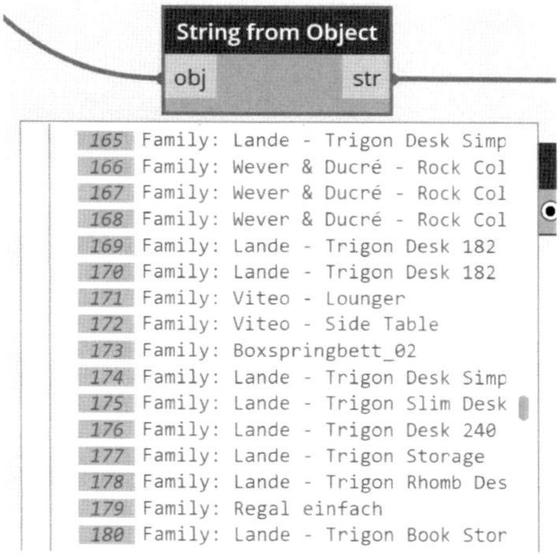

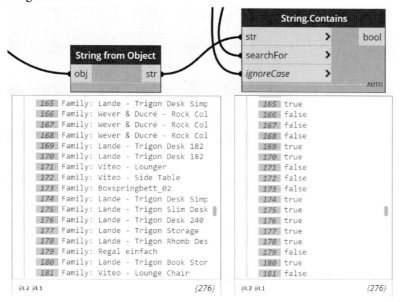

Figure 8.40 – Finding families that start with the same word

As shown in the preceding diagram, I found a bunch of families, beginning with the word **Lande**. We will find all families starting with that word by writing inside the code block's placeholder and hitting **Run**. The **String.Contains** node will do the work for us and return some results. Let's see them.

You'll get a list of trues and falses. That's the way the **String.Contains** node informs us about the match, or otherwise, of the inputs provided. Take a look at the following screenshot:

Figure 8.41 – String.Contains output

I've placed the output lists of those nodes side by side to better look at what's going on. Take a look, starting with the list on the left, at the strings containing the word **"Lande"**. Those strings will be the true ones in the list to the right. You can help yourself by looking at their indexes, starting from index 165. Now that we know what string contains the word we are looking for, we want to use another OOTB node to filter those results.

8. Now, search for the **List.FilterByBoolMask** node. That node comes with two inputs:

    a) **list**, which is self-explanatory. It's a list of "something." It could be elements, strings, or numbers, a list of any object you need to filter out.

    b) **mask**, which must be a list of Boolean values. And we just got one!

    All that this node does is separate an input list into two. The first one will contain all elements that have a corresponding index of trues. The second one will contain the corresponding false ones. Take a look at the following diagram. It shows a more straightforward example of how **List.FilterByBoolMask** works:

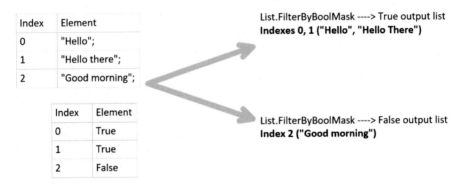

Figure 8.42 – List.FilterByBoolMask example

I hope the diagram helps you better understand the logic of that node. I know that the concept of using a list of Booleans as a mask to filter another list may be a bit complex to understand, but once you use it a few times, you'll start being more confident with it. It's not that complex anyway!

9. Now, we want to connect that node to our previously placed ones. The first input of the **List.FilterByBoolMask** node, **list**, must be connected to the list of elements we found a few steps ago. So, please connect the **All Elements of Type** output to it. Then you want to connect the list of Booleans we got earlier. The correct configuration of this part of the script has to look something like this:

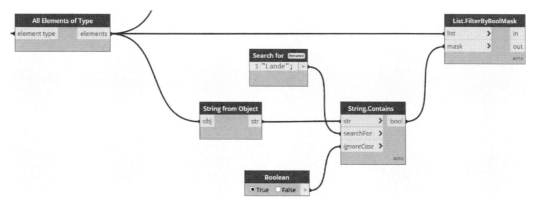

Figure 8.43 – How to connect the List.FilterByBoolMask node

We now have separated, in my case, the families containing the word **"Lande"** from the ones that do not. Very well. We're halfway there. The remaining part of the script will deal with the **replacing** operation.

Take a look at the output preview window of the **List.FilterByBoolMask** node. It shows two lists, an **in List** and an **out List**. Of course, the **in List** contains the elements coming from the true mask, and the **out List**, the false mask. Let's pause for a second to think about what we have done so far:

- Get element types.
- Transform them into their string representation.
- Find any matches using a **String.Contains** operation ("Lande").
- Then, use a Boolean mask to get element types, again

You may be wondering why we retrieved elements, converted them into strings, and then got elements again? We did that only because, in order to search for a string, you need to use strings. You can't use any other object type. Then we got elements again and not their string representation because, later on, we want to replace their element type names. We can't use their string representations to update their names as there is no correlation between the real element type object and those strings. I hope this makes sense to you. If not, it soon will!

OK. Let's now follow these steps to complete the script:

1. Search and place the following nodes:

    a) **Element.Name**, which takes an element object as input and outputs its string representation (again!)

    b) **String.Replace**, which does the same thing as the previous **String.Contains** node, but this time it helps us replace what we need

    c) The code block, which we will use to specify the replacement

2. Take a look at the following diagram. This is how you should arrange those nodes:

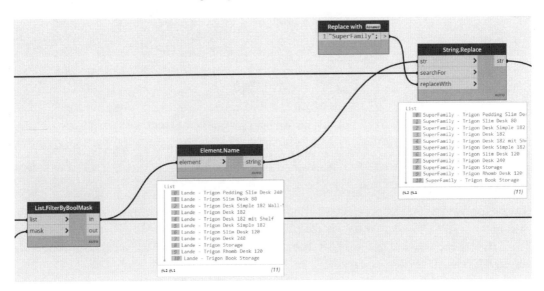

Figure 8.44 – How to arrange the newly placed nodes; Element.Name and String.Replace

As you can see, we connected the **in** output of the **List.FilterByBoolMask** node to the input of the **Element.Name** node. As we said previously, in order to work with strings, you need strings, and that node, **Element.Name**, provides strings.

3. Once you do that, connect the **string** output to the **str** input of the **String.Replace** node. That's the list of strings we need.

4. Next, we want to connect the **searchFor** input with the previously renamed **Search forCode** block, the one I used to write **"Lande"**.

5. The last thing to do is to connect the **replaceWith** input with a new renamed code block. I've typed in `"SuperFamily"`, but of course, you can type any string you want.

We are almost done. We only have a couple of things left. Let's start by placing a new node, this time not an OOTB one, called **Element.SetName**. The node comes with the **Clockwork** downloaded package. I want to thank **Andreas Dieckmann** for sharing their package with the Dynamo community. I also recommend you follow him on social media. His Twitter account is `@a_dieckmann`. The package, as you'll see, is full of awesome nodes. Check them out. We will also use some others in the last section, when we talk about regular expressions. More on that later.

Now we want to connect this node, **Element.SetName**, from **Clockwork** to two previously placed nodes. Take a look at the following diagram:

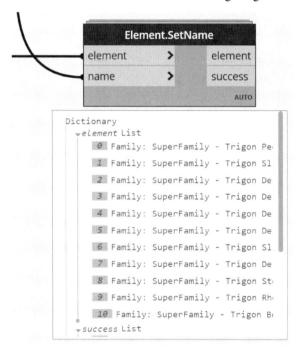

Figure 8.45 – Element.SetName node from Clockwork

6. As the input names suggest, the first one, **element**, needs to be connected with an element object type and not with its string representation. That's the reason why we converted elements into strings and vice versa. Proceed and connect it to the **in** output of the **List.FilterByBoolMask** node.

7. Then, connect the **name** input to the **str** output of the **String.Replace** node. Here we're passing the list of replaced strings. This node, **Element.SetName**, will deal with all of the converting object types for us. And that's one of the good reasons for using custom packages. They save us time. But be aware; not every package you find inside **Package Manager** is as good as this one. Now we're ready to hit **Run** one more time and see what's changed inside Revit!

When you run the script, it may take a few seconds to complete. It depends on how many families you changed the names of and your computer hardware. Also, you'll notice that from time to time, Dynamo, unfortunately, will freeze and crash. *We can't prevent this, but a good thing to do is to hit the Ctrl + S keys on the keyboard to save as often as possible.*

Moving on, script completed, great work! You're on the right track to acquiring new powerful Dynamo skills. The following is a screenshot of the Revit family names we changed with this script:

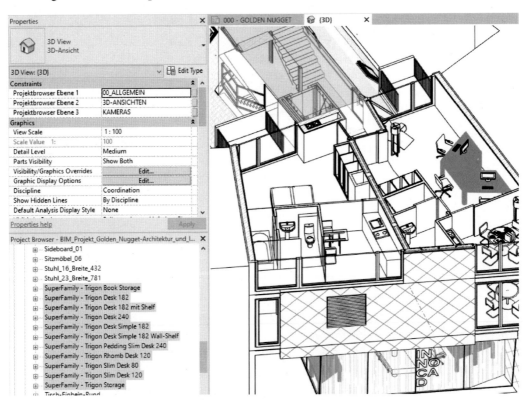

Figure 8.46 – Screenshot of the Revit UI showing the changed family names

I've highlighted them in magenta because I was curious to see what families I changed. It seems "Lande" has something to do with desks.

In this section, we learned how to search and replace strings. You're going to work with strings quite often, especially when developing something that involves a UI, like the data-shape one we talked about, or when working with family names, as in the last exercises, parameters, types, and so on. In any case, strings are used by developers all the time. The following are a few examples of where we use strings on some of the most common apps:

- All search bars you see on almost any application are strings; Google searches, LinkedIn searches, even the Dynamo library search uses strings to do something like **String.Contains**, which we explored previously.

- Telegram messages are strings.

- Gas stations change the price on their displays almost every day. They probably use some variables, and those variables are strings.

- The vocal commands we use with Alexa, or Cortana, or Google Assistant are all strings.

In this section, we learned how to use **String.Contains** and **String.Replace**. You will see that you'll use them all the time when working with strings. In addition, we also learned one important node to filter results from a list, **List.FilterByBoolMask**. That node though can also be used in many other ways, and not only to filter strings.

Let's now jump to the last section of this chapter, where we will deal with *regular expressions!* However, keep in mind that it is not mandatory to follow this last section, but I suggest you at least read it. It shows something that may appear like magic, but in the end, it is a way of working with strings with more efficiency, speed, and control. We can use regEx to find patterns inside our lists of strings. With regEx, we can search, for example, for strings starting with four letters, with two numbers in the middle, and a closing comma. With regEx, we can find any pattern that comes to our mind without hardcoding **String.Contains** everywhere. I'll see you in the next section.

Getting to know regular expressions

As we said previously, regEx, or regular expressions, can check, match, replace, and manage strings. A regular expression consists of encoded strings that we can use to find patterns in large amounts of data. Using regEx can save us many hours of work instead of using string operations, like the ones we learned in the previous sections. Also, this section will not be a deep dive into regEx as it deserves a book on its own.

Let's get started by opening Dynamo and creating a new file. If you've followed the previous section, you should have Clockwork already installed. If you didn't, open **Package Manager** and install the **Clockwork** package as it includes a few nodes that allow us to use regular expressions. As an example, let's see how we can take advantage of regEx to parse phone numbers. Let's say we have a list of phone numbers, and we want to check whether or not they match the following convention:

3 digits, 1 dash, 4 digits, 1 dash, 4 digits

A match to that structure could be something like **123-1234-1234**, or something like **368-0951-0016**. A non-match, instead, could be something like **4465-1112-3254** because it starts with four digits and not three as we wanted. Let's see how we can do that inside Dynamo:

1. Start by placing the **Regex.ContainsRegularExpressions** node inside the workspace environment. This node, as mentioned previously, comes with the **Clockwork** package.

2. Then, generate a list of strings made by random numbers and separated by a dash symbol. I've created the following list of numbers. All you need to do is to place a code block and type `["165-5555-1264", "5123-444-5966", "90112-696-588", "665-1654-4555", "852-4912-6691", "022.3365.4958"];`.

   It is unnecessary to use the same strings, but I suggest you do that to follow the exercise as it only takes a few seconds.

3. Next, place a node called **String**, which will convert anything we write inside it as a string.

   You're probably wondering why we don't just use code blocks and type something inside double quotes as we did previously? Because, to write a regular expression, we need to use special characters such as \ [ ] { }, and to use them inside code blocks, we will also need to type escaping character symbols every time we use them. If we need to type \d, which, for regEx, represents any digits, we need to use double backslashes to let Dynamo know that we want to use the backslash as part of our string. Anyway, do not worry about those technical details. Just trust me and do not use a code block for that. Instead, right-click on the workspace environment and type `String`, find the node, and then place it.

4. Once you have placed the **String** node, type \d inside it.

5.   Now, connect those three nodes, as shown in the following diagram:

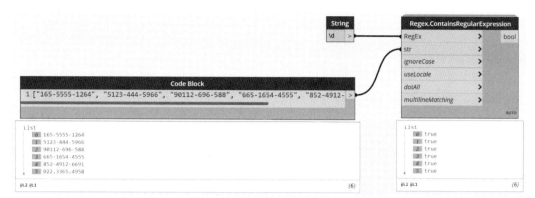

Figure 8.47 – Connecting those three nodes to start practicing with regEx

To summarize, we first created a list of six items. Each item represents a string made of numbers and a few symbols. We pretend that these are phone numbers, and we want to check whether they match the rule: *3 digits, 1 dash, 4 digits, 1 dash, 4 digits*. Next, we placed a node called **Regex.ContainsRegularExpression** and connected the list of numbers to the **str** input of that node. Then, we incorporated an OOTB node called **String** and typed \d inside it.

If we were working, as we did before, with string operations, we would first need to check whether each item in the list has a dash symbol and then use the Boolean mask to filter the results. Next, we would need to perform a lot more operations and create an enormous script to check whether or not those follow the rule we wrote earlier. And don't get me wrong, there is no problem at all in doing that. The end result will be the same as using regular expressions. The thing is that it will take a lot more time to complete the script and to make it work. Also, the script will be full of if statements and Boolean masks. *But we are pro users (or at least we pretend to be pro), and we don't want to waste time and create an infinite script just to check strings.*

6.   Now, if you hit **Run**, you should see a list of trues. That's because, for regEx, the expression \d means any digits, and without specifying anything else, regEx tells us that every item in the list has digits. Hence, every item matches the regular expression.

But that's just the more straightforward regular expression that came to my mind. Don't think that every regEx is like that. I told you before that those regular expressions are like geoglyphs. So, what regEx should we use to match the previous rule? I want to write something that checks the following:

- It should start with three digits.

- A dash symbol should follow those three digits.

- Then it should have four more digits, followed again by a dash symbol.

- And it should end with four digits as well.

If you're thinking, well, why don't we repeat \d three times, then use a dash symbol, then \d four times, and so on? *If you think that, you're on the right track!* The regEx you probably want to write should look like this:

\d\d\d-\d\d\d\d-\d\d\d\d

Let's write that inside the **String** node and hit **Run** again to see whether it works.

I got these results:

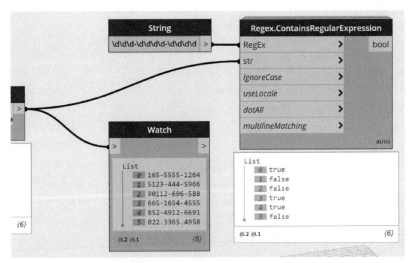

Figure 8.48 – Regex.Contains results with the new regular expression string

As you can see from the previous diagram, this expression works pretty well in terms of checking whether or not each item follows the naming rules. Also, I've placed a **Watch** node to move the output preview window of the list of strings closer to the regEx one. Those **Watch** nodes do nothing. They're helpful because you can move them around without moving the original node. It's like having a copy of the preview window you can bring with you in the workspace as needed.

OK, so the regular expression worked, but let's be honest, it doesn't really feel like pro syntax, does it? The one we used before is called a *character shorthand*. Indeed, the regular expression syntax comes with lots of shorthand to help us write concise and elegant expressions. But the one we wrote before isn't really concise and elegant. Let's see how we can improve the expression and be closer to the pro style.

We could use something like this: `^\d{3}-(\d{4}[-]?){2}`.

This syntax uses **capturing groups**, **quantifiers**, and **metacharacters**. Curly brackets enclosing numbers are a type of quantifier. Also, the question mark symbol is another type of quantifier, and *it means zero or more* for computers. But for us humans, zero or more means it's optional. Curly brackets themselves are considered metacharacters. Then we have the rounded brackets, which are considered capturing groups. Capturing groups are a way to view multiple characters as a single instance. Then we can apply quantifiers to those groups to specify how many times they should occur, for example. Previously, we wrote a bunch of `\d\d\d`... to specify three digits, then a dash, and so on. We could have used capturing groups to do this in a more pro-style way.

However, let's read this syntax one piece at a time:

`^\d{3}-(\d{4}[-]?){2}`

- `^` means at the beginning of the line.
- `\d{3}` means any digit, precisely three times.
- `-` matches that dash symbol literally.
- `(` is the start of the capturing group. And by the way, you can use multiple capturing groups if necessary.
- `\d{4}[-]?`: This part of the expression means any digits, precisely four times, with an optional dash symbol.
- `)` is the end of the capturing group.
- `{2}` is a quantifier, and means precisely two times, and it refers to the previous capturing group. We simply said, match four digits and an optional dash symbol, exactly two times.

Did you write the regEx inside Dynamo too? If you didn't, go ahead and test it out. The following diagram shows the output result using the syntax we just described:

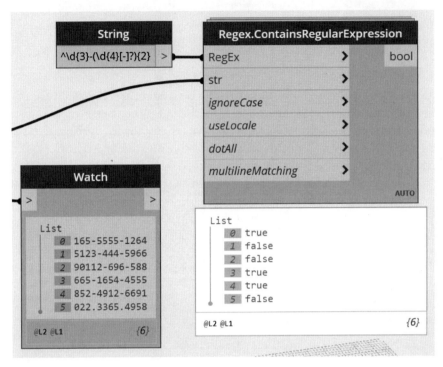

Figure 8.49 – Testing the new regular expression by capturing groups and quantifiers

As you can see, it works pretty well! I hope you do not have a headache now. I know regEx can be complex, but I want you to understand its potential as I can't give you a complete picture of regular expressions here. Hopefully, you'll start to use regular expressions in the future and learn along the way, like I have done the past few years. I've used online courses and books to help me out. I suggest you do the same. Maybe you can start with the Packt website to find more learning content.

Summary

Figure 8.50 – Curiosity is the key to learning something new

That's a wrap for this chapter! In this chapter, we learned about lists and indexes, selecting elements, and managing levels. We now know that levels and indexes are like streets and house numbers when it comes to precisely locating an item or list. Then we explored a few exercises relating to if statements, what they are, and how they work. And the end of the chapter was all about strings and how to manage them. We did a few exercises, including concatenating, searching, and replacing. And last but not least, we started to understand what regular expressions are, why they are helpful, and why you should learn them as they work basically in any programming language out there.

Besides pointing you in the direction of this learning content, my main objective is to make you curious about things. *Curiosity is the key to understanding something new and increasing your knowledge. If you're curious, you can learn anything.*

In the next chapter, we will learn how to place family instances inside the Revit model using Dynamo. We will do that by exploring the logic needed to develop those kinds of scripts, using points, lines, and Revit elements' coordinates. I'll see you in the next chapter!

9

Using Dynamo to Place Family Instances

Hi there! In this chapter, we will leave Power BI aside for a moment and use the skills we gained in *Chapter 8, Deep Dive into Dynamo Data Types*, to create a new script that places families automatically inside our Revit model. Have you ever needed something like that?

I've needed it a lot of times. Here at La SIA, an Italian engineering and architecture firm, we complete several types of projects. We work in both the private and the public sector, and we provide design services for the architectural, MEP, and structural fields. Among all our projects, a big part of them is related to the telecommunications sector. We generally produce hundreds of Revit models per week. We often need new Dynamo scripts to automate model-checking and validation, as well as scripts to place families within the Revit model.

To give you a practical example, when we model communication devices, we need to connect them to the main steel structure using structural connections. The thing is that those structural connections are always placed at a certain angle and are offset from the telecommunical device itself. And when something is *always placed in a certain way*, that means *its placement could be automated*. Today, our BIM Specialists can place structural connections in just a few seconds using a few scripts. Dynamo itself does all the hard work of calculating the points and coordinates. The engineers only need to verify that everything went well after the placement. *Although Dynamo is a powerful friend, you can't trust it all the time!*

So, in this chapter, we will use variables and math operators to calculate the placement of particular families and go through two exercises to understand the logic behind those operations (we will not develop a script to place structural connections, though).

The first exercise will focus on the very basics of placing families within the model using Dynamo. We will use an empty model and place certain families on a segmented line just to understand the basic geometry entities of Autodesk Dynamo. When we become more familiar with those concepts, we will move on to the second exercise, where we will use a completed Revit model and place families using the geometry retrieved from them. We will learn how to use advanced geometries such as topology, edges, and vertexes other than lines and points.

In this chapter, we will cover the following topics:

- The fundamental nodes for working with geometries
- How to manipulate geometries using topologies, edges, vertexes, lines, and points
- How to develop a script that automatically places some family instances on calculated coordinates

The first script, as we mentioned previously, aims to cover some basic knowledge regarding manipulating Dynamo geometries and using those geometries to place families. Let's start by creating the script and become familiar with that kind of operation. Let's jump right in!

Technical requirements

One more thing before we start: make sure that you have Revit 2021 with Dynamo 2.4 or higher installed. Please open the software to check your Dynamo version; click on **Manage** from the top menu and select **About**. Also, make sure that you have installed the **Clockwork** package.

The files for this chapter can be found here: `https://github.com/PacktPublishing/Managing-and-Visualizing-Your-BIM-Data/tree/main/Chapter09`

Creating the first family placement script

Let's start by learning how to work with points and coordinates using Dynamo!

A point in Dynamo is an object made up of three numbers. Those numbers represent its X, Y, and Z coordinates. It's that simple.

Open Dynamo and follow these steps to understand the theory we are discussing here:

1. Place an OOTB node inside the **Point.ByCoordinates** workspace environment, as shown in the following screenshot:

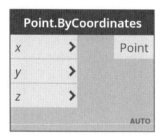

Figure 9.1 – Point.ByCoordinates OOTB node

Ensure that you place the node that requires three coordinates and not just two (just X and Y), as it will be placed on a two-dimensional surface. Here, we want to work with three-dimensional points.

2. Next, place the **Integer Slider** node. This node allows us to use a slider to move through a range of integers. When you place one, please copy and paste it two more times as we want to connect it to the three available coordinates of the **Point. ByCoordinates** node.

3.   Now, let's switch to the 3D environment of the Dynamo workspace. You can do this by clicking on the geometries icon at the top-right of the UI or by using the shortcut *Ctrl + B*, which will let you move in and out of the 3D environment. When you do that, you should see that the node's opacity is reduced; that means you are now in the 3D environment. Use the pan, orbit, and zoom commands to find the point at the center of the 3D grid, as shown in the following screenshot:

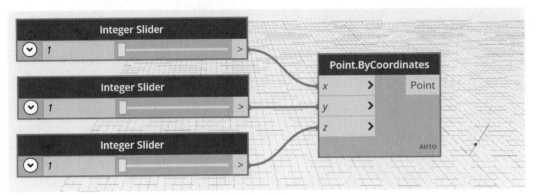

Figure 9.2 – Finding the point at the 3D environment gird's center

If you didn't do this on your first try, don't worry – that's normal. Try to navigate the 3D environment a few times before moving on. So far, we have only explored the environment of the nodes.

4.   Try to find a camera position so that you can see both the nodes and the point in the background. From here, make sure that you use **Automatic mode** from the bottom-left of the Dynamo UI and play with **Z Integer Slider** for a moment. Do you see the point moving up and down as you move the slider handle? That's awesome, isn't it?! *Congratulations, you are manipulating geometry using Dynamo!* But don't get too excited. That's a pretty simple thing to do. If you see the point moving out of your screen too quickly, you may want to set a different unit of measurement from the Revit project units settings.

5.   Now, let's do something a bit more interesting. We want to create a line using a starting point and an ending point. So, please go ahead and place the **Line. ByStartPointEndPoint** node.

6. Next, duplicate the **Point.ByCoordinates** node, including its **3 Integer Sliders**. Then, connect the outputs of the point nodes to the **startPoint** and the **endPoint** inputs, as shown in the following screenshot:

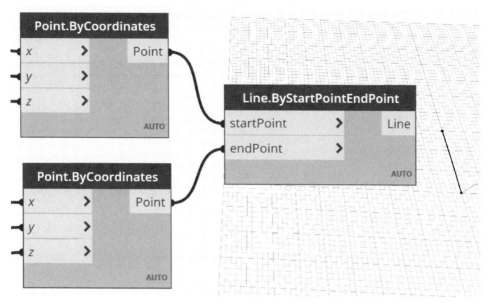

Figure 9.3 – Creating a line using the Line.ByStartEndPoint node

7. Please also move the X or Y coordinate of the second **Point.ByCoordinates** node so that the line can be created.

If we leave the coordinates of those two points at **0, 0, 0**, Dynamo can't create the line as its starting point coincides with the ending one. So, leave the first point at **0, 0, 0** and the second one at **0, 15, 0**, for example. When you do that, you should see a line appear in the background.

8. Now, we want to split that line into, let's say, 10 segments. To do that, we want to use the **Curve.PointsAtEqualSegmentLength** node. Although we read the word Curve in the node's name, Dynamo considers **Lines** and **Curves** as the same geometrical entities. Even if a Line is perfectly straight, it is considered as a Curve object. Connect the **curve** input of this node to the **Line** output of the **Line. ByStartPointEndPoint** node.

9. Then, place a **Code Block** and type, for example, the number **10**. Next, connect **Code Block** to the **divisions** input of the **Curve.PointsAtEqualSegmentLength** node, as shown here:

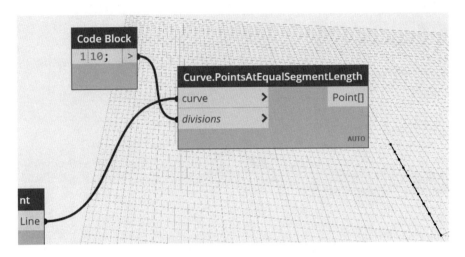

Figure 9.4 – How to connect the inputs of the Curve.PointsAtEqualSegmentLength node

After you connect those nodes, you should see the line in the background divided into 10 segments. We will use those new points to place some families in the Revit model to become familiar with the logic of the family placement scripts.

The first thing you must always do when placing families is load one. *Did you know that Dynamo can load a family directly from your computer to the Revit model?* As we mentioned in *Chapter 8, Deep Dive into Dynamo Data Types*, in the *Learning IF statements and variables* section, pretty much all you can do with your mouse in Revit, you can do in Dynamo. So, the algorithm for this part of the script should be as follows:

a) Load the Revit family.

b) In the meantime, draw the line and divide it into a few segments.

c) Now, extract the coordinates of the points of that divided line.

d) Place a family instance on each point.

To do that, we will need to use the Clockwork package again! If you followed *Chapter 8, Deep Dive into Dynamo Data Types*, you should have already installed it on your PC. If not, please download the package by clicking on **Packages** from the top menu, and then **Search for a Package**. From here, type Clockwork, search for it, and install it.

10. Now, we're ready to place the **clockwork** node. Let's search for a package called `Document.LoadFamily`. This package will allow us to load the family we want. It's important to also to switch the running mode from **Automatic** to **Manual** at this point.

11. Now, choose a family from your default Revit library folder (you can choose whatever you want) and copy it to the desktop. This will simplify finding it later. I've chosen a Revit chair. If you don't remember, you can find the Revit default library path at `C:\ProgramData\Autodesk\RVT 2021\Libraries\`.

12. Now, let's place another OOTB node called **File Path**. This node will allow us to select a file outside of the Dynamo environment. Place the node and connect it to the path input of the **Document.LoadFamily** Clockwork's node.

13. Now, we can hit **Run** and check the output preview window of the **Document. LoadFamily** node. Take a look at the following screenshot:

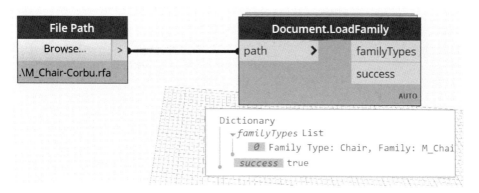

Figure 9.5 – Family successfully loaded

That node gives us two outputs. The first is a list of family types included inside the `.rfa` file we specified in the **File Path** node, while the second is a boolean value. If the operation completes without errors, the result is **true**. We will use that **true** to decide whether to continue with the script's execution. And to do that, we will use something we learned in *Chapter 8, Deep Dive into Dynamo Data Types*: IF statements.

14. Let's continue by placing the **If** node. By placing it, we can take advantage of the **IF statement** logic to continue with the script's execution. So, add that node and connect it like so:

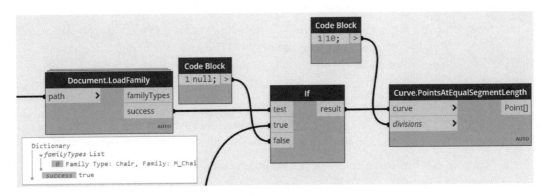

Figure 9.6 – Rearrangement of the last nodes

Why did we move **Curve.PointsAtEqualSegmentLength** after the **If** node? We moved it because it will only execute if the test input is **true**. And that's what we want. We don't want to continue performing complex calculations if something is wrong.

Although we are not performing complex calculations, I want you to understand the logic here. You will develop scripts that perform complex calculations in the future, and you will want to stop the script's execution immediately if something goes wrong. Doing so will prevent you from wasting time calculating something that we already know is wrong. And how do we do that? We use the IF statement logic!

15. However, let's move the **Curve.PointsAtEqualSegmentLength** node after the **IF statement** logic and connect the **curve** input to the **result** output of the **If** node. The following screenshot shows how to connect those nodes:

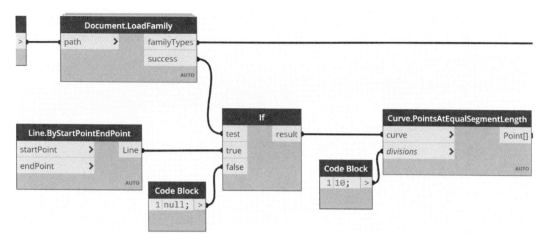

Figure 9.7 – How and where to connect the If node and Curve.PointsAtEqualSegmentLength

16. Next, connect the **test** input of the **If** node to the **success** output of the **Document. LoadFamily** node.

17. Then, connect the **true** input of the **If** node to the **Line** output of the **Line. ByStartPointEndPoint** node that we just placed.

We're all set now. To place our families, we will need two things:

a) The family type we want to place

b) A list of points to use for the placement

We have both of these. We can use the **Point** list from the output of the **Curve. PointsAtEqualSegmentLength** node to place the families!

18. Search for and place the **FamilyInstance.ByPoint** node and connect it, as shown in the following figure:

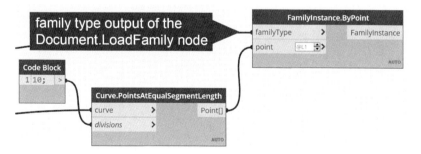

Figure 9.8 – How to connect the FamilyInstance.ByPoint node

Also, make sure to set **@L1** to the point input of the **FamilyInstance.ByPoint** node, as shown in the previous figure. Perfect! Now, we only need to hit **Run** and check the Revit model.

Awesome! Everything worked as we hoped. The following screenshot shows my result inside the Revit model:

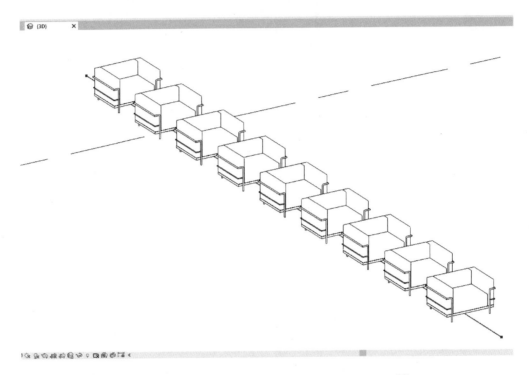

Figure 9.9 – Placement of family instances on a segmented line

If you don't see this result, I suggest that you double-check the Revit project units settings. My project units are set to meters. If I had set it to millimeters, Dynamo would have placed just one chair because it wouldn't have enough space to place all the chairs. The distance between the segmented line's points would have been too small for Dynamo to place all the remaining families.

I hope you enjoyed creating this fun script. In this section, we learned how to take advantage of the **IF statement** node to decide whether to continue with the script's execution. We also learned how to create points and lines and divide them into segments to extract a list of points to be used for the family placement. We also learned how to load a family document inside the Revit file thanks to the Clockwork nodes!

Figure 9.10 – The feeling when you place families using Dynamo and it works!

I am super happy to continue this chapter with a new family placement script – an upgraded version of the one we just created. Here we learned how to create a line starting from two points. Then, we segmented that line to extract 10 different points and used them for the placement. The next script will be a bit more complex because we will use a complete Revit model, not just an empty one. Let's jump to the next section.

Creating the second family placement script

We are now ready to work with a real Revit model and not just lines and points placed in a space. In this exercise, I would like you to use the Revit model you prefer, so long as it has these characteristics:

- It has multiple floors.
- It has multiple windows.

If you don't have a model to start with or have a model with one or more missing requirements, then don't worry – you can download one using the link provided in the following section. During this exercise, I will use the Revit Architecture Advanced Sample Project. Enjoy!

Environment setup

Please read the following instructions as they are fundamental for correctly executing this script. We will need the same tools that we used for the first script – Revit 2021 with Dynamo 2.4 or higher installed. If you need to check your Dynamo version, please open the software, click on **Manage** from the top menu, and select **About**. Also, make sure that you have installed the Clockwork package.

If you need a Revit model to start with, you can download one from the following link: `https://cutt.ly/ImxxNLM`.

From that page, you can choose between several Revit models. I've downloaded the Architectural Advanced Sample Project named `rac_advanced_sample_project.rvt`, but you can download the one you like the most, so long as it complies with the previously listed requirements.

Enough with the setup. Let's get started!

Introducing the second script

Let's start by opening our Revit model. I'm going to open up the Revit model, `rac_advanced_sample_project.rvt`, that I previously downloaded. As you can see, the model has three floors, plus a roof level:

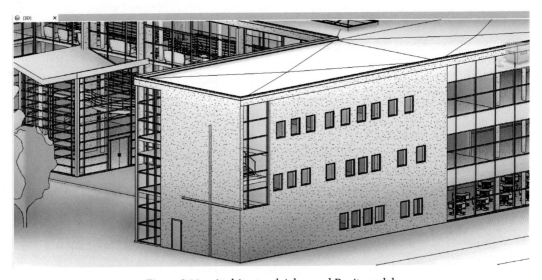

Figure 9.11 – Architectural Advanced Revit model

The whole project has a C-like footprint and many windows distributed on different levels on the shorter side of the building. The algorithm of our script will proceed as follows:

- Collect all of the window elements.
- On each window, extract the geometries.
- Then, use the geometries to calculate a point on top of the window frame.

- Next, place a family instance on each calculated point.
- Check the results in Revit!

Before continuing, you should check the Revit project units settings as it will be better to work with meters or feet. If you want to use smaller units such as millimeters, please convert the calculated values accordingly during the script's development. Now, let's open Dynamo and start the script by dealing with windows first!

Placing a family instance on each window

This section will develop a new part of the script that will allow us to place family instances on each window. The script will contain three parts:

- Retrieving all of the geometry information
- Calculating the placement points
- Placing the family instances

Let's get started.

Retrieving the geometries

In this section, our goal is to develop the first part of the script: retrieving geometries. The process is quite simple – Dynamo "asks" Revit to provide all of the family instances that belong to the Windows category. Then, will we use those elements as input for the geometry extraction OOTB nodes.

When you open Dynamo, make sure that you set the running mode to **Manual**. Next, perform the following steps:

1. Place two OOTB nodes called **Categories** and **All Elements of Category**, as shown in the following screenshot:

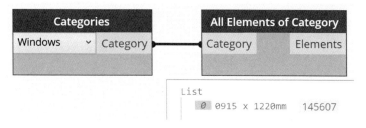

Figure 9.12 – Place those two nodes to select every window inside the Revit model

2.   Once you have placed those nodes, hit **Run** and check the output preview window to see if Dynamo selected those elements correctly.

You should notice a list of type names, followed by a green rectangle with a number inside it. The green rectangle means that each item in that list is an element of the Revit model, and it has a specific element identification number (ID). If you see that, you're good to go. If you don't, you may want to double-check the model or the nodes you just placed.

3.   Next, we want to retrieve all of the windows' geometries as we need to calculate a specific point for each one. To do that, we'll use the **Element.Geometry** node. When placing it on the workspace environment, connect its input to the **All Elements of Category** output and hit **Run**. You should see the geometry of your windows appear on the Dynamo background, as shown here:

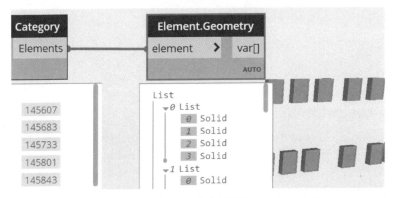

Figure 9.13 – The Element.Geometry node highlighting the window's geometries

If you look at the previous screenshot, you will see that the output preview window of the **Element.Geometry** node shows separated lists, one for each window. Inside each list, there are four solids. We will need to find the best solid that works for us. The solid we want to select needs to be distributed on the vertical plane.

4.   To select the correct solid, we can randomly click on some of the lists included in the **Element.Geometry** output preview window. Let's look at the following screenshot:

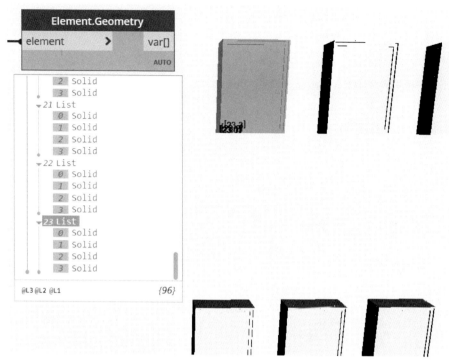

Figure 9.14 – Highlighting a Dynamo geometry by selecting a list of solids

On my computer, the list at **index 23** contains the four solids. If you click inside the **index 23** list and select each **Solid element** one by one, you should see a smaller part of the geometry being highlighted, instead of seeing the whole window geometry being highlighted (think, for example, of a window frame being highlighted).

In my case, the solid that I want to work with is at **index 1**, as it will allow us to calculate the midpoint of the top part of the window's frame. The following screenshot shows the solid I am talking about:

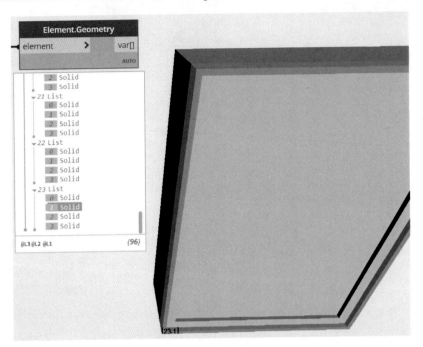

Figure 9.15 – The window's frame solid highlighted

I've also switched to the 3D background of the Dynamo workspace to zoom in on the window geometry. You can use the *Ctrl + B* shortcut or hit the geometries icon at the top-right corner of the Dynamo UI to do this.

Now, we want to check if each **Solid element** at **index 1** of each list highlights the same part of the window's geometry. Select index 1 contained in other lists. Here, every window has, at **index 1**, the solid of the window's frame.

5.   Now, we are ready to filter the **Element.Geometry** output and get all the elements at index 1 of every list. We did the same thing in *Chapter 8, Deep Dive into Dynamo Data Types*, when we worked with lists and indexes. (If you need a refresher on lists and indexes, I suggest that you re-read that chapter!) At this point, we need to place the **List.GetItemAtIndex** node. As we did in *Chapter 8, Deep Dive into Dynamo Data Types*, we will use that node to select multiple items from a list of lists. Place the node and connect its `list` input to the **var[]** output of the **Element. Geometry** node.

6. Next, we want to specify the index of the elements to get. As we mentioned previously, we will use **index 1**. So, go ahead, place a **Code Block**, and type **1** inside it. Next, make sure to set **@L2** on the list input of the **List.GetItemAtIndex** node. This will ensure we get every item at **index 1** from every list of the window's geometries. The following screenshot shows the results:

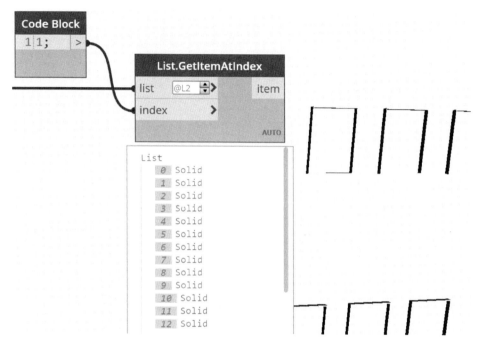

Figure 9.16 – We correctly got the frame geometry of each window

As you can see, I've also hidden the solids we wanted to discard. To do that, you need to click on the **Element.Geometry** node, which contains all of the solids, right-click on it, and deselect **Preview**.

7. Now that we've selected the window's frame, we want to use the lines and points of those geometries to calculate our points. To do that, let's place all of the nodes shown in the following screenshot:

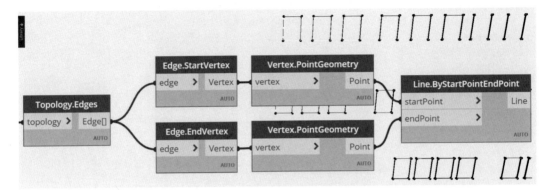

Figure 9.17 – Extracting lines from solids

In Dynamo, there is a hierarchy when we speak of geometries. I don't want you to get bored with the technical details, but you should know that we use topologies when querying 3D geometries. With the topology, we can query vertexes, points, and so on. To get more information about the hierarchy of geometry entities in Dynamo, please check out the following link: `https://cutt.ly/fQiZTIW`.

Let's recap what we just did. If you take a look at the previous screenshot one more time, you can see that the following occurred:

- We started with a list of solids.

- Then, we converted those solids into topologies.

- Then, we used those topologies to extract edges and vertexes.

- Finally, we drew lines using **Line.ByStartPointEndPoint**.

Now, we need to find a few more points on the geometry of the windows. Then, we'll be good to go!

As the output of the **Line.ByStartPointEndPoint** node contains many items, and as we need to identify a line from the upper part of the geometry, we should only select one window for now and focus on that. By doing this, we can identify the line we are looking for. Once we've done that, we will be ready to do the same for every other window. I hope that makes sense to you too; if not, it will in a minute!

8. Let's start by right-clicking on each recently placed node and deactivate its preview. Unfortunately, Dynamo doesn't allow us to deactivate the preview of multiple nodes at once. We need to do this one by one. Go ahead and deactivate all of the previews of those nodes. You can start from **Topology.Edges**. The result should look like this:

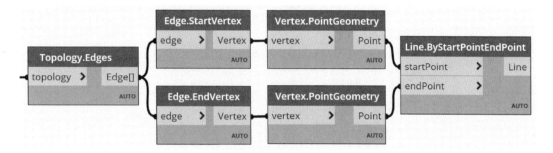

Figure 9.18 – Nodes after deactivating their previews

As you can see, after deactivating their previews, all of the nodes have changed their colors from brown to gray.

9. Next, we want to grab the lines of one window. You already know that when we want to select elements from a list, we use **List.GetItemAtIndex**. So, let's do that. As I did previously, I'll use **index 23** because, in my case, it corresponds to the first window of the Dynamo 3D background. The following screenshot shows the result after hitting **Run**:

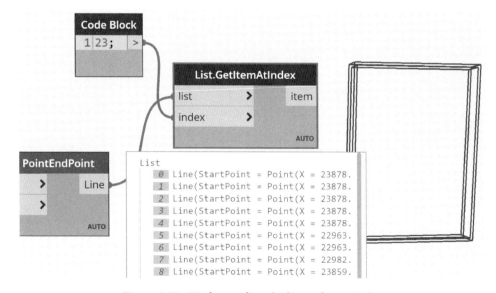

Figure 9.19 – Understanding the lines of one window

When you hit **Run**, you can switch to the 3D environment to move the window's lines closer to the camera. *From now on, we don't want to hide the node's previews.*

10. At this point, let's place another **List.GetItemAtIndex** and select only one line from the list. Let's start with the line at **index 0**, and let's check if the highlighted line works for us. Also, change the execution mode to **Automatic**.

At index 0, this is what I found:

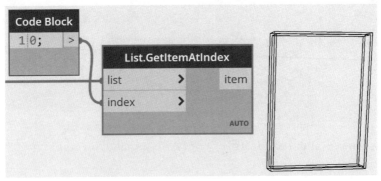

Figure 9.20 – We're highlighting one line at a time using List.GetItemAtIndex

When you click on the **List.GetItemAtIndex** node, you should see a blue stroke around it, meaning it is in a *selected state*. And if it's in a selected state, whatever geometry contains that node will be highlighted in blue on the Dynamo 3D background, as shown in the preceding screenshot. If you need a refresher on the node's states, you may want to reread *Chapter 5, Getting Started with Autodesk Dynamo and Data Gathering*.

11. Anyway, in my case, at **index 0**, I can see a vertical line on the left-hand side of the window geometry. So, let's update the Code Block's number to **index 1**, then **index 2**, and so on. In the end, we will find our line!

12. The line I was looking for can be found at **index 4**. Easy peasy. Take a look at the following screenshot:

Figure 9.21 – Line found at index 4 using the rac_advanced_sample_project.rvt file

Finally, we found the line at **index 4**. We're now ready to do the same on every other window. Let's remove the last **List.GetItemAtIndex** node – the one we placed only to highlight one line at a time – as we don't need it anymore.

13. Let's use the index we found just now and set **@L2** as the **list** input of the **List. GetItemAtIndex** node as we want to grab all lines at **index 4** of all windows. Look at the following screenshot:

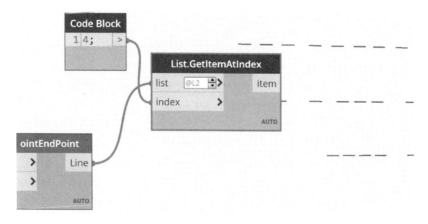

Figure 9.22 – Selecting all the upper lines of each window geometry

Here we are. As you can see, we selected the correct lines. Now, we want to use those lines to calculate a list of new points, which we will use, at the end of this chapter, to complete the third part of the script, which is placing family instances.

Calculating the points

Do you remember that we used a node to divide a line into 10 segments during the first family placement script? To extract our first point now, we will use a similar node:

1. This one is called **Curve.PointAtParameter** and requires two inputs: **curve** (a list of lines) and **param** (a parameter that the lines will be evaluated on). As we want to extract the midpoint of those lines, we can type 0.5 as the **param** input, as shown in the following screenshot:

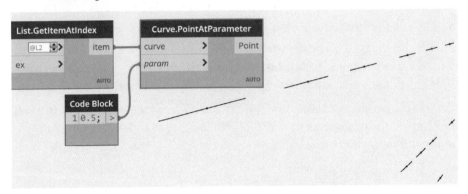

Figure 9.23 – Using Curve.PointAtParameter, we can calculate the midpoint of each line

So, by typing **0.5**, it's the same thing as saying 50%. And that's what we need to calculate midpoints. Now that we have all the midpoints of all the lines, we can make a few simple calculations and find the placement point of our family instance. As we did in the previous exercise, we know that points have three coordinates: X, Y, and Z. Let's learn how to extract those coordinates from the **Point** output of the **Curve.PointAtParameter** node.

2. This is pretty simple to achieve. Search for and place the following nodes:

-   Point.X
-   Point.Y
-   Point.Z

    Those nodes will give us the separate coordinates of a list of points. Now, we want to manipulate the Z coordinate and create new points using the extracted X and Y coordinates.

3. Once you've placed those nodes, connect them to the **Point** output of the **Curve. PointAtParameter** node.

4. Next, we want to do the following to complete the placement point calculations:

- Place a **Code Block**.

- Write three variables that we will use to calculate the placement point.

    Let's start with the following variables:

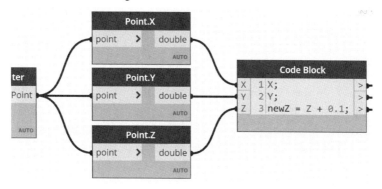

Figure 9.24 – Writing the three variables as shown

The first two variables are X and Y, and we use them to pass the original values of those coordinates without changing anything. Then, we write **newZ** as a calculated value in which we pass the **Z + 0.1** formula. This formula will take whatever value is coming from the list of Z coordinates and add 0.1. In my case, this is 0.1 meters. In a few steps, we will use **XY** and **newZ** to create a new list of points where **X** and **Y** stay unchanged, while **Z** is 10 centimeters higher than the previous one.

Before we create the new list of points, take a look at the **Code Block** output preview window:

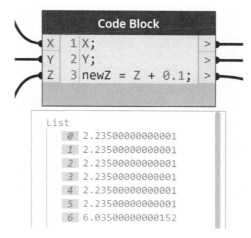

Figure 9.25 – Output preview window of Code Block

As you can see, the calculated **newZ** values have quite a lot of decimal numbers. Let's fix that. Usually, in computer science, we use a library to perform more advanced operations with numbers, integers, and so on. In this case, we want to round the decimals to two values only, for simplicity's sake.

Luckily, in Dynamo, there are plenty of OOTB nodes that come in handy. The one we will use now is a library called **Math**. With the **Math** library, if you type **Math** inside the Dynamo library's search bar, you'll find many operations such as **And**, **Or**, **Exponentials**, **PI**, **Max**, **Min**, and so on. These operations are out-of-the-box functions that we can use right away with the default version of Dynamo.

To round out our **newZ** values, though, we will need to use a node called **Math. Round** and provide it with two inputs: a list of values to round and the number of decimals to use. Please note that there are two **Math.Round** nodes and you need to place the one asking for two inputs: number and digits. Let's learn how to correctly use the **Math.Round** OOTB node and complete the script.

5. Let's place the **Math.Round** node and provide, to its number input, the list of values coming from the **newZ** calculated variable.

6. Next, place a **Code Block** with the number **2** typed in to specify that we want two decimals only. When you're done, hit **Run** and check the results. You'll see that all of the previews values with many decimals are now rounded to two decimals only. Well done!

7. Now, we're ready to create our new list of calculated points. Let's place a node we already know, **Point.ByCoordinates**. Ensure that you place the node with three inputs (X, Y, and Z), and not the one with two inputs. Next, let's pass the **X**, **Y**, and **newZ** variables to the node we created inside **Code Block**. The result should look like this:

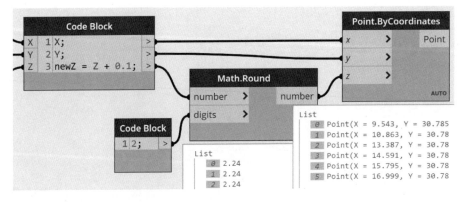

Figure 9.26 – After rounding the newZ values, we can create the new list of points

Awesome! We've successfully created the new calculated list of points.

8. Now, hit **Run** and check the 3D views of the Dynamo 3D background and the Revit model itself. The following screenshot shows my Revit 3D view:

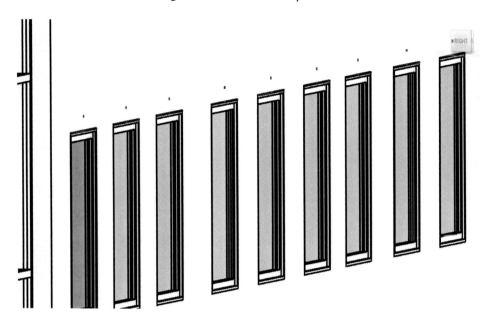

Figure 9.27 – Revit windows with the new calculated points highlighted in blue

Dynamo is fantastic. It will highlight what we're doing in the Dynamo environment inside any Revit view!

Now for the final part: placing the family instances.

Placing the family instances

We're all set now. All we have to do is choose a family and provide it to the Dynamo script. Of course, you can choose whatever family you like, but I've already prepared a family you can use:

1. First, switch to **Manual** mode.

2. Then, place the usual nodes to insert the family instances with the Clockwork package:

- **Document.LoadFamily**

- **FamilyInstance.ByPoint**

- **File Path**

3. When placed, you can connect everything, as shown in the following screenshot:

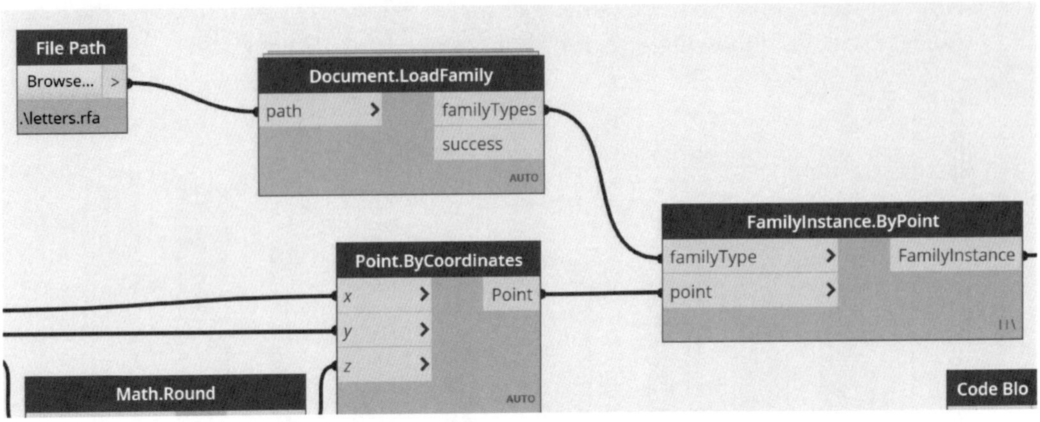

Figure 9.28 – Placing families using FamilyInstance.ByPoint from Clockwork

4. I've already selected a family using the **Browse** button of the **File Path** node. You can use any family you like, but if you want, you can download the family from here: `https://github.com/PacktPublishing/Managing-and-Visualizing-Your-BIM-Data/tree/main/Chapter09`.

5. Do not forget to set the auto-lacing of the **FamilyInstance.ByPoint** node to **Longest**. Right-click on the node and select **Lacing**, then **Longest**. This will ensure that the node will calculate each element of the two input lists. When you're done, go ahead and hit **Run**!

6. Now, let's switch back to the Revit 3D view and see what we have achieved:

Figure 9.29 – Family instances correctly placed using Dynamo!

As you can see, the families have been placed 10 centimeters above each window. An important note here is that those families, after being placed, have also been rotated. This is due to the hosting plane of the Revit view. If the script place flipped families, you could add those optional nodes to fix that:

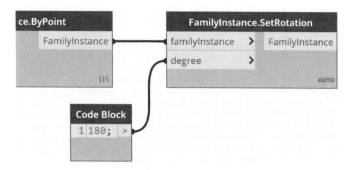

Figure 9.30 – How to rotate families

Of course, using Dynamo, we can decide if a family needs to be rotated or not, depending on the view and orientation of the family. We didn't do that here because it depends on various factors, and we can't create a script that works in any case. If you need to do that in the future, you have to figure out the best algorithm to achieve the desired result. And right now, you have all the knowledge needed for that! So, don't be afraid, try something, make mistakes, and learn! That's the best and fastest way to improve your Dynamo skills!

In this section, we learned how to use more advanced geometry concepts to place our family instances. We retrieved the geometry of each window and used that to make a simple calculation and place a family on top of them. Of course, you can calculate anything now. Think about cameras, lighting fixtures, tables, cars, and so on. The important thing I want you to understand here is that if we can calculate a point in the Revit space, we can use that to do anything, including placing families and removing families!

Summary

Now, let's recap what we learned in this chapter. We tested ourselves by developing two scripts.

In the first one, we learned about the essential nodes needed to calculate an abstract geometry such as a line, divide it into segments, and extract points for the family placement node.

After that, we started the second script by using an actual Revit model. While developing the script, we used all of the nodes we explored in the development of the first script, but we also learned how to use Revit elements to calculate the points we wanted. Here, we extracted geometries using the window category. Then, we manipulated those geometries using the topology, edge, vertex, and point nodes. At the end of this chapter, we placed the family we wanted on each window of the model, and also we learned how to rotate them using the OOTB **FamilyInstance.SetRotation** node.

I hope you had fun with this chapter!

In the next chapter, we will learn how to extract the model's data from multiple Revit models at once. Let's get right into it!

10

Gathering a Revit Model's Data from Multiple Models at Once

Welcome to *Chapter 10, Gathering a Revit Model's Data from Multiple Models at Once*! In this chapter, we will learn how to get data from multiple Revit models. We will do that in "ninja mode" – by that, I mean when we complete the script, we will launch it from an empty Revit model; then, Dynamo will open several Revit models in the background, gather their data, and print everything inside an Excel file. That's how a real ninja would do this! By the end of this chapter, we will be able to use the Dynamo player to launch a script and allow Dynamo to do the calculations in the background. Although it may seem like a complex thing to do, it isn't. We already explored all of the required nodes to export data from the Revit model to Excel in previous chapters, including *Chapter 5, Getting Started with Autodesk Dynamo and Data Gathering, Chapter 8, Deep Dive into Dynamo Data Types,* and *Chapter 9, Using Dynamo to Place Family Instances*. In addition to what we covered in those chapters, we will integrate our script with new nodes. In particular, we will use a few new packages, so get ready for that! I want to simulate a real case study here, doing things in a slightly more organized way and keeping everything crystal clear for future colleagues.

We will work with groups, and we will rename them according to our needs. Also, between the new packages, we will use another one that we named a couple of times previously but we never implemented: **Data-Shapes**. *This package will allow passing user inputs into the Dynamo script without the need to even open Dynamo!* Isn't that awesome?! After launching the script, the **Data-Shapes** package will create a pop-up window, asking the user for a few inputs, and then pass the user inputs to Dynamo and execute the rest of the script in the background.

The workflow will work as follows:

- Start a new empty Revit model.
- Open the Dynamo player to start our script.
- Ask the user for a few inputs.
- Collect and pass those inputs to the Dynamo script.
- Open a bunch of Revit models in the background.
- Get their data, one by one.
- Print the data in different Excel sheets.
- Check the results.

To summarize, we will cover the following topics in this chapter:

- Creating the data collector script
- Exporting the datasets to Excel
- Adding the user interface

As you can see, we have a lot to cover in this chapter, so let's get started!

Technical requirements

To follow this chapter, we will need to have installed the following software:

- Autodesk Revit 2021
- Dynamo BIM for Revit 2.4 or higher

We will also need to install the following Dynamo packages:

- Clockwork

- Data-Shapes

- Rhythm

And last but not least, please download the Revit models from the following folder: `https://github.com/PacktPublishing/Managing-and-Visualizing-Your-BIM-Data/tree/main/Chapter10`.

We won't waste any time by building new Revit models. Instead, we will use these models to get data and print the information in Excel. I've used the Autodesk sample models for that operation and made a few changes to work with Power BI later. However, if you already feel like you can start working independently, you can choose a few Revit models you made previously. It's up to you. And of course, if you decide to start with your Revit models, you can always come back and download mine if you become stuck somehow.

Creating the data collector script

Let's start by opening Revit to create a new empty model. We will use an empty model just to start Dynamo, as we will ask Dynamo to open multiple Revit models in the background.

Follow these simple steps to start things out:

1. Open Dynamo and create a new script file.

2. Although it's empty, save the file in a folder on your PC.

> **Important Note**
> It's good practice to keep a saved file and make sure to save the file regularly as Dynamo can sometimes freeze, and you will lose your work. It's happened to me several times, and it's not a pleasant feeling, to be honest!

3. Set the running mode to **Manual** for now.

Perfect – we're ready to continue. The first thing I would like to do is collect model information, and once we have that, we can send that data to a new list of items. We will do that for every category of information we will collect from those models. In the end, we will have a list made up of several sublists that contain plenty of data. That data will be sent to different Excel sheets. *In this way, we have an organized Dynamo script and an organized Excel file, which is always a good thing!*

Collecting information from multiple models

As you may already know, model information in Revit consists of all of the data attached not to a single-family instance but the entire Revit model. Those attributes are, for example, project information, location information, and so on. Let's start our script by collecting some:

1. As we want to open multiple Revit files, we need a node that allows that. In this case, place a node named **Applications.OpenDocumentFile**. This node comes from the Rhythm package (developed and maintained by John Pierson, an expert in design technologies) and it contains several helpful nodes.

   The node wants several inputs, but they are all optional except for one, as you can see by the italic font in the following screenshot:

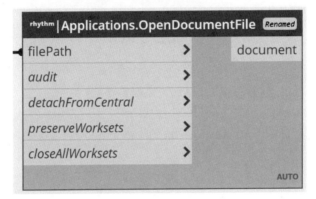

Figure 10.1 – Inputs written in italic font are optional

   Keep in mind that when you see inputs written in italic font, it means they're optional. In this case, those optional inputs are related to work sharing models, and we don't need them right now.

2. Next, place the following four nodes (try not to look at the following screenshot and connect them on your own first):

a) **Directory Path**

b) **Directory from Path**

c) **FileSystem.GetDirectoryContents**

d) **Code Block**

So, place the nodes while trying not to look at the screenshot. If you get stuck, go on and take a look, of course!

3. Be aware that you also need to type the following string inside **Code Block**:

```
"*.rvt"
```

By writing the previous string, you're saying, *"Get every file with a .rvt extension and exclude everything else."* And that's what we need.

4. Now, take a few minutes to figure out how to connect those nodes. I hope you did it right! But in case you didn't or need help, you can take a look at the following screenshot:

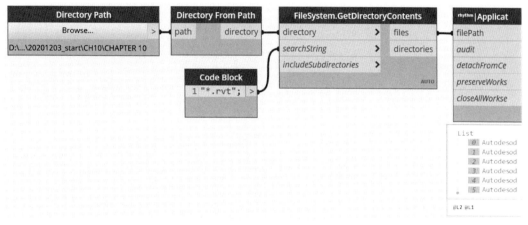

Figure 10.2 – How to connect the four nodes to the Application.OpenDocumentFile node

To summarize, we used a **Directory Path** node to specify the folder where we saved the Revit models we previously downloaded. Next, we retrieved a **Directory** object from the **Directory Path** node. Then, we passed the **Directory** object to the **FileSystem** node, in conjunction with **Code Block** as the **searchString** input, to search for Revit files. Lastly, we provided the **Files** output of the **FileSystem. GetDirectoryContents** node to the **Application.OpenDocumentFile** node to open our Revit documents.

5. We have now connected Dynamo to the Revit documents in the background, and we're ready to get their data. Let's continue by placing two more nodes:

a) **Element Types**

b) **Collector.ElementsOfTypeInDocument**

The first thing to do here is choose **ProjInfo** from the **Element Types** node drop-down list. Then, we must connect the **Element Types** output to the **elementType** input of the **Collector.ElementsOfTypeInDocument** node. Then, we want to connect the **Document** output of the **Application** node to the **Document** input of the **Collector** node.

6. Once done, hit **Run**. The following screenshot shows the correct result:

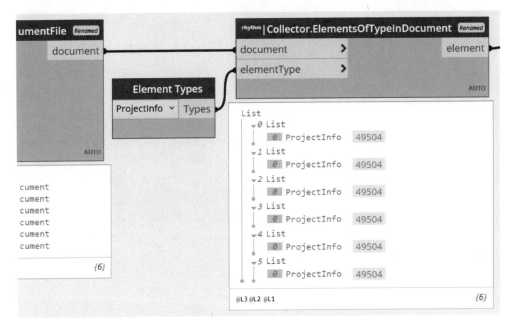

Figure 10.3 – ProjectInfo elements as the outputs of the Collector node

As you can see, we have six models open in the background, and we retrieved their six **ProjectInfo** elements. Each contains all of the project information we need. Let's get that now.

7. As we're dealing with elements and need to retrieve element parameters, let's place the **Element.Parameters** node. The following screenshot shows the connected node:

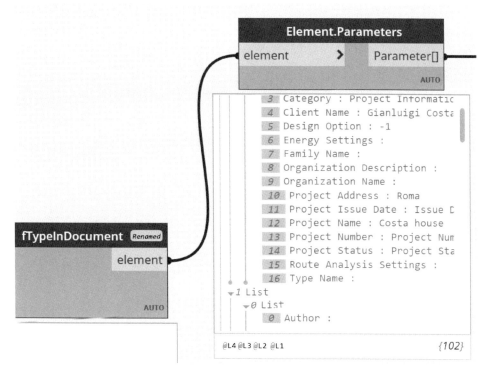

Figure 10.4 – Using Element.Parameters to get a list of parameters from an element

If you check the output preview window of the **Element.Parameters** node, you should see six lists with the project information we needed. From each of them, we want to get a few items. In my case, I need to pick the following:

a) **Project Address**

b) **Client Name**

c) **Project Name**

8. How do we get items from a list? We can use **List.GetItemAtIndex**. Let's place one, along with a **Code Block** node, to specify the indexes we want. Those items are located at indexes **10**, **4**, and **12**. We also want to specify the level to use. Set the **list** input of the **List.GetItemAtIndex** node to **@L2**, as shown here:

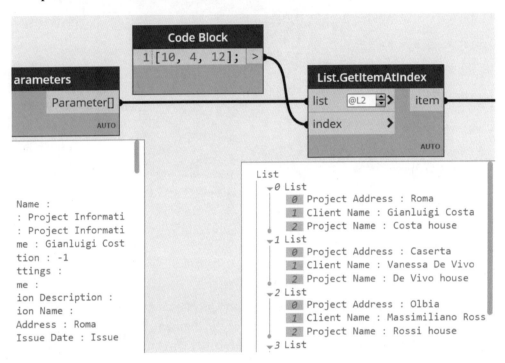

Figure 10.5 – Once we have specified the indexes, we can retrieve the items we need

That's awesome! We successfully got that information from every Revit model open in the background. We now know where the model is located, who the client is, and the project's name. As you can see, I've simplified the information to provide a more straightforward approach; I want you to learn the logic behind the algorithm and not deal with complex data right now. In this way, you'll know how to face more complex datasets in the future.

You have probably noticed from the output preview window that we got the parameter values we needed, but we also got the name of the attributes at the same time. And that's not good. Later on, we want to provide Power BI with the parameter values only. We can't give Power BI the **Project Address: Roma** string. Instead, we only want to send the **Roma** value. It seems that we might need to use some sort of string manipulation here. What do you think? I'm thinking about **RegExes**, of course!

9. So, search for and place the following nodes:

    a) **Regex.FindRegularExpression**

    b) **String**

    c) **String from Object**

10. We have a few strings at this point, including both the name of the attribute and the value itself. The strings are as follows:

    a) **Project Address: Roma**

    b) **Client Name: Gianluigi Costa**

    c) **Project Name: Costa house**

    We need a regular expression that takes every character after the comma, right? We want to get **Roma**, **Gianluigi Costa**, and **Costa house** only, without the parameter names. The RegEx for this is as follows:

```
: ( . * ) $
```

Let me explain what happened here. The syntax we used works as follows:

- : matches the colon character.

- (represents the start of the capturing group.

- . matches any characters except line breaks.

- *matches 0 or more of the preceding tokens.

-) closes the capturing group.

- $ specifies that we want to match everything we wrote before until the end of the string.

The correct output should look like this:

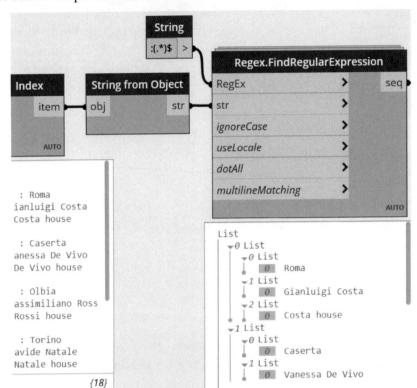

Figure 10.6 – Using a RegEx to get the partial string we need

You have probably noticed the **String from Object** node. This is essential as the output of **List.GetItemAtIndex** is not a list of strings, and we need to convert it into a string data type.

Now, we have two things to fix:

- We want the same Revit model values grouped in the same list and not in separate ones, as shown in the previous screenshot.

- Then, we want to eliminate the space before each value. If you take a closer look at the previous screenshot, you'll see that each value starts after a space key, and we don't want that.

To group the same Revit model values, we want to use the **List.Flatten** node. As the name suggests, this node will flatten the levels of the input lists by a specified amount. Let's see how it works. The **List.Flatten** node is pretty applicable when it comes to eliminating unnecessary levels.

Please notice that the **amt** input is written in italics, which we now know means that it is optional. If you leave it blank, the node will flatten everything to a single list by default. But since we have data coming from multiple models, we don't want to flatten everything into a single list of values as we won't know where a Revit model's data starts and ends later. Let's set **@L2** on the **List.Flatten** node:

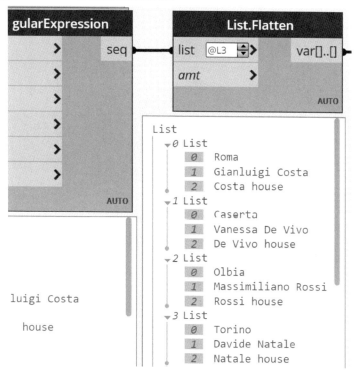

Figure 10.7 – Now, every dataset is grouped into separate lists

We did this correctly by using the **List.Flatten** node. It's pretty simple to use and very helpful. You'll use the **List.Flatten** node a lot in the future, so you'd better learn how to use it!

Next, we want to remove the space before each string. Note that we could have done this with a slightly upgraded regular expression, but I want you to learn something new when it comes to "cleaning" strings. In computer science, every operation related to "cleaning" strings has, sooner or later, got something to do with white spaces. White spaces are unnecessary spaces for a specific string, whether before or after a particular text. Think, for example, about a user signing up on a website, and they mistakenly place one or two spaces before their username. Developers often do automatic trimming operations to solve that. And guess what – Dynamo has OOTB nodes to help us with that. Let's place the **String.TrimWhitespace** node and provide the **List.Flatten** node to it, on the **str** input.

The following screenshot compares the two lists:

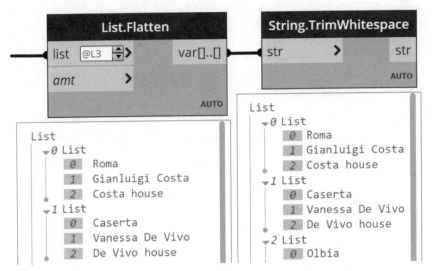

Figure 10.8 – String.TrimWhitespace will remove unnecessary spaces before and after strings

By using **String.TrimWhitespace**, we removed any unnecessary spaces around those strings, and all of the values are finally "cleaned":

Figure 10.9 – Much whitespace, very clean

With the last operation, we completed our steps to get project information. We learned that we could open multiple Revit models in the background using a few custom packages. We also understood how to get, clean, manage, and organize project information properly. But we've just scratched the surface here. The following section will be more elaborate as we need to gather much more data from the Revit models.

Collecting information about Rooms

Now, it's time to focus on element information. I am talking about all of the information that is associated with a single-family instance, such as their categories, family names, family types, and some other attributes. After we get those, we want to group them and get ready for the Excel export. There are plenty of categories in those sample models, and as this will not be a 1,000-page book, we will just focus on three categories during this exercise. Of course, the things you'll learn about those three categories will apply to any other category. Remember, we want to understand the logic and not waste time with pointless and complicated datasets.

Let's get started:

1. The first thing we must do is collect information about **Rooms**. For that purpose, we need the **Collector.ElementsOfCategoryInDocument** node, which we used previously to collect project information, and the **Categories** node, as we are no longer dealing with element types. So, search for and place the following:

   a) **Collector.ElementsOfCategoryInDocument**

   b) **Categories**

   From the **Categories** node choose **Rooms**.

2. Next, get their parameter values. If we find those values to be messy, we will use regular expressions again to fix everything! I know that's not your hope too, but regular expressions are powerful weapons when dealing with strings!

3. I am sure you know what node to place after a list of elements to get their parameter values. It's **Element.Parameters**. Place one and connect it. Also, remember to connect the **Document** output of **Applications.OpenDocumentFile** to the **Document** input of the **Collector.ElementsOfCategoryInDocument** node. Now, hit **Run**!

Let's take a look at the following screenshot:

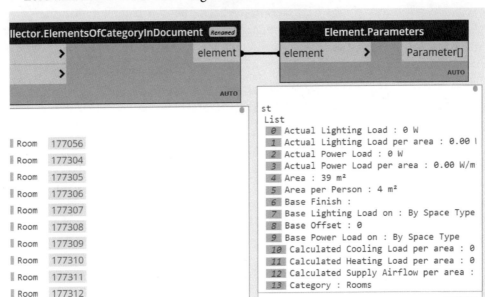

Figure 10.10 – We received a lot of items after using Element.Parameters on Rooms

Take a look at the output of the **Element.Parameters** list. Using the Revit models provided in the *Technical requirements* section, you should have the same number of items; that's more than 16,000 items, as you can see by the bottom-right of the output preview. Keep in mind that we are only working with six Revit models. I created a script 1 year ago that retrieves information from more than 1,000 Revit models simultaneously, and that's a bit frightening, to be honest, but we achieved the desired results.

4. Let's get the items we want from each list. I want you to get the following parameter values:

a) **Category**

b) **Area**

c) **Level**

d) **Name**

5. Please go ahead and create a **List.GetItemAtIndex** instance and a **Code Block** instance to specify the indexes (I won't tell you what indexes to get as you already know how to get them, as we did that plenty of times during this chapter and the previous ones).

6. Don't forget to set **@L2** to the **List.GetItemAtIndex** node, and also click on the **Keep list structure** checkbox. We need this option enabled to group the **Rooms** data in separate lists for each Revit model.

Now, you should see the following results:

Figure 10.11 – We received Category, Area, Level, and Name for each Room, for each Revit model

You'll also notice a bluish background on the list input when you enable **Keep list structure**, as shown in the previous screenshot. That's a visual confirmation that we enabled the **Keep list structure** option.

7. Looking at each Room's data, you'll notice a similar situation to what we had the project information previously. We have attribute names and values on the exact string. And that means only one thing: *it's now time to use a RegEx, my friend!* The boring thing, though, is that we could use the same regular expression as earlier. Let's place the nodes, as shown here:

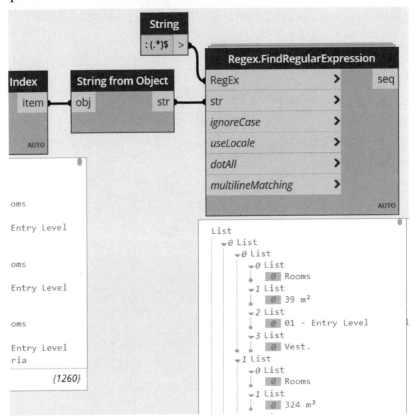

Figure 10.12 – We used a regular expression to get the end part of each string

We also used **String from Object** to convert a list of objects into strings before passing it to the regex node. Then, to avoid using whitespace trimming again, I wrote a slightly modified regular expression:

```
:  (.*)$
```

We have to use the same regex we used previously in the first section, *Collecting information from multiple models*, but we want to place a space after the comma this time. This will help us avoid whitespaces.

8. Now, let's use **List.Flatten** to group and organize our strings. Take a look at the following screenshot:

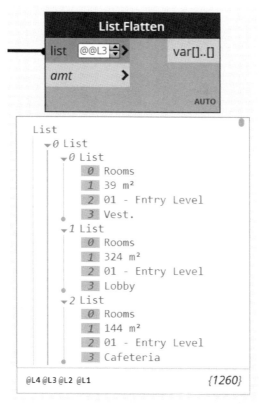

Figure 10.13 – Using List.Flatten will allow us to organize our lists of strings

Note that you need to set **@L3** this time and enable **Keep list structure**. By doing so, we will get all **Rooms** data in separate lists, by Revit model. If you didn't, **Save** the Dynamo script again!

We did it. We collected **Rooms** data and organized it into separate lists. In this section, we collected information similarly to how we collected the project information. This time, though, we learned how to get information about the different elements, starting from their category. The following sections will do the same to two more categories: **Levels** and **Sheets**.

Collecting data from Levels

We will collect **Levels** data now. The goal here is to retrieve attributes such as name, elevation, and a few more. Before we begin, I want you to organize the nodes, as shown here:

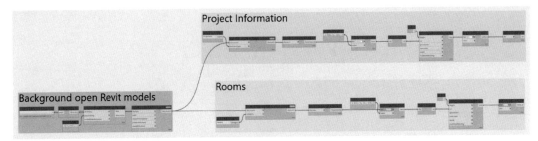

Figure 10.14 – Organizing the nodes into groups by their scope

You can group multiple nodes by selecting them, right-clicking, and choosing **Create a Group** or by pressing *Ctrl* + *G* on your keyboard. I've used a 72 font size because I want to read the group names when I've zoomed out as we place many nodes in this script.

Now, let's copy/paste the nodes we used to collect the **Rooms** data. You can left-click on the **Rooms** group, then press *Ctrl* + *C* and *Ctrl* + *V* to paste the copied group. Move it just below the **Rooms** group, as shown in the following screenshot:

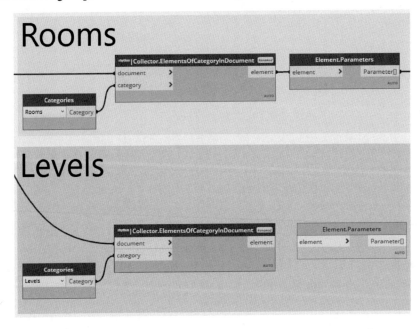

Figure 10.15 – Copying and pasting the Rooms group to create the Levels group

As you can see, I've disconnected the **Collector.ElementsOfCategoryInDocument** node from the **Element.Parameters** one as we need to filter out some of the elements from the **Collector** output list. We also have family types in that list, but we want to deal with just the instances for obvious reasons. We want to collect all the information about families that have been placed in the 3D environment (instances), not the family types coming from the family library catalog (types).

9.   Now, let's hit **Run** and check out the output preview window.

Dynamo takes a few minutes to gather the data (remember that we're working on six Revit models simultaneously). The waiting time will depend on your PC hardware. If you feel like your PC is getting a bit tired, you can restart it. Most of the time, it helps to refresh the RAM!

The output of **Collector.ElementsOfCategoryInDocument** should look as follows:

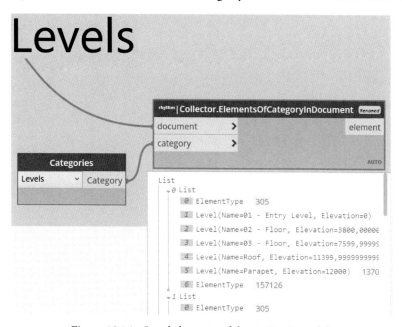

Figure 10.16 – Level elements of the six Revit models

As you can see, we have some additional elements we don't want, such as element types. We need to find a way to filter out the results. We often use **List. FilterByBoolMask** for that, so let's see how.

10. To filter out our results, let's use the following nodes:

a) **String from Object**

b) **Code Block**

c) **String.Contains**

d) **List.FilterByBoolMask**

Those nodes should be arranged like so:

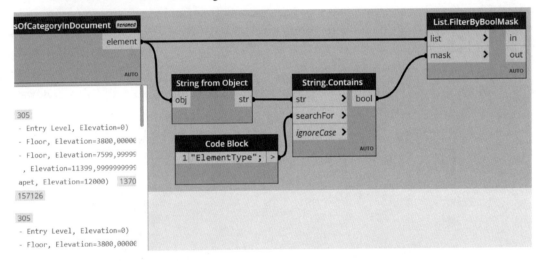

Figure 10.17 – How to filter the results from the list of Level elements

I've used a string containing the word **"ElementType"** to filter the unwanted element types. Also, to group the new nodes with the **Levels** group, you want to select the new nodes, the group, and then right-click on one of the nodes and click on **Add to Group**.

11. Perfect – we now have our list of **Levels**. From here, connect the **Elements. Parameters** node. Note that you need to connect the **Out** output of the **List. FilterByBoolMask** node to make it work. The **Out** output contains the correct list of **Level** elements. When you hit **Run**, I would like you to check the output list and get the following parameters:

a) **Category**

b) **Elevation**

c) **Name**

12. Then, connect **List.GetItemAtIndex** and write the correct indexes, as shown here:

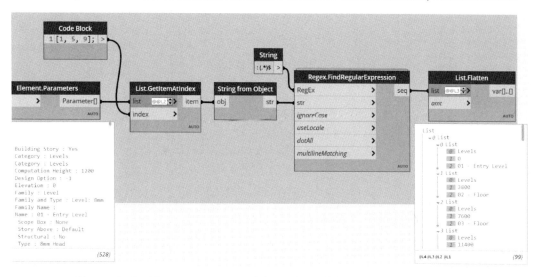

Figure 10.18 – The remaining part of the nodes will deal with the cleaning tasks

Perfect – we now have **Levels** information too. As you can see, the script is getting bigger and bigger. And by the way, here, we're just gathering some of the available information. *Now that we understand how to get project and elements data, group nodes, and filter the results we want, we are unstoppable!* In the next section, we will do the same by collecting Revit **Sheets** data.

Collecting information from Sheets

As we did with **Rooms** and **Levels**, the algorithm to gather **Sheets** data works similarly. To get started, let's copy/paste the **Level** group, move it below **Rooms**, and rename it. The following screenshot shows the whole script so far:

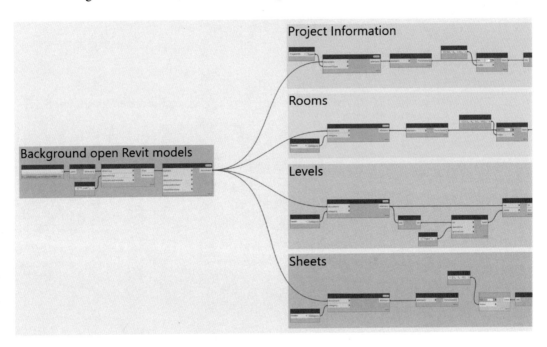

Figure 10.19 – We've created five groups, each with a specific function

It would be best if you organized your script the same way. We have to be as organized as possible because it will help us quickly find any issue that may come up during development and because, in the future, we may need to update or add more functions to the script. If everything is messy, we will have a hard time updating the script.

Now, let's focus on collecting data from Revit **Sheets**:

1. After copying and pasting the **Levels** group, please change the category from the drop-down list of the **Categories** node by selecting **Sheets**.

2. Next, make sure to disconnect the output of the **Element.Parameters** node, as we need to check the position of the attributes we want to retrieve.

3. When you disconnect the node, press **Run** and check the output preview window of the **Element.Parameters** node, as shown here:

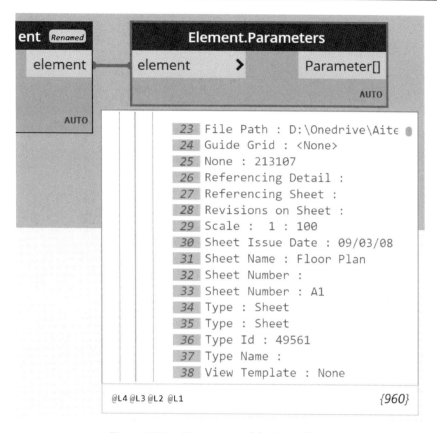

Figure 10.20 – Parameters of the Revit Sheets

The Revit **Sheets** have multiple parameters. You can think of creating a script that will collect all of the information related to sheets. In this way, you can track the number of sheets, issue dates, authors, and much more helpful information. You can think to create an entire dashboard only on **Sheets**, **Views**, and **Schedules** to manage and control our BIM models. In this exercise, we want to gather the following data:

a) **Category**

b) **Sheet Name**

c) **Scale**

4. After finding the correct indexes of those attributes, please connect the remaining parts of the nodes. The following screenshot shows the results:

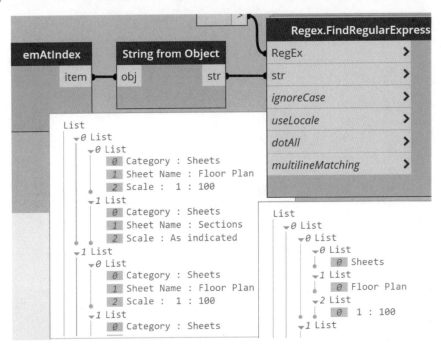

Figure 10.21 – Collecting the Category, Sheet Name, and Scale of the Revit sheets

The preceding screenshot shows that the regular expression worked great, even if the **Scale** attribute contains two commas. The reason is that the regular expression starts at the beginning of the string, so everything after the first comma is captured. However, one thing to fix is the **Scale** value because there is an additional space before the value itself.

5. To fix that, we know we need to use the **String.TrimWhitespace** node, as we did when gathering **Rooms** information. Let's place the node after **List.Flatten**, as shown in the following screenshot:

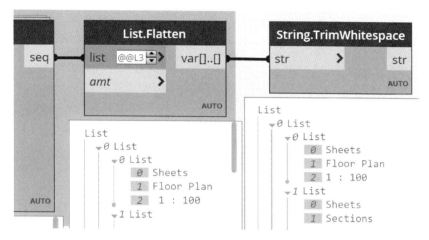

Figure 10.22 – The String.TrimWhitespace node will remove all of the unnecessary spaces

Perfect – everything is looking good. The last thing we must do is add the **String. TrimWhitespace** node to the **Sheets** group.

6. You can select the node and the group, then right-click on the node and choose **Add to group**, as shown here:

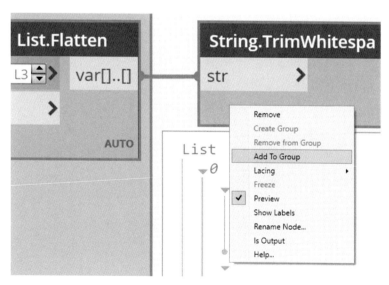

Figure 10.23 – Selecting both the group and the node, and then right-clicking on the node and choosing Add to Group

This last operation completes the data gathering tasks of our script. We collected data on **Project Information**, **Rooms**, **Levels**, and **Sheets** too. The following section will be the last one that puts everything together before we export the data to an Excel file. Let's see how that works.

Adding the filename to each list

Finally, we need to add information about the filename to every list we have so far. This is important because we are working with multiple Revit models, and we need to identify when a dataset starts and when it stops inside the Excel sheets. We need one more column of data to do that. When printed on Excel, each row of information will belong to one file only. And this is the best way to know what data belongs to what model.

We want to add a new group of nodes, starting from the directory contents we created at the beginning of this exercise. By converting the directory content's list into strings, we will extract the filename and add that to each list of data that's been collected so far. Let's learn how to do that:

1. Place a **String from Object** node just above the **FileSystem.GetDirectoryContents** node. The following screenshot shows what I mean:

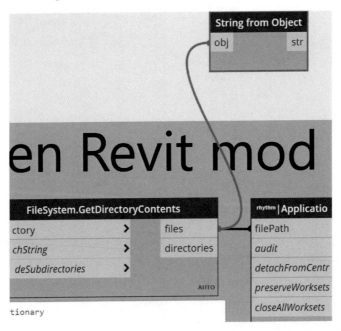

Fig. 10.24 - Use a String from Object node to convert the file paths to strings

Perfect – we now have a list of strings that contains file paths. Before continuing, please select the **Application.OpenDocumentFile** node, right-click on it, and choose **Freeze**. In this way, we're not asking Dynamo to compute everything every time we run the script. At the moment, we need to focus on the file paths.

2. Now that we've collected the file paths as strings and we only want to extract the filenames, it's time to use a new regular expression! Place the **Regex. FindRegularExpression** node, along with a **String** node.

3. Next, use the following regular expression:

```
([^\\]+$)
```

This expression works as follows:

- (represents the beginning of the capturing group.

- [^ is a negation set. This means that we want to match everything that is not included in the set.

- \\, where the first backslash is an escaping character. The second is just a backslash.

-] represents the set closure.

- +$ means one or more of the preceding tokens, until the end of the string.

-) represents the capturing group closure.

To me, the most astonishing thing about regex is that with five or six symbols, we can instruct the computer to perform complex operations on strings. It's insane. I love it! On the contrary, if we'd used string operations, we would have ended up placing lots of nodes on the Dynamo workspace environment. And we don't want to waste time nor space.

4. Hit **Run** and check the output preview window of the **Regex. FindRegularExpression** node. As expected, the results are the filenames only, and that's fantastic!

Now, we want to insert each of the filenames into the correct sub-list. Before continuing, unfreeze the **Application.OpenDocumentFile** node but freeze each **Collector** node of every group except for **Project Information**.

5. Select the **Collector** nodes at the beginning of the **Rooms**, **Levels**, and **Sheets** groups, and then right-click on each and **Freeze** them. *Also, save the Dynamo script.*

6. Now, search for a node called **List.AddItemToFront** and place it after the regex. The following screenshot shows how to set up the node:

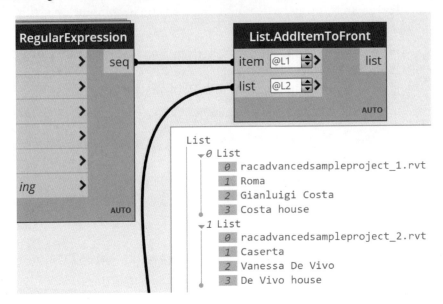

Figure 10.25 – List.AddItemToFront will insert an item into each sublist

To achieve the preceding output, you need to connect the regular expression output to the item input. Then, you need to connect the **String.TrimWhitespace** output to the list input of the same **List.AddItemToFront** node.

Also, make sure that you correctly set the levels of the **Item** and **List** inputs. Set **@L1** on the **item** input and **@L2** on the **list** input. Those settings will place each filename inside each different sublist. As you can see, the first model, **racadvancedsampleproject_1.rvt**, is located in Rome, the second in Caserta, and so on. Now, we have to do the same to every group we created previously.

7. Move the **List.AddItemToFront** node closer to the end of the **Project Information** group as we will use that node when inserting data into the Excel file later.

8. Now, before placing a new **List.AddItemToFront** right after the **Rooms** group, we need to place two more nodes. If you take a look at the last **List.Flatten** node of the **Rooms** group, you'll see that it is organized into four levels, not three like the **Regex** output list. As we want to add an item to many lists and sublists, we need the levels of the two lists to match in length and item numbers. Think about it this way: we have six pencils and we want to insert them into 50 different boxes. That's impossible, right?

To solve that, we want to do *"something"* that duplicates our *"pencils"* (the filenames) as many times as there are boxes (the rooms). And not only that, but we also want to keep the list structure because we're dealing with multiple Revit models simultaneously. All we need to do is place two nodes: **List.Count** and **List. OfRepeatedItem**.

Note that the item input of the **List.OfRepeatedItem** node must be connected to the **Regex.FindRegularExpression** node we placed in *Step 4* to extract the filenames.

9.   Next, place **List.AddItemToFront** and connect everything, as shown in the following screenshot:

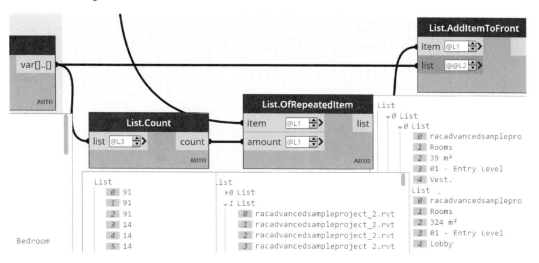

Figure 10.26 – List.OfRepeatedItem will duplicate our filenames by provided amounts

Let me explain what happened here. The **List.Flatten** node of the **Rooms** group contains data about each Room in each model. That data is organized into four levels. With the **List.Count** node, we're counting how many items we have inside those lists, and we're using that count to provide different numbers to the **List. OfRepeatedItem** node, which has the job of repeating an item a particular amount of times. If you look at their outputs, we can see that we need to repeat the filename of the first model 91 times because it contains 91 rooms. Next, we replicate 91 times the filename of the second model, 91 times the filename of the third model, 14 times the fourth model, and so on. I hope this makes sense to you now.

10. Next, don't forget to set the following levels to each node:

- **List.Count**:

  a) **list** input to **@L3**

- **List.OfRepeatedItem**:

  a) **item** input to **@L1**

  b) **amount** input to **@L1**

- **List.AddItemToFront**:

  a) **item** input to **@L1**

  b) **list** input to **@L2**, checking the **Keep list structure** button too

  That last operation was tricky, but we could solve this issue in a few minutes with a bit of problem-solving!

11. Now, unfreeze the **Collector** node of the **Levels** group.

12. The last node of this group also has four levels. So, we need to do the same thing we just did. We need to repeat our "pencils" (the filenames) several times. Let's copy/paste the **List.Count**, **List.OfRepeatItem**, and **List.AddItemToFront** nodes and connect them, as shown in the following screenshot. Then, hit **Run**:

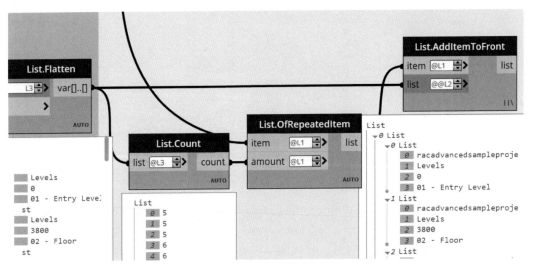

Figure 10.27 – Copying and pasting the last nodes just after the Levels group

The last node of the **Levels** group, **List.Flatten**, has four levels, so without changing the settings of the levels (**@L1**, **@L2**, and so on) to the inputs of the copied nodes, we should be able to achieve the desired result.

13. Now, it's time to save the script! We can also unfreeze the **Collector** node of the **Sheets** group and do the same copy/paste we just did. Go ahead and connect the nodes, just as we did with the **Levels** group. When you place and connect each copied node correctly, the result should look as follows:

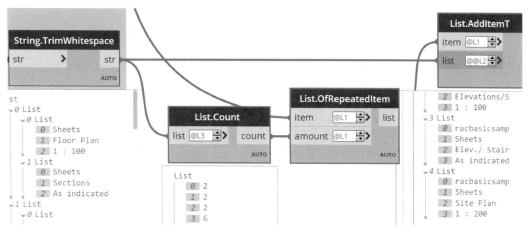

Figure 10.28 – Copying the three nodes right after the Sheets group

Awesome! We've added the filename to each list of each Revit model. Everything will make more sense in a few minutes when we export the data to Excel. One last thing we must do before moving on is add those nodes to each group. Select them, select the group, then right-click on one of those nodes and choose **Add to Group**. Before continuing with the export part of the script using Microsoft Excel, let's recap what we learned in this section:

Figure 10.29 – Excel-lent meme

We just learned when to use the **List.OfRepeatedItem** node. The main reason for using it is when we have lists with different lengths and level structures. Then, we learned how to add information to the front of each sublist using the **List.AddItemToFront** node. And as you're probably thinking, yes, there is also a node called **List.AddItemToEnd** in case we have to insert data at the end of our lists. *In the next section, we will focus on exporting those datasets to Excel the right way!*

Exporting the datasets to Excel

Here we are – we have a script that collects various datasets from multiple Revit models. Now, it's time to write those datasets to Excel. The goal is to separate that information into different Excel sheets. Remember, we want to be as organized as possible, and we don't want to export all of the data into a single Excel sheet. The sheet could be very long if we use complex Revit models, and Excel isn't a good solution for extended datasets. And by extended, I mean 100,000+ rows. That would cause problems later on when working with Microsoft Power BI. So, let's learn how to do that:

1. The first thing we must do is create a new Excel file on our PC.
2. Next, switch to Dynamo and save the file if you haven't done that recently.
3. Now, place the **Data.ExportExcel** OOTB node. The node takes six inputs, one of which is optional. Let's start by providing **filePath** first. To do that, we want to place a **File Path** node and connect it to the **filePath** input of the **Data.ExportExcel** one.
4. After that, we want to create a **Code Block** and type **Project Information** as a string to connect it to our **sheetName** input. We will use this **Code Block** to connect the **startRow** and **startCol** inputs.
5. Next, write the number **0** below the **Project Information** string. Then, connect it to those two inputs, **startRow** and **startCol**, as shown here:

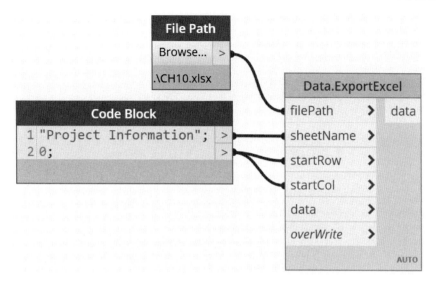

Figure 10.30 – Connecting the outputs of Code Block to sheetName, startRow, and startCol

Great! Now, it's time to feed **Data.ExportExcel** with some data.

6.   All we have to do is connect the last node of the **Project Information** group to the data input of the **Data.ExportExcel** node. When you're done, hit **Run** and check out the following screenshot:

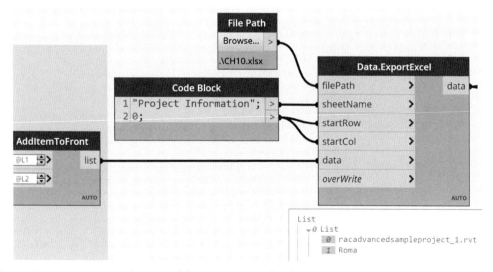

Figure 10.31 – Connecting the List.AddItemToFront node of the Project Information group to the Data.
ExportExcel node

When you hit **Run**, you should see the Excel file opening. The information has been written on a sheet named **Project Information**, as we specified in **Code Block**. Each line includes data coming from a single Revit model. And that's great because this is the best format to provide to Power BI later on.

7. At this point, we want to add some sort of intelligence to the Dynamo script as we need to write multiple datasets to multiple Excel sheets. I want to add *"something"* that writes information in a queue. I want to write **Project Information** on the first sheet. Only when this task is completed do I want Dynamo to continue writing the **Rooms** information to the next sheet, and so on. I don't want to run the script and execute all of the writing tasks altogether as it may overload my PC or, even worse, freeze the Dynamo script. Of course, this is not the case because we're working with six simple models, and we're collecting relatively little data. But it can happen with more complex models or datasets. And of course, we don't want that. We want to avoid those situations as much as possible. Let's take a look at the following screenshot to see what I mean:

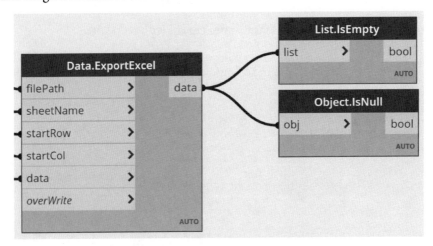

Figure 10.32 – Placing the List.IsEmpty and Object.IsNull nodes

As you can see, the **List.IsEmpty** and **Object.IsNull** nodes check if a list is empty or has null values. Why do we want to check that? We want to ensure that the preceding nodes are working correctly. By checking if there are empty lists or null values, we can control whether to write that information in the Excel file and decide to stop the script's execution in case of any problems. Place those two nodes, connect them to the **Data.ExportExcel** node, and hit **Run**.

8. As those two nodes provide Boolean values, we can check if they're both false. The following two nodes to place are called **List Create** and **List.AllFalse**. Place and connect them, as shown in the following screenshot:

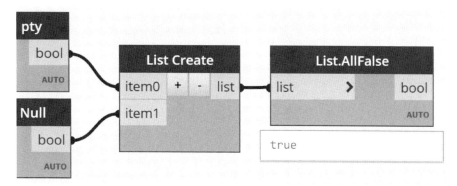

Figure 10.33 – Code Block and List.AllFalse will check if the incoming lists are false

List Create will group those two lists of boolean values, while **List.AllFalse** tells us if every value is a false Boolean. Next, we want to check if **List.AllFalse** returns true or false. If the result is true, you can move on and write the data to Excel. If it's false, stop the script.

9. Now, let's group those nodes, as shown here:

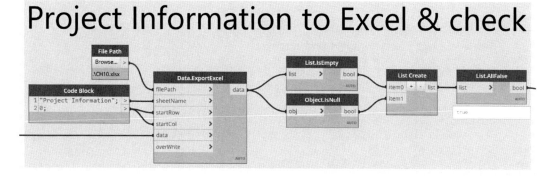

Figure 10.34 – Creating a new group with the last few nodes

10. I've named the group **Project Information to Excel & check**. As we only want to continue the script's execution if the result is true, we need to place an **If statement** node. This node will get some **Test** input, which is the **bool** output of the **List. AllFalse** node we just created.

11. Next, on the **True** input, let's connect the last node of the **Rooms** group; that is, **List.AddItemToFront**.

12. While on the **false** input, let's write **null** inside **Code Block** and connect it. In case of any problems, the **If statement** node will pass a null value to the **Data. ExportExcel** node, causing the script to stop. The following screenshot shows the connected **If statement** node:

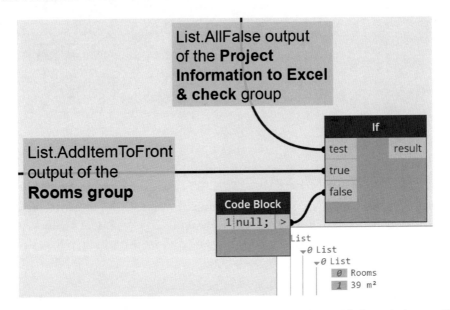

Figure 10.35 – If the List.AllFalse node outputs true, we can continue with the script's execution

As shown in the previous screenshot, the **If statement** node will pass the data that's connected to the **true** input if **test** is true.

13. Now, we want to copy/paste the **Project Information to Excel & check** group. Once you've done this, move it after the **If statement** node we just created.

14. The first thing we must do here is rename the group to **Rooms to Excel & check**.

15. Now, change the **sheetName** input we wrote inside **Code Block**. Modify the string to "Rooms"; . By doing so, we are creating a new Excel sheet named **Rooms** and feeding the sheet with the **Rooms** data we collected previously.

16. Also, since the data we want to feed to the **Data.ExportExcel** node is organized into four levels, we need to manipulate it a bit to solve writing problems that may occur. Place **List.Flatten** between the **If statement** node and the **Rooms to Excel & check** group.

17. Set the input of the **List.Flatten** node to @L2. Then, connect the **List.Flatten** output to the **Data.ExportExcel** data input.

The arrangement of those nodes is shown in the following screenshot:

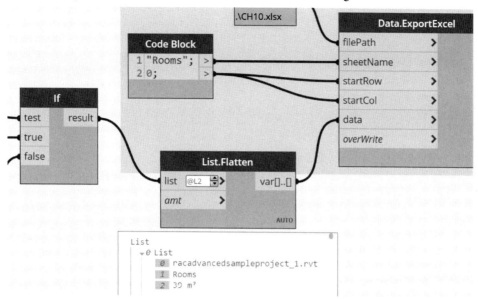

Figure 10.36 – Using List.Flatten to remove the extra fourth level

Why did we remove the fourth level of the **If statement** output? The reason is that **Data.ExportExcel** will only write the last few datasets of our list to the Excel file. This means it will only write information about the last Revit model. However, the **List.Flatten** node will solve this issue flawlessly.

18. Let's take a look at the Excel file now. Open the last sheet containing the last dataset we wrote, **Rooms**:

298	racbasicsampleproject_2.rvt	Rooms	24 m²	Level 1	Hall
299	racbasicsampleproject_2.rvt	Rooms	70 m²	Level 1	Living
300	racbasicsampleproject_2.rvt	Rooms	2 m²	Level 1	Mech.
301	racbasicsampleproject_2.rvt	Rooms	1 m²	Level 2	Linen
302	racbasicsampleproject_3.rvt	Rooms	27 m²	Level 2	Master Bedroom
303	racbasicsampleproject_3.rvt	Rooms	7 m²	Level 2	Master Bath

Fig. 10.37 – The Rooms sheet of the Excel file

The first column shows what Room belongs to what Revit model, and that's great!

19. Also, let's check the **List.AllFalse** node of the **Rooms to Excel & check** group. The result should be true.

Ready for another writing operation? We have **Levels** and **Sheets** left. Let's go.

20. Select the **Rooms to Excel & check** node, including the **If statement** node, its **Code Block**, and the **List.Flatten** node. Copy everything, paste it, and move it, as shown in the following screenshot:

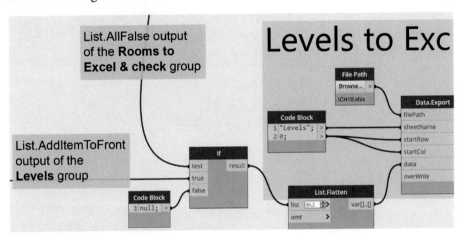

Figure 10.38 – Copying the whole group, along with the If statement, Code Block, and List.Flatten nodes

As you can see, we renamed the copied group to **Levels to Excel & check** and changed the **sheetName** string to **Levels**. Please go ahead and do that. Leave the **List.Flatten** node as **@L2** and hit **Run**.

21. The data has been correctly written in a new Excel sheet named **Levels**. Awesome! Now, we have to write the **Sheets** group. Perform the same operations that we did for the **Levels to Excel & check** group for the **Sheets** group. For this, you must do the following:

- Copy/paste the **Levels to Excel & check** group, including the **If statement**, its **Code Block**, and the **List.Flatten** nodes.

- Rename the copied group **Sheets to Excel & check**.

- Change the string that feeds the **sheetName** input of the **Data.ExportExcel** node.

- Leave **List.Flatten** on **@L2**.

22. The following screenshot shows the completed arrangement of this last group of nodes:

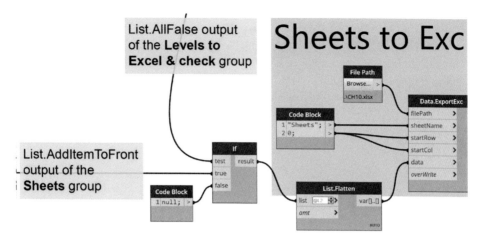

Figure 10.39 – Sheets to Excel group

With the **Sheets to Excel & check** nodes, we have finished writing the Excel tasks! All you have to do is save the Dynamo file if you haven't recently, then hit **Run** and check the Excel file to see if everything is working correctly. And as expected, everything looks good so far:

Figure 10.40 – Using Dynamo to export data from multiple Revit models meme

This section taught us how to manage, organize, and export data from multiple Revit models to Excel. We took advantage of the **If statement** node to check whether a list contains null or empty values. In this way, we also learned how to stop the script's execution in case of any problems. This time, we checked if there were null or empty lists, but you can do any check you like. In the future, I am sure you will come up with new, unique workflows so that you have complete control over your script's execution. It's now time for the last section of this chapter. We want to create a simple user interface that will allow us to execute this script without opening Dynamo!

Adding the user interface

We're now ready to complete the script. I think it's about time to add the icing to the cake! Adding a user interface to a script adds value to our work. It will allow the script to be used by colleagues and peers who don't have Dynamo skills or don't want to open a script to make changes or update variables. All they have to do is press a button from the Dynamo player interface. Then, the Dynamo player will launch the script. If we have developed a user interface, it will come up, asking the user for a few inputs.

We are going to add a few nodes to the beginning of our script. Our goal is to create a simple user interface that asks the user for a directory path. Then, it will pass the directory to the script so that it can be executed. Pretty simple, yet powerful.

Let's learn how to do that:

1. The first thing you must do is install the **Data-Shapes** package if you didn't at the beginning of this chapter.

2. Next, let's **Freeze** the first node of our script. Go to the **Background open Revit models** group, right-click on the **Directory Path** node, and **Freeze** it. We are doing this because there is no need to calculate our datasets and print them in the Excel file. We only want to focus on the UI.

3. Now, let's place the **MultipleInputForm++** node. You can find it by right-clicking and typing its name or searching for it in the Dynamo library, which can be found to the left of the Dynamo UI.

4. Please don't be scared – the node has many inputs to feed, but they're almost all optional. Let's take a look at them one by one:

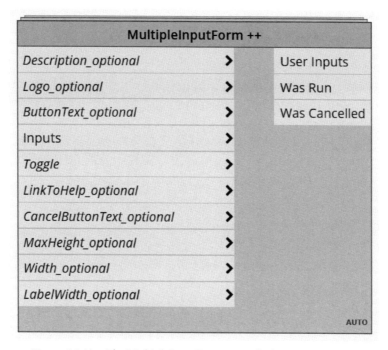

Figure 10.41 – The MultipleInputForm++ node from Data-Shapes

As you can see, the node has several inputs. Let's describe them:

a) **Description_optional** is an optional input and it allows you to add a description to the UI. Maybe we need the user to read some instructions first, and this is the right place to do that. We need to provide a string to it.

b) **Logo_optional** works similarly to the **Description_optional** input, but instead of providing a string, we need to provide an image to make it work.

c) **ButtonText_optional** allows us to customize the **Ok** button. If we don't provide anything, default text will be used.

d) **Inputs** is where the magic happens. We will deep dive into it in a few minutes.

e) **Toggle**, even if it's written in italics, isn't optional. The toggle wants a Boolean value to allow the node to be executed. Providing it with a true value will run the node.

f) **LinkToHelp_optional** is optional, and it places a URL on the UI. I've used it several times because it opens a web page and gives you more space to write instructions than **Description_optional**.

g) **Description** is helpful when we want to place just a few rows of instructions.

h) **CancelButtonText_optional** works similarly to **ButtonText_optional**. It allows you to customize the **Cancel** button in case a user mistakenly runs a script.

i) **MaxHeight_optional** and **Width_optional** are both optional, but I use them every time because they allow us to customize the size of the UI window, and that's a significant feature.

j) **LabelWidth_optional** will regulate the label's width, as the name suggests, but I never use it as the default value works every time.

5. Okay, let's start with the **Description** field. Add a **Code Block instance** and write a string inside it. I wrote, *"This script gathers data from multiple Revit models, please select a Directory."*

6. Next, add a logo to our script. I've used a .png image. If you want, add an image to that input by placing a "**File Path**", selecting the image, and connecting the node to the **Logo** input.

7. For the **ButtonText** input, I've placed a new **Code Block** and wrote the following string: "**Let's go!**". Of course, you can write anything you like. If you don't, a **Set Values** string will appear by default.

8. On the **Inputs** input, we want to place the following nodes:

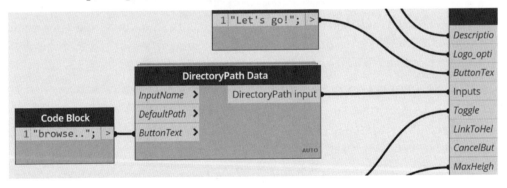

Figure 10.42 – Placing DirectoryPath Data and Code Block

As you can see, we can't feed the **Inputs** input with an OOTB **Directory path** node. We have to use one made by the developers of the **Data-Shapes** package to make it work. Place a node named **DirectoryPath Data** and connect a **Code Block instance** to its **ButtonText** input. I wrote "**browse..**" but you can customize it as you want.

9. Now, let's place one last **Code Block** and type what's shown in the following screenshot:

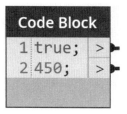

Figure 10.43 – Placing a Code Block instance with true on the first line and 450 on the second

Great – we're almost done! Let's type `true` and `450` inside **Code Block**. Then, we can connect the **true** output to the **Toggle** input and **450** to both the **MaxHeight** and **Width** inputs.

10. With that, everything is set! Before unfreezing the script, let's try this UI and see how it looks. Please go ahead and hit **Run** when you're ready. The following screenshot shows both the nodes' arrangement and the UI:

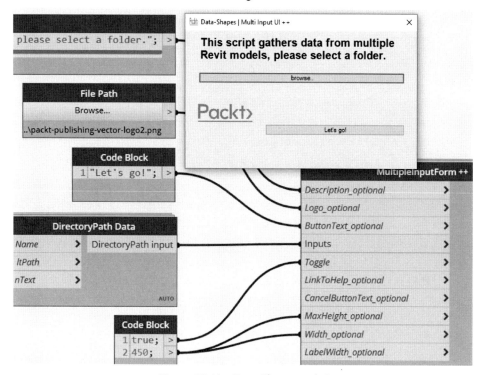

Figure 10.44 – Data-Shapes rocks!

As you can see, the UI we just created has all of the inputs we provided. It has a description, a logo, and customized buttons. Let's try it out. Close the UI by clicking on the X icon at the top right. Save the script, close Dynamo, and restart Revit.

11. Now, open Revit and Dynamo again and open the script. The first thing we must do is delete the node we previously froze, **Directory Path**.

12. Next, connect the **User Inputs** output of **MultipleInputForm++** directly to the **Directory From Path** node, as shown here:

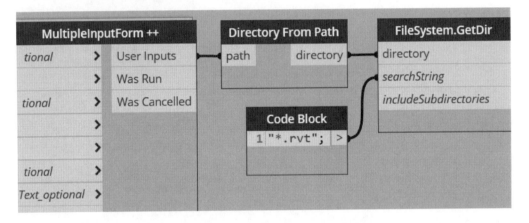

Figure 10.45 – Connecting MultipleInputForm++ to the Directory From Path node

We don't need the **Directory Path** node as we're asking the user to choose a path with the **DirectoryPath Data** node from **Data-Shapes**.

13. When you do, hit **Save** and close Dynamo.

14. We want to launch the script without opening Dynamo; instead, we want to use the Dynamo player. So, let's go back to Revit, open the **Manage** tab, and go to the Dynamo icon. To its right, you'll see another Dynamo icon named **Dynamo player**. Click on that.

15. Now, if you're not familiar with the Dynamo player, don't worry – it's pretty straightforward. When you open it for the first time, you'll see a default list of scripts. All the Dynamo player does is point to a folder and show you all of the scripts in that folder. Of course, it doesn't know where we saved our Dynamo script, so let's click on the first folder icon at the top left of the Dynamo player UI, as shown in the following screenshot:

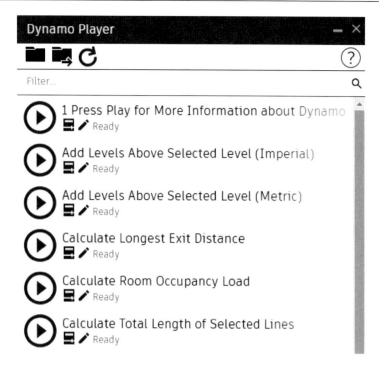

Figure 10.46 – Clicking on the first folder icon at the top left

16. Now, a new window will appear. Here, we need to select the folder where we saved our Dynamo script. So, please go ahead and select the folder. Then, click **Ok**.

17. When you click on **Ok**, you'll be taken back to the Dynamo player list, which shows all of the scripts included in that folder. We're now ready to click on the play icon to run the script.

18. After clicking on the play icon, you'll see the Data-Shapes UI! All we need to do now is browse the folder where we saved the Revit models, click on the **Let's go!** button, and Dynamo will do the rest.

19. Wait a few seconds for Dynamo to complete the data-gathering process and print the results to Excel.

In the end, you'll see an Excel window that contains all the datasets we have retrieved so far, as shown here:

15	racadvancedsampleproject_3.rvt	Levels
16	racbasicsampleproject_1.rvt	Levels
17	racbasicsampleproject_1.rvt	Levels
18	racbasicsampleproject_1.rvt	Levels
19	racbasicsampleproject_1.rvt	Levels
20	racbasicsampleproject_1.rvt	Levels
21	racbasicsampleproject_1.rvt	Levels
22	racbasicsampleproject_2.rvt	Levels
23	racbasicsampleproject_2.rvt	Levels
24	racbasicsampleproject_2.rvt	Levels

| | | Sheets | **Levels** | Rooms | Project Information | | ⊕ |

Figure 10.47 – Excel window showing the exported datasets

Congratulations! You were able to export data coming from multiple Revit models at the same time! That's fantastic.

In this section, we learned how to add a simple yet powerful UI to our script. We learned what kind of data type to provide to each input of **MultipleInputForm++**. Using just a few nodes from the **Data-Shapes** package, we were able to create a window that will pop up every time a user starts our script. Isn't that awesome?!

Now, let's recap what we learned in this chapter.

Summary

In this chapter, we covered quite a lot of things. We learned how to use Autodesk Dynamo to create a script that opens multiple Revit models in the background. By the way, I made a similar script last year, and I've used it to gather data from more than 1,000 Revit models simultaneously. I was so proud of that!

We learned how to retrieve all we wanted from our BIM models during script development by collecting models, rooms, levels, and sheets information. We can query any of the families contained within the model, whether they are family instances or loaded families that haven't been placed yet. Then, we learned how to add the filenames to each list to see where a model's data stops and where the next one begins. Then, we understood how to organize those datasets for Microsoft Excel, exporting different datasets into different sheets.

Also, as the icing on the cake, we learned how to add a simple user interface to our script, allowing colleagues who may not know how to use Dynamo to use it.

I'll see you in the next chapter, where we will take all of the datasets we've retrieved so far and create an excellent dashboard on Power BI. I'll see you later!

Further reading

In this chapter, we used three downloaded packages made by three design technology experts. Keep in mind that those packages take time to develop, and those guys provide them for us to use for free. Contact them on socials and thank them if you get the chance. My chance is now. I want to thank the following people:

- Andreas Dieckmann (Clockworks):
- `https://twitter.com/a_dieckmann`
- John Pierson (Rhythm):
- `https://twitter.com/60secondrevit`
- Mostafa El Ayoubi (Data-Shapes):
- `https://twitter.com/data_shapes`

Their work helps hundreds of users every day. Thanks – keep up the excellent work!

11
Visualizing Data from Multiple Models in Power BI

Here we are – chapter 11! This chapter will use the previously gathered data from multiple Revit models to create great Power BI dashboards.

During the previous *Chapter 10, Gathering a Revit Model's Data from Multiple Models at Once*, we collected a lot of information from six different Revit files. This time, we will use those datasets to create other charts to have a dashboard that will give us a consistent and complete overview of every project.

Also, we will learn how to take advantage of the project addresses to create a Power BI map showing the location of each model. In the end, this will be great also for presenting our work to clients, partners, and colleagues.

Today, indeed, I use Power BI to show our work to partners and clients to show the result of managing and visualizing vast BIM datasets

This chapter will talk about importing data, formatting, creating charts, and visualizing project locations on the map.

The following is a list of the topics we will cover in this chapter:

- Preparing the datasets
- Importing and formatting
- Creating charts
- Visualizing the location of projects on the map

Let's now jump straight into Power BI!

Figure 11.1 – Brace yourselves, Power BI is coming!

Technical requirements

This chapter is pretty straightforward. We only need to have Microsoft Power BI Desktop installed as this will be the primary tool here. If you have followed the previous chapters, you should already have it. If not, install Power BI using the following link:

```
https://powerbi.microsoft.com/en-us/downloads/
```

When you click on the link, scroll down and find the section **Microsoft Power BI Desktop**. Right below this section, you'll see a **Download** button. When you click on the **Download** link, you should see a pop-up message that asks you to open the Microsoft Store and start the download. Do that and come back when you're ready.

Importing and formatting the datasets

OK. Our journey to build Power BI charts starts with Microsoft Excel. Let's open up the Excel file we generated in *Chapter 10, Gathering a Revit Model's Data from Multiple Models at Once*. Before we start using it, however, we need to make a change to the Dynamo script. I don't know if you noticed, but the scale we exported from the Sheets category shows decimal values and not the actual scale. If you saw it, great! Kudos to you! If you don't, don't worry, I'll show you how to fix that in a minute.

So, if you open the Excel file, you'll see that each scale value of each sheet is wrong, the reason being is that when we print something such as 1:100 to Excel, it will be interpreted as numbers to divide. So, Excel will calculate the result of the operation 1:100, and it will type 0.011111.

However, we won't need to add any node to the script to fix the issue. We only need to remove one. Let's follow these steps, and then we will talk about the "computer science" reasons behind this issue:

1. Open the data collector script.

2. Find this part of the script:

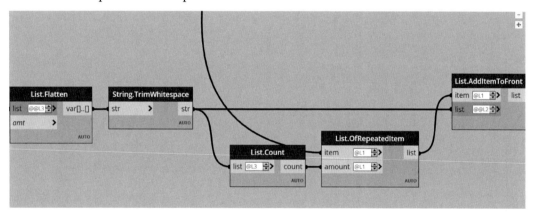

Figure 11.2 – Sheets group of the data collector script

As you can see, the part of the script indicated in the preceding screenshot can be found at the end of the Sheets group of nodes.

3. All we need to do is to connect the **List.Flatten** node directly to the list input of the **List.AddItemToFront** node. When you do that, move the **String.TrimWhitespace** node below.

4.   The following screenshot shows the end result:

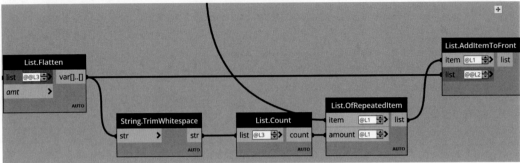

Figure 11.3 – Connecting the List.Flatten output to the list input of the List.AddItemToFront node

The problem has been resolved! Let's now run the script and check the results.

Following script completion, if you go to the **Sheets** page, you'll notice now that every scale value has been inserted correctly. Now we don't have any decimals left.

Why is that? Do you remember that we removed the space in front of each string by using the **String.TrimWhitespace** node? Well, in this case, we left the space only in front of the scale values. If we remove the space, Excel interprets the string **1:100** as a division sum to calculate. If we add a space in front of the scale so that the string will be " **1:100**", Excel interprets this as a text and won't perform any calculations. Computer science can be weird sometimes, can't it?

I am sorry about this slight deviation. Let's now go back to our workflow!

Importing the datasets

As we were saying, the first thing to do is work on Excel to create a few tables. Then, all we need to do is open Power BI, import the datasets, and check those tables.

Let's do this as follows:

1.   Open the file we just regenerated using Microsoft Excel.

2. Go to the **Sheets** page. Open the page and select every row, as shown here:

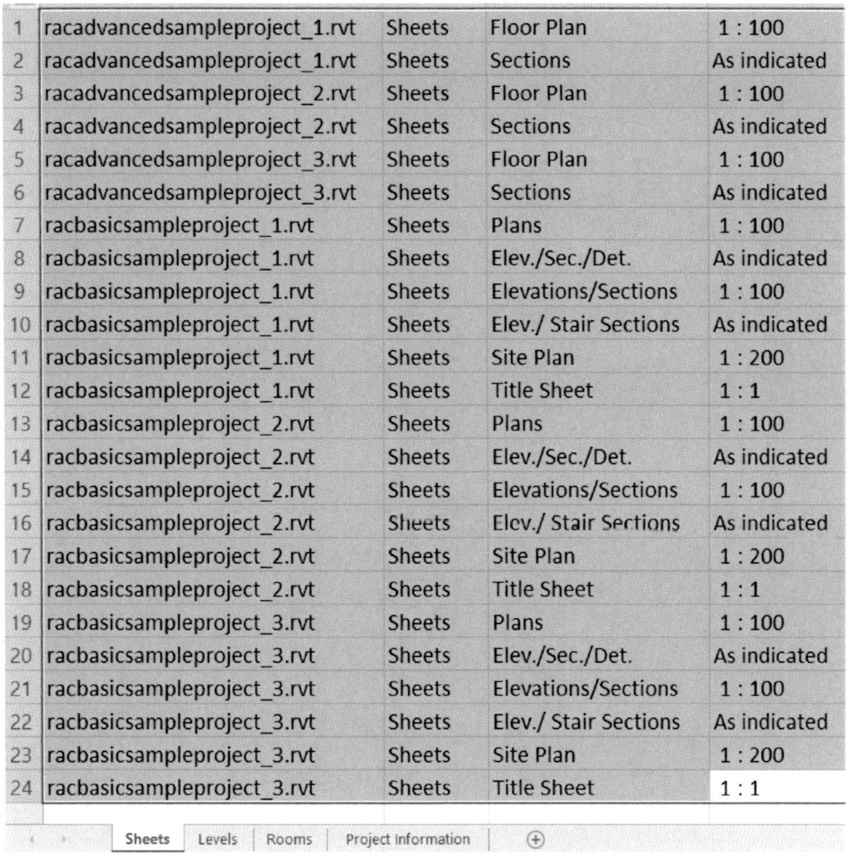

1	racadvancedsampleproject_1.rvt	Sheets	Floor Plan	1 : 100
2	racadvancedsampleproject_1.rvt	Sheets	Sections	As indicated
3	racadvancedsampleproject_2.rvt	Sheets	Floor Plan	1 : 100
4	racadvancedsampleproject_2.rvt	Sheets	Sections	As indicated
5	racadvancedsampleproject_3.rvt	Sheets	Floor Plan	1 : 100
6	racadvancedsampleproject_3.rvt	Sheets	Sections	As indicated
7	racbasicsampleproject_1.rvt	Sheets	Plans	1 : 100
8	racbasicsampleproject_1.rvt	Sheets	Elev./Sec./Det.	As indicated
9	racbasicsampleproject_1.rvt	Sheets	Elevations/Sections	1 : 100
10	racbasicsampleproject_1.rvt	Sheets	Elev./ Stair Sections	As indicated
11	racbasicsampleproject_1.rvt	Sheets	Site Plan	1 : 200
12	racbasicsampleproject_1.rvt	Sheets	Title Sheet	1 : 1
13	racbasicsampleproject_2.rvt	Sheets	Plans	1 : 100
14	racbasicsampleproject_2.rvt	Sheets	Elev./Sec./Det.	As indicated
15	racbasicsampleproject_2.rvt	Sheets	Elevations/Sections	1 : 100
16	racbasicsampleproject_2.rvt	Sheets	Elev./ Stair Sections	As indicated
17	racbasicsampleproject_2.rvt	Sheets	Site Plan	1 : 200
18	racbasicsampleproject_2.rvt	Sheets	Title Sheet	1 : 1
19	racbasicsampleproject_3.rvt	Sheets	Plans	1 : 100
20	racbasicsampleproject_3.rvt	Sheets	Elev./Sec./Det.	As indicated
21	racbasicsampleproject_3.rvt	Sheets	Elevations/Sections	1 : 100
22	racbasicsampleproject_3.rvt	Sheets	Elev./ Stair Sections	As indicated
23	racbasicsampleproject_3.rvt	Sheets	Site Plan	1 : 200
24	racbasicsampleproject_3.rvt	Sheets	Title Sheet	1 : 1

Sheets   Levels   Rooms   Project Information   (+)

Figure 11.4 – Selecting all of the available rows on the Sheets page

As you can see, you only need to use your mouse to select every cell on the **Sheets** page.

3. Once everything is selected, click on **Format as Table**. You can find this in the
    Home tab, inside the **Styles** group. The following screenshot shows where to find
    the button:

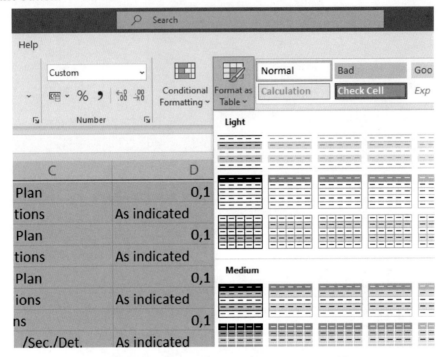

Figure 11.5 – Formatting the selected cells as a table

From here, select one of the available choices. It doesn't matter what color you pick
since, inside Power BI, we won't use the colored tables. Instead, we want to use the
Format as Table feature to name our tables and use their names to find and import
them in Power BI.

4. When you click on one of the available color choices, pay attention to the window
    that pops up. It wants to know whether our table has headers. As our table didn't
    have headers, make sure to uncheck it and then click **OK**.

5. Now we need to rename each column as we didn't specify heading names previously. You'll see on top of each column the name **Column1**, **Column2**, and so on. Let's go ahead and rename those. Starting with **Column1**, I've made the following changes:

- **Filename**

- **Category**

- **Sheet name**

- **Sheet scale**

6. Perfect! Now we need to rename the table itself. The important thing is to choose a cell inside the table. It doesn't matter what cell it is. Any cell will work. Just select one with the left mouse button. Now you should see a new menu appearing after the **Help** menu. Click on this new tab, **Table Design**.

7. When you open it, on the left side, the first group of attributes is called **Properties**. Above that, we can do two things:

a) Specify a new table name.

b) Resize the table.

Inside the **Table Name** textbox, overwrite whatever is written inside it. I'll rename the table to `table_sheets`. I recommend that you use no spaces and all lowercase characters.

8. Now, our **Sheets** page contains a renamed table with headings. Awesome!

9. Now we need to do the same to all of the other pages. Repeat *steps 1 to 8* on all the other pages. I want you to use the following column names:

- Levels (rename as **table_levels**)

    A. **Filename**

    B. **Category**

    C. **Level elevation**

    D. **Level name**

- Rooms (rename as **table_rooms**)

    E. **Filename**

    F. **Category**

    G. **Room area**

    H. **Room level**

    I. **Room name**

- Project Information (rename as **table_projectinfo**)

    J. **Filename**

    K. **City**

    L. **Client name**

    M. **Project name**

10. Well done! We have now completed the table settings in Excel and we're ready to switch to Power BI.

By repeating these steps, we set column names and table names for each of our Excel pages in a few minutes. In this section, we learned how to create tables inside Excel using the dataset we generated previously. Also, we learned how to avoid the division operation in Excel when we export the scale values. We now know that if we insert a space in front of each string, Excel will interpret it as a text and not an operation to calculate! Next, we will import the datasets into Power BI and pave the way for creating the charts.

Formatting the datasets

The following steps will guide us in terms of importing the datasets into Power BI. Let's start by performing the following steps:

1. Open Power Bi Desktop.

2. Then, in the top-right corner, click on the pointing down arrow, right next to **Get data**, and then select **Excel**, as shown in the following screenshot:

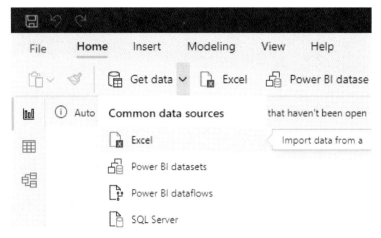

Figure 11.6 – Selecting Excel from the Get data drop-down menu

3. Next, browse your PC folders to find the previously generated Excel file and click **Open**.

4. From here, you should see the Power BI **Navigator** window. On the left, we have a list of tables and sheet names. Select all of the tables we created previously:

- **table_levels**
- **table_projectinfo**
- **table_rooms**
- **table_sheets**

5. When you check them, go ahead and click **Load** in the bottom right of the **Navigator** window.

6. Give Power BI a few seconds to load the tables. When this is done, you will see the tables on the right side of the Power BI user interface, right under the **Fields** panel. Before creating any chart, let's check the datasets we imported by clicking on the **Data** icon on the left of the UI. There are three buttons:

- **Report**
- **Data**
- **Model**

7. Go ahead and click on **Data** to open the table contents view. You should see something like the following:

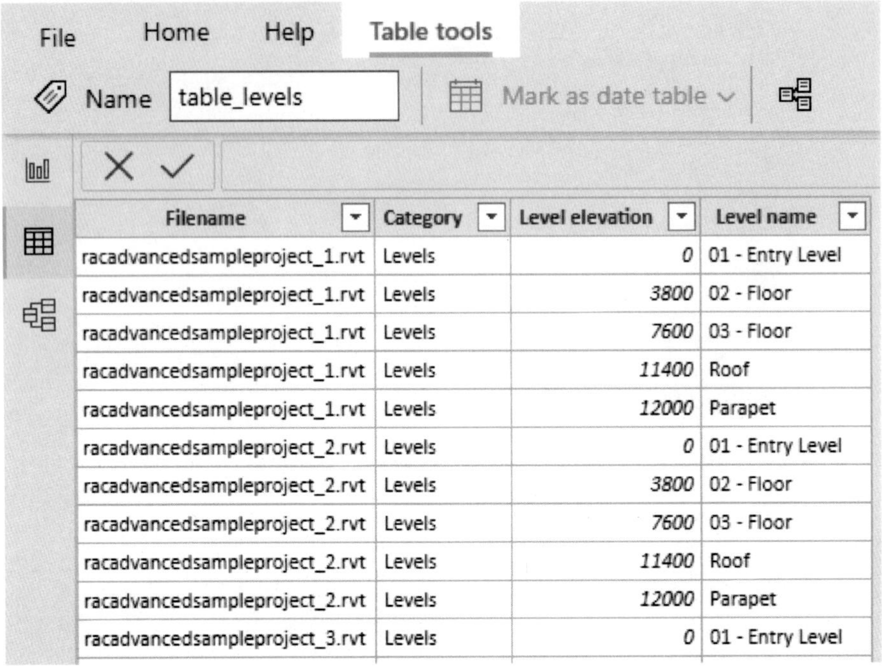

Filename	Category	Level elevation	Level name
racadvancedsampleproject_1.rvt	Levels	0	01 - Entry Level
racadvancedsampleproject_1.rvt	Levels	3800	02 - Floor
racadvancedsampleproject_1.rvt	Levels	7600	03 - Floor
racadvancedsampleproject_1.rvt	Levels	11400	Roof
racadvancedsampleproject_1.rvt	Levels	12000	Parapet
racadvancedsampleproject_2.rvt	Levels	0	01 - Entry Level
racadvancedsampleproject_2.rvt	Levels	3800	02 - Floor
racadvancedsampleproject_2.rvt	Levels	7600	03 - Floor
racadvancedsampleproject_2.rvt	Levels	11400	Roof
racadvancedsampleproject_2.rvt	Levels	12000	Parapet
racadvancedsampleproject_3.rvt	Levels	0	01 - Entry Level

Figure 11.7 – Power BI Data view to check the dataset formatting options

As you can see from the preceding screenshot, my **Level elevation** column has values in millimeters, whereas I want to show these values in meters. Let's see how to fix that quickly.

8. While in the **table_levels** data view, we simply need to create a new column that takes the **Level elevation** values as input and divides them by 1,000. Of course, this is the case here as I have millimeter starting values and I wish to convert them to meter values. You should use different numbers in the calculations if working with feet and inches. The first thing to do is to click on the **Home** tab and then click on the **New column** icon, as shown here:

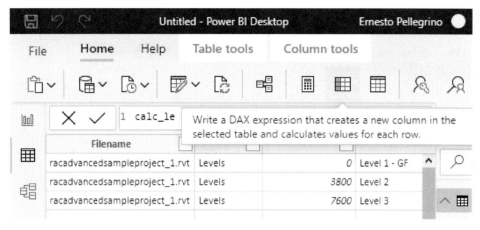

Figure 11.8 – Clicking on the New column icon

9. When you click on the **New column** icon, you should see that a new column is created immediately and a string saying `Column` = appears on top of the table in a white rectangular space. That space is where we put our formula.

10. Now, rename the `Column` string to something like `calc_level_elevation_to_meters`. Remember to rename it according to your Revit model measurement units.

11. Then, hit the space bar and incorporate an equals sign to start writing the formula, exactly as we would do with an Excel formula. It's more or less the same thing.

12. Now we should start with the table's name as a string without any symbol or special character. Therefore, type `table_levels`.

13. Then, type opening and closing square brackets. Inside those, we want to write the column's name we are looking for, in this case, `[Level elevation]`.

14. The complete formula should be as follows:

```
calc_level_elevation_to_meters = table_levels[Level
elevation] / 1000
```

The following screenshot shows that by using this simple formula, we correctly converted millimeter values into meters:

Level elevation ▼	Level name ▼	calc_level_elevation_to_meters ▼
0	Level 1 - GF	0
3800	Level 2	3,8
7600	Level 3	7,6
11400	Level 4	11,4
12000	Level 5	12
19400	Level 6	19,4
24400	Level 7	24,4
28400	Level 8	28,4

Figure 11.9 – Level elevation values transformed into meters

Perfect! At this point, let's move on to the table_rooms column. Take a look at the Room area column. Other than the area itself, there is also the measurement unit on the right side of the string, m². And that's the problem here. Power Bi recognized the values as strings. When we build the charts, I would like to know the total area of the rooms – per building, floor, or anything else, and if we work with strings, we can't perform sum operations. I hope you remember that when we talked about strings and operations allowed on strings in *Chapter 8, Deep Dive into Dynamo Data Types, we learned that when we sum two or more strings, we are concatenating strings.*

However, here we don't want to concatenate strings but sum the area of the rooms. How can we do that? We need to find a way to extract only numbers from the **Room area** column. And guess what, we could use **RegEx** for that! But actually, no, not in this case.

We won't use regular expressions this time as we need to install additional Python libraries and frameworks, and that's too much for a simple exercise like this one. I told you that regular expressions deserve an entire book, as the topic is vast and can also be quite complex! Anyway, you now know that we can use the Power BI **R script** console to execute Python scripts. To resolve this issue this time, we will take advantage of one of the Power BI built-in programming languages, **DAX**. DAX stands for *Data Analysis Expressions*, and all you need to know is that this programming language, like **M** and **R**, helps power users who want to go beyond the default operations. But enough talking, let's perform the following steps to create a new column with area values only:

1. The first thing to do is to open the **Report** view by clicking on the **Data** view icon to the left of the user interface.

2. Then, click on the **Transform data** button at the center of the top menu. You can't miss it.

3. A new window will open up. The window is called **Power Query Editor**, and from here, we can create the area values column that is required. Click on the **Add Column** tab on top of the PQE ribbon.

4. Then, click on the **Custom Column** button on the left side of the ribbon, as shown here:

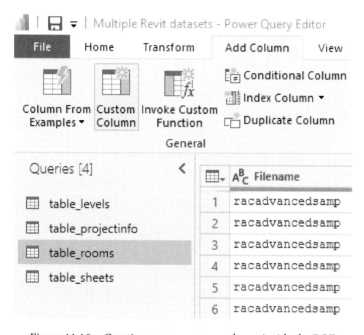

Figure 11.10 – Creating a new custom column inside the PQE

5. When you click on the **Custom Column** button, write the following code inside the **Custom Column** formula textbox:

```
Text.Combine(List.RemoveNulls(List.Transform(Text.
ToList([Room area]),each if Value.Is(Value.FromText(_),
type number) then _ else null)))
```

DAX has many OOTB functions and methods to help us achieve data manipulation operations, like any programming language. I can't explain all of the code details here, but I want you to know that all it does is take a specified column ([**Room area**]) and processes each included value. If it's text, it skips it. If it's a number, it keeps it. I hope this makes sense to you, too!

6. When you type the function, also specify the new column name, as shown in the following screenshot:

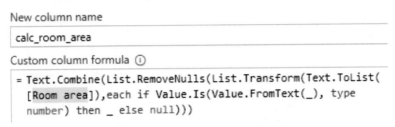

Custom Column

Add a column that is computed from the other columns.

New column name

calc_room_area

Custom column formula ⓘ

```
= Text.Combine(List.RemoveNulls(List.Transform(Text.ToList(
  [Room area]),each if Value.Is(Value.FromText(_), type
  number) then _ else null)))
```

Figure 11.11 – Custom Column name and formula

7. As you can see, I wrote `calc_room_area` as the column name. Now, hit the **OK** button to execute the DAX function. *Both the column name and the formula are case-sensitive!*

8. At this point, the PQE shows a new column named **calc_room_area** containing only numbers. From here, there is one final thing to do. We need to tell Power BI that those values are numbers because they don't have a specified data type. So, let's select the newly created column and then click on **Detect Data Type**. The button can be found inside the **Any Column** group, as shown here:

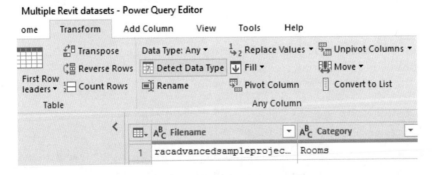

Figure 11.12 – Detect Data Type button

This feature will auto-detect the data type of the selected column, and as those are just numbers, Power BI will automatically set **Whole Number** as the data type.

9. Perfect! Now, without leaving the PQE, go to the **Home** tab and click on the **Close & Apply** button. It will apply the previous operations to the tables and save the results in Power BI. You can find the button on the far left-hand side of the **Home** tab.

Our room table is now ready. Let's switch to the Power BI dashboard.

10. Next, let's go to the **Data** view and open the **table_rooms** table.

11. From here, select the new column, **calc_room_area**, and enable the thousands separator by clicking on the comma symbol at the center of the top ribbon, as we did a few minutes ago. The following screenshot shows all of the steps:

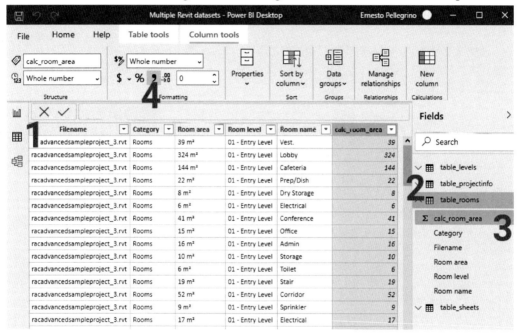

Figure 11.13 – How to add the thousands separator

Perfect! Now you can check the other tables to see whether everything looks good. Everything is set up, but I suggest you look at the other tables and get more familiar with the **Data** view. When you're done, let's also open the **Model** view to see whether Power BI automatically detected the **Filename** links between our tables. You can find the **Model** view icon right under the **Data** view icon to the left of the Power BI user interface.

12. In the **Model** view, you should see the following boxes:

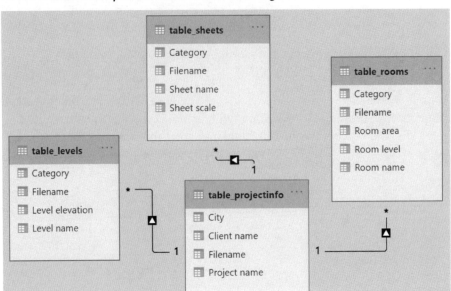

Figure 11.14 – Power BI Model view

It's essential to link the **Filename** columns to one another. In this way, we will be able to create dynamic charts. I mean, when we create the map and donut charts later on, if we interact with one of the values on the map chart, the donut will update accordingly, and vice versa. In my case, Power BI already detected the connection. That's because we assigned the same column heading name to all of our tables. *And that's why you should always be coherent with your datasets, especially if you work with more extensive datasets.*

If your Power BI, for some reason, didn't find the connection on its own, you can proceed to fix the issue in one of two ways:

1. Double-check the column names in the Excel file. Make sure that every table has the string **Filename** written the same way. Remember that strings in Power BI are read as case-sensitive, so uppercase and lowercase characters will result in different words.

2. If the tables in the Excel file have the string **Filename** written the same way, you can help Power BI understand the links. All you have to do is to drag the **Filename** column from one table and drop it to the **Filename** column of another table, as shown here:

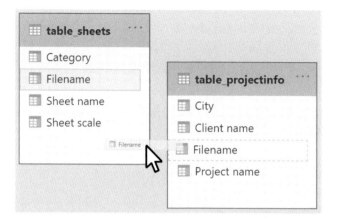

Figure 11.15 – Drag and drop the column names between tables to establish links

When you do that, Power BI will know that the filename of the **table_sheets** table and the filename of the **table_projectinfo** table show the same type of values. Repeat the process for any table that has no **Filename** link.

Awesome! We're now ready to build and customize our charts. I know those last steps might be tedious, but they are key to setting everything up to make the charts work!

Figure 11.16 – Power BI meme

In this section, we learned how to import multiple tables from an Excel file in Power BI. We understood to open the **Data** view to perform formatting operations, such as converting millimeter values into meters for the Revit levels' elevations. Then, we learned how to use the Power Query Editor to perform more complex formatting operations, such as capturing just numbers on strings containing square meter symbols. This was key as the charts we are going to build will never recognize those values as numbers. Next, we learned how to link columns between tables if Power BI didn't automatically get it on the first try. Although Power BI is a pretty powerful tool, sometimes it cannot recognize links between tables, so we need to set the links manually. In the next section, we will create some cool-looking charts. Let's go!

Creating the charts

Now the fun begins! We have imported a dataset coming from multiple Revit models, and we have done an excellent job with the "cleaning" stuff so far. Let's now create the charts one by one and customize them in terms of fonts, colors, and shapes.

Creating the table chart

The first chart we will create is the table chart, which is simple yet powerful. To create the chart, perform the following steps:

1. The first chart to drop is **Table**. Click on the table icon under the **Visualizations** pane on the right-hand side of the Power BI user interface.

Figure 11.17 – Placing the table chart

As you can see, the table chart is pretty straightforward. We will use it to create a small table containing values such as the model's name, the client's name, and the location.

2. Once you place the table chart, go to the **Values** panel and insert the following columns:

- **Filename**

- **Client name**

- **City**

The following screenshot shows where to find them. You just need to drag and drop each column under the **Values** field.

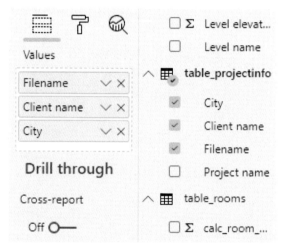

Figure 11.18 – Inserting Filename, Client name, and City under the Values field of the table chart

Great! Now, switch to the format panel. Looking at the preceding screenshot, you can click on the little paint roller icon, just above and to the right of the **Values** field, to open the formatting panel.

3. Here, there are several formatting options grouped by category. We explored some of them in *Chapter 2, Understanding Data Centers*, and *Chapter 3, Warming Up Your Data Visualization Engines*. It's not mandatory, but if you like, you can refresh your memory by giving those chapters a quick re-read! However, let's start by customizing the **Style** option. If you expand the section, you should see a drop-down list of styling options. I've selected the **Sparse** style, but you can obviously choose whatever style you wish.

4. Next, I've customized the column header's background color. The following screenshot shows where to find the option:

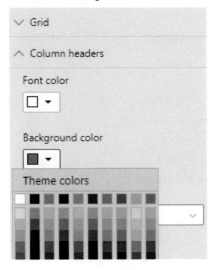

Figure 11.19 – Column header background color

I've selected a dark gray instead of the default black. This looks slightly easier on the eye than the pure black background.

5. The last option to customize is the background. Activate the **Background** option if it isn't activated already and select the black color. You will find an On and Off switch right next to it. Then, I like to apply transparency of **98%**.

6. Done! The first piece of our dashboard is complete. Look at the following screenshot:

Filename	Client name	City
racadvancedsampleproject_1.rvt	Gianluigi Costa	Roma
racadvancedsampleproject_2.rvt	Vanessa De Vivo	Caserta
racadvancedsampleproject_3.rvt	Massimiliano Rossi	Olbia
racbasicsampleproject_1.rvt	Davide Natale	Torino
racbasicsampleproject_2.rvt	Giorgia Bonanno	Lecce
racbasicsampleproject_3.rvt	Valeria Calabrese	Catania

Figure 11.20 – The Table chart is complete

Your chart should look like the one indicated in the preceding screenshot, if you used the same style and colors, of course.

Creating the stacked column chart

The next chart I would like to create will show how many rooms per project there are. We could use several types of charts to achieve that, but in this case, I will go ahead and use the stacked column chart. If you hover over the icons of the **Visualization** pane, you should find it on the first row, occupying the second position. Now, in order to bring the chart to life, follow these steps:

1. To populate the chart with data, begin by dropping the project name on to the **Axis**.

2. Then, drop the filename on to the **Legend**.

3. And finally, drop the room name on to the **Values**. Please note to use the **Room name** column and not the one we calculated previously. The reason is that we want to count how many rooms we have per project and sum their area.

The fields should be used as shown in the following screenshot:

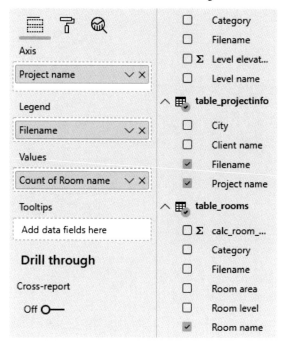

Figure 11.21 – Placing the right columns on to the right field

Awesome! Now let's go to the format panel and customize the formatting options. The following screenshot shows the complete setup:

Figure 11.22 – Updating the formatting options

As you can see, I've only enabled the **X axis**, **Y axis**, **Total labels**, **Background**, **Tooltip**, and **Visual header** options. All of the other options are turned off.

4. Next, let's expand the **X axis** group and scroll down until we find **Title**. Turn it off.

5. We also want to do the same for **Y axis**. By turning off **Title**, we won't see it on the chart as the chart itself is pretty straightforward, and there is no need for the title in this case.

6. One last thing to do is to set the same background as we did previously. Go ahead and expand the **Background** section, incorporate a black color, and a transparency of **98%**.

Our chart is now complete! Take a look at the following diagram:

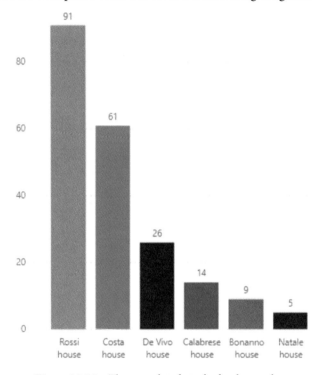

Figure 11.23 – The completed stacked column chart

As you can see, the Rossi house has the greatest number of rooms, with Natale having the fewest. Poor Natale; he should buy a bigger house!

Jokes aside, if you don't like the colors of the stacked column chart, you could update them. To do that, simply go to the formatting panel (paint roller icon) and expand the **Data colors** options to customize them.

Creating the donut chart

The next chart to build is the donut chart. Like the pie chart, the donut chart is excellent for showing parts of a whole of the same category, as we learned in *Chapter 3, Warming Up Your Data Visualization Engines*. To create a donut chart, follow these steps:

1. Click on the donut icon under the **Visualization** pane. You will recognize it immediately by the shape of its icon and because it's right next to the **Pie chart** icon.

2. After placing one donut chart, drop **City** on to the **Legend** field, and **calc_room_area** on to the **Values** field.

3. Then, make sure to check the **calc_room_area** calculation settings. We want it to be set to **Sum** to know the total room area for any building in a specific city.

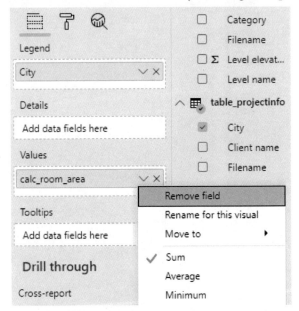

Figure 11.24 – Checking the calculation settings of the calc_room_area values

Indeed, we're using **City** here to group the area values. Imagine having multiple Revit models located in different cities, and for each city, we have five or more models, and not just 1. This chart would be awesome for providing an overview of the total square meters of all buildings grouped by city, region, country, and so on.

4. Now, let's go to the formatting panel. From here, let's turn on just **Detail Label**, **Title**, **Background**, and **Tooltip**.

5. Under the **Detail Label** options, I've selected **Category, percent of total** as I want to see the city (category) and its total room area percentage.

6. Now, let's modify the **Inner radius** property under the **Shapes** section. I've selected a radius of **75** as I like the donut chart to be a bit slimmer than the default one, but this is entirely up to you.

7. Next, we want to keep and customize the title here. I wrote `Area of rooms by city`.

8. Last but not least, let's also customize the **Background** section by setting a black color and a transparency of **98%**.

This is the final result:

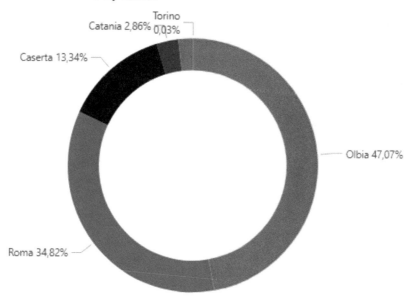

Figure 11.25 – Donut chart complete

Fantastic! We've completed another cool-looking chart. By looking at it, we can immediately see that the buildings with the greater area extension are located in Rome and Olbia. Regarding the totals between our projects, buildings in Rome and Olbia occupy 34 and 47 percent of the total area, respectively, while Catania, Lecce, and Turin account for less than 5%.

As you can see from this chart and the preceding one, I've exaggerated those numbers by manipulating the original Revit model data. I wanted to create a dashboard containing numbers that vary slightly from one another, even if the Revit models come from the same Autodesk samples! In the end, there is no way that the Rossi house has 91 rooms! Who needs 91 rooms after all?!

Creating the scatter plot chart

Now, let's create a scatter plot chart. This is a fantastic chart as it shows the correlation between two parameters of a specific dataset. In this example, we will use it to correlate the previously calculated room area and the elevation of our buildings. *The question is, is the building occupying a larger area also taller?* Let's find out!

1. After placing the scatter plot chart on the Power BI canvas, by clicking on its icon right before the **Pie chart** icon, let's drop in some data.

2. Drag and drop **City** from the **table_projectinfo** column on to the **Details** field.

3. Next, drop **calc_level_elevation_to_meters** on to the **X axis** field.

4. Then, drop **calc_room_area** inside the **Y axis** field.

    By default, Power BI calculates the sum of the values we use in our chart's field. This time, we want to change that before moving to the format panel. Let's pause for a second to think about what values we're using. We selected the elevation of the Revit levels and the area of the rooms. But if we sum the elevation of levels, we end up with a number that does not correspond to the height of our buildings. If we have a building with three floors, for example, the default sum operation will calculate the height of the first floor from the ground, plus the height of the second, also from the ground, and the height of the last one from the ground too, which is incorrect. To fix that, Power BI comes with a variety of predefined calculations:

5. Let's click on the pointing down arrow right next to **calc_level_elevation_to_meters** and select **Maximum** from the list, as shown here:

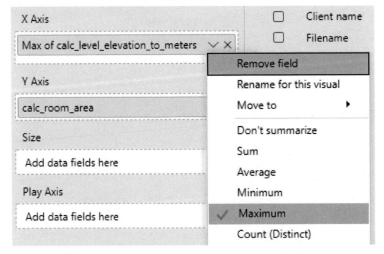

Figure 11.26 – Using the Maximum option for the level's elevations

Perfect! Now our scatter plot data makes more sense.

6. At this point, we can open the formatting panel. The groups to keep on are **X axis**, **Y axis**, **Category labels**, **Title**, **Background**, and **Tooltip**.

7. Next, expand the **Y axis** section and select **None** from the drop-down list of the **Display units** setting. By doing so, we will see the numbers on the *y* axis in units of thousands. If you don't set that, you'll see **5K** and **4K**, instead of **5,000** and **4,000**. I prefer the second option.

8. Then, expand the **Shapes** section and adjust the **Size** and **Marker shape** options as you like. I am using **12** for the size and a circle as the shape.

9. Now it's time to change the title. I've used **Building height vs room area**. Expand the **Title** section and update it accordingly.

10. The last thing to do is the background. Update it using the black color and the same transparency we used previously for the other charts.

The following screenshot shows the end result:

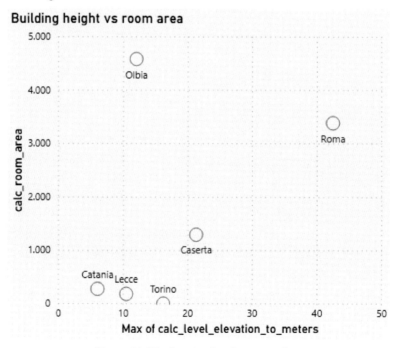

Figure 11.27 – Scatter plot chart complete

Another fantastic chart is complete. One thing to also remember here is that we can change the size of the circles if we so wish. Let's suppose we had the total number of family instances per project. We could have used that number to increase or decrease the circle size. Pretty cool!

Creating the map

Now it's time to create the map chart. Perform the following steps:

1. Let's start by clicking on its icon, as shown here:

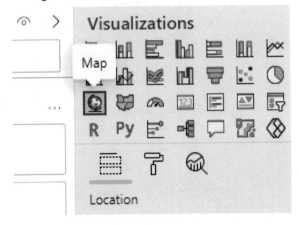

Figure 11.28 – Placing the map chart

Everybody is familiar with maps, right? We use them all the time, so we can say with a fair degree of certainty that the map chart is straightforward to understand. Here, we're using it by inserting city names, and that isn't exactly technical, I should say. A common application of those charts is to insert latitude and longitude, a better way for specifying locations on Earth. However, Power BI uses BING as its default search engine, and as everybody uses Google maps, BING is often underestimated, but it is pretty powerful. Anyway, just by providing the city names, BING should be able to find our sites regardless.

2. Let's drop **City** into the **Location** field, **Client name** into the **Legend** field, and **calc_room_area** into the **Size** field.

3. Next, on the formatting panel, turn on the **Category labels**, **Title**, **Background**, and **Tooltip** sections.

I've updated the colors of the map symbols to match the ones on the other charts. Unfortunately, there is no way to transfer colors from one chart to another in Power BI (yet). However, lucky for us, there are plenty of tools out there that can be of assistance. I use one named **Just Color Picker**, now at version 5.5. When you open it, you can use your mouse to pick any color on your screen. It's a quick solution when it comes to spotting a color code and typing it on another chart. This is what it looks like:

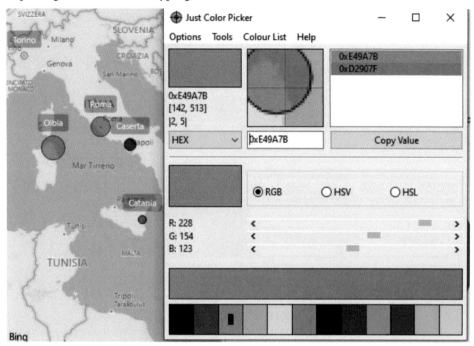

Figure 11.29 – Using Just Color Picker, we quickly get color codes

Google it to try it out. It's free. Also, don't forget to select HEX from the drop-down list right under the colored rectangle in the top-left corner. Power BI uses hexadecimal codes for coloring.

4. Moving on, let's set the transparency to **75%** percent on the **Category labels** section.

5. Now, expand the **Bubbles** group and set the size of the map symbols. I've used **0**.

6. Then you can customize the **Map styles** options by expanding its section. From there, you have two options. The first one is the style, while the second is the **Show labels** on and off switch.

7. Then, update the title of the chart using something like **Buildings location by total rooms area**.

8. The last setting is the background – black, **98%**.

The following is a diagram of the completed map chart:

Figure 11.30 – Map chart complete

Excellent, the map is complete and looks good! The complete report can be visualized here: `https://cutt.ly/dWL4X6K`.

We're gaining new skills and having fun by practicing more and more on Power BI with those Revit datasets. I started using Autodesk Revit back in 2010, and nobody used it as a database. It was a great and promising competitor for 3D modeling of Graph of tArchicad, which was used a lot more then. Anyway, during 2012/2013, I experimented with the Revit database to extract data from the models. From there, I tried many, many times to connect the Revit data to an external online database. I used Access, Azure, and many more online services, most of which I don't even remember anymore. I worked on most of those experiments with *Manuel Bottiglieri*, and with him, we found an excellent solution using Azure, Sharepoint, and a few other Revit plugins.

Figure 11.31 – The "What do we want?!" meme

It's great to see that today, 10 years later, Manuel has found a new, improved solution for streaming data from Revit, and he also coded it himself! Not only that, but we can also now grab that data, manipulate it a little, and visualize it on fantastic charts. Isn't that awesome? Well, it is to me!

Summary

That concludes this chapter. During the exercises, we learned many things! First, we learned how to solve the scale numbers issue by placing a simple space in front of each value. By doing so, Excel will not execute the division operation but interpret those values as strings. Then we covered a few more Excel steps on how to prepare the tables for Power BI. After that, we understood how to format the data in Power BI using the PQE and the DAX language to create custom columns and extract the part of the strings we needed. Then, we learned how to correlate the columns of data to one another and build a number of charts, including the scatter plot, the stacked column, and the map chart. In the next chapter, the fun continues with Power BI by analyzing a dataset started by me and produced by the book's readers themselves!

12
Having Fun with Power BI

Hi there, and welcome to chapter 12! This is sadly the last chapter of the book. We will use it to explore even more features and workflows of this fantastic business intelligence tool – Microsoft Power BI. Forget about construction, buildings, and BIM data. We will use a fun dataset here to explore some new Power BI tools and a new way to stream data into it! We want to master how to manage data in Power BI. We don't care whether the data relates to our projects. *This chapter will indeed use a dataset created by the readers of this book themselves.* Yes! I made a form to collect users' data and create a streaming link directly into Power BI. Do not worry. I won't ask for personal information, such as your name, email, or address. I just want to create a "live" dataset designed and visualized by you, the readers. However, I will approve each reply to the form for security reasons to keep everything clean and professional. The form includes questions such as what's your country, what's your age, your job, and a few others. As I have just said, no personal information will be asked, and it will take just 30 seconds to complete it.

In this chapter, I will explain how the form has been created so you can replicate its workflow within your company. And I am sure you will like it! Think, for example, about creating a form that asks a few questions relating to Autodesk Revit or Dynamo.

You could organize the questions on different difficulty levels and assign points to them. In this way, you could quickly identify who, between your colleagues, needs more help and who doesn't. Or maybe you could use it to see how new employees perform on those tools or perhaps others. You could have historical data and take advantage of that data to make informed business decisions.

This chapter will cover the following topics:

- Learning how to build the form

- Understanding how to import the dataset

- Completing the Google form

- Importing the data and creating the charts

Before we start, let's first cover the technical requirements.

Technical requirements

This chapter also uses Power BI as the primary tool, so ensure that you have it installed. If required, you can find it here: `https://aka.ms/pbidesktopstore`.

Also, we will use some free online services from the Google office suite, such as Google Sheets and Google Forms. Create a Google account if you don't already have one. You can do this here: `https://cutt.ly/pW9Tut7`.

Once you have both Power BI Desktop installed and a Google account, you're ready to start.

Building the form

This section will teach you how to build your form and prepare it to stream data to Power BI. I've also tried to replicate the workflow using services such as Microsoft Flow and OneDrive, but I then chose Google services to complete it. The reason is that to achieve the same workflow, you will need a Microsoft business account as Micorosft Flow can't be accessed by users with personal accounts.

To be honest, this is a bit disappointing, as many people perhaps don't have a business account to try out those services. Microsoft Flow is fascinating as it could allow the creation of smart widgets to place on our phones, and that's pretty cool. Flow belongs to a software family type called **IFTTT**. IFTTT is an acronym, and it means **IF THIS THEN THAT**. Like any other IFTTT tool, Microsoft Flow can be connected to various online services, such as emails, spreadsheets, databases, sensors, and many different fantastic kinds of stuff. I suggest you learn more about this as they are becoming smarter and smarter each year. It's unbelievable the things you can automate with those.

However, Google services will work just as well as Microsoft in this exercise. The workflow I am talking about is quite simple, and it can be summarized in three steps:

1. Create a Google form.
2. Print the answers to a Google Sheets file.
3. Publish the dataset to the web.

Figure 12.1 – Google services meme

Let's now start by building the Google form:

1. First, log in to your Google account and then open the Google Drive web application by going here: `https://www.google.com/drive/`.

2. Now, create a **Google Form** file by clicking on the +**New** icon in the top-left corner of the web application user interface, as shown here:

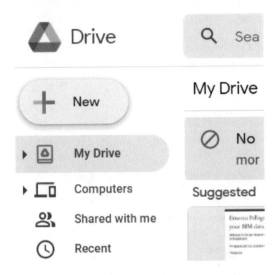

Figure 12.2 – Creating a Google Forms file

When you click on the +**New** button, you can select **Google Forms** from the drop-down list and click on **Blank form** to create a new empty file.

3. You will see a new page opening on the browser. When it opens, you can rename the file by filling in the title in the top-left textbox. You can also add it to your favorites if you check the star icon on its right.

4. The Google form is divided into three sections: **Questions**, **Responses**, and **Settings**. The opened page should look like the following:

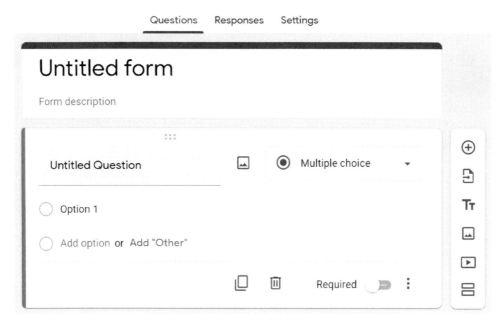

Figure 12.3 – Google Form empty file

5. Customize the form title and description by replacing the placeholders, as you can see from the top-left of the preceding screenshot.

    Keep in mind that this title is different from the title we talked about in *step 3*. The title in *step 3* represents the filename, and only you can see it inside your **Google Drive** folder (as long as you don't share the Google Drive folder itself). Instead, this title is the form's title and will be visible to anyone who receives the link to answer your questions.

6. If you take another look at the preceding screenshot (*Figure 12.3*), you can see that to the right, there is a **Multiple choice** option selected. Click on that button and you'll see the following list:

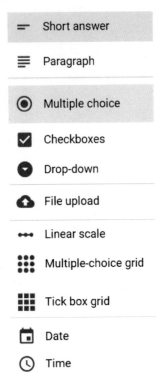

Figure 12.4 – Google Forms type of questions

Google, by default, provided us with a lot of question types. You can use **Multiple choice**, **Checkboxes**, **Short answer** or **Paragraph**, **Date**, and even ask the user to upload files through the form. Kudos to Google for that!

7. Great! Now let's create three questions, and then we will cover a few other things inside the **Responses** page and **Settings** as well.

For this exercise, I've renamed the title of the form to **Holiday wishes** and pretended to ask questions about visiting European cities. I've started with multiple-choice types of questions. Of course, you can create any form you want, as this is just to show how Google Forms works. We won't use this dataset in Power BI as I've already prepared one, and we will talk about it at the end of this section. The following screenshot shows my first multiple-choice question:

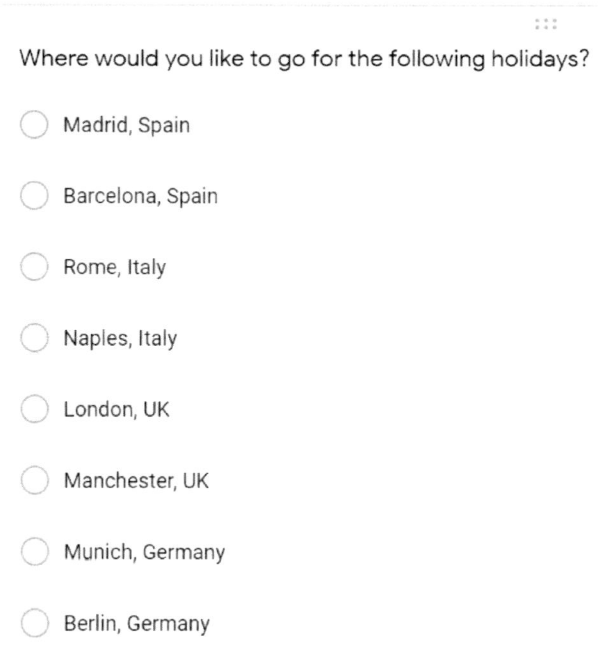

:::

Where would you like to go for the following holidays?

◯   Madrid, Spain

◯   Barcelona, Spain

◯   Rome, Italy

◯   Naples, Italy

◯   London, UK

◯   Manchester, UK

◯   Munich, Germany

◯   Berlin, Germany

Figure 12.5 – Multiple-choice question

The screenshot shows the Google Form UI when we develop the questions. In this case, you will see a list of available choices and pick one of them.

8. OK, so the first question was multiple-choice, and it asks *Where would you like to go on your next holiday?*. To add a second question, click on the + icon on the vertical menu at the right of the main panel, as shown here:

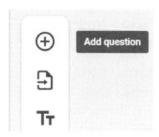

Figure 12.6 – Adding a new question to the Google form

9. When you click on that, a new question box appears. As we did for the first question, you have to choose the type between the available options in the drop-down list.

    I selected a drop-down type of question and asked *Choose the closest answer that best suits you*. Then, I created a few options related to the main activity they would like to do during this holiday.

    When you select a question, a few icons in the bottom-right corner allow us to duplicate or delete the question, or make it mandatory. Refer to the following screenshot:

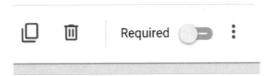

Figure 12.7 – Duplicate, delete, and the Required toggle switch

As you can see from the preceding screenshot, when you click on a question box to activate the changes, you will see them appear at the bottom of the box.

10. Now, go to the **Settings** page. Scroll up on the **Google Form** page and click on **Settings**. It's the third option on the menu.

Figure 12.8 – Settings menu

The preceding screenshot shows where to find the **Settings** menu.

Here, there are a few settings divided into different categories. We won't cover everything here as this is beyond the scope of this chapter. We will explore the fundamentals in terms of allowing the data to travel to Power BI! However, if you want to take a few minutes and expand those settings, they are pretty straightforward to understand.

11. While on the **Settings** page, expand the **Presentation** category, as shown in the following screenshot:

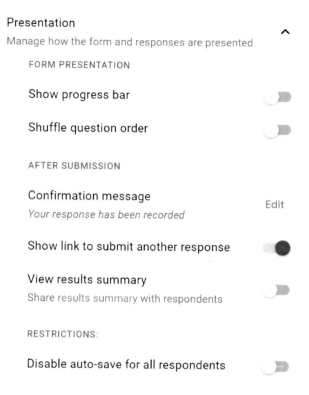

Figure 12.9 – Presentation settings

12. Under **Presentation**, you can activate various settings, such as showing a progress bar or shuffle the order of the questions. Click on **Edit** to customize **Confirmation message**.

There is already a placeholder sentence that says *Your response has been recorded*, but this is something that a robot will say.

13. Change that to something more user-friendly, such as *Thanks for your replies, see you later!*. Anyway, I just wanted to show you how to edit the message that pops up when someone completes your form.

14. Now we come to the essential part of the Google form that interests us. Let's open the **Responses** page. From here, click on the green icon right before the one with three vertical dots. You can't miss it; it's on the right-hand side of the UI, and it pretends to look like an Excel icon.

A new window will appear. That's the response destination's settings. You have two options that you can set, as shown here:

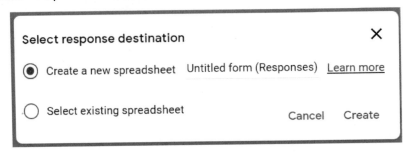

Figure 12.10 – Response destination's settings

15. Choose the one you want. I created a new spreadsheet and renamed it by replacing the **Untitled form** placeholder with `Holiday Wishes`.

16. Click on **Create** and you will see a new tab open with the newly created Google spreadsheet. As the questions are long, you can apply the **Wrapping text** option to the column headers. Take a look at the following screenshot:

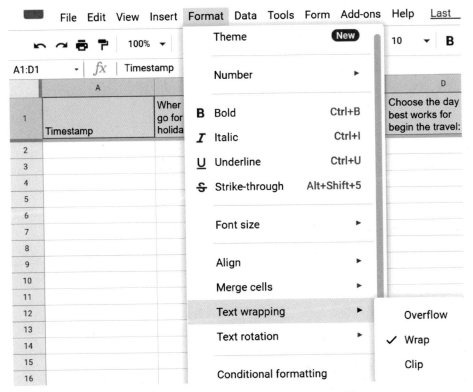

Figure 12.11 – Wrapping text on a Google spreadsheet

17. Select the column headers, click on the **Format** menu, **Text wrapping**, and then choose **Wrap**, as indicated in the preceding screenshot.

18. Perfect! Now our Google form is ready to accept responses. Let's simulate a few of them by opening the form on another page. Keep the Google spreadsheet page open and go back to the previous form page. Click on the **Send** button in the top-right corner of the page. It has a dark blue background.

19. All you have to do is click on the second **Link** icon right after the **Email** icon, as we don't want to send it via email at the moment. The following screenshot shows the generated link that we need to copy and paste inside another browser tab:

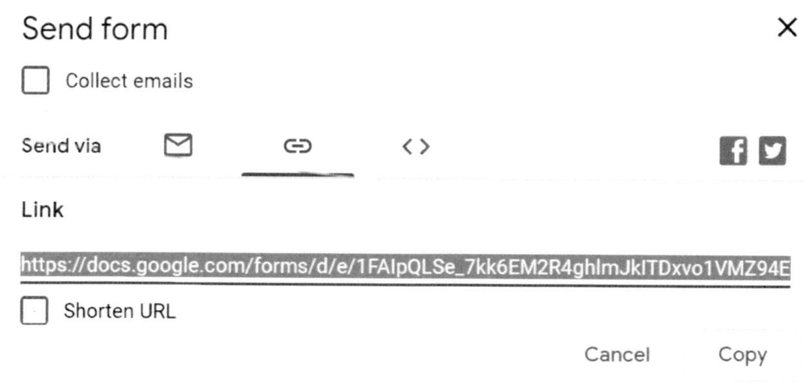

Send form   ✕

☐   Collect emails

Send via   ✉   ⊝   < >   f ▸

Link

https://docs.google.com/forms/d/e/1FAIpQLSe_7kk6EM2R4ghImJkITDxvo1VMZ94E

☐   Shorten URL

           Cancel   Copy

Figure 12.12 – Send form window

Great! Let's grab the link and paste it into another tab. Then, complete the form a few times to see the responses appear on the Google spreadsheet page.

Once you have completed the form a few times, open the Google spreadsheet. If you closed it by mistake, no worries. Go to the **Responses** page and click on the Excel-ish icon we used a few minutes ago, as shown here:

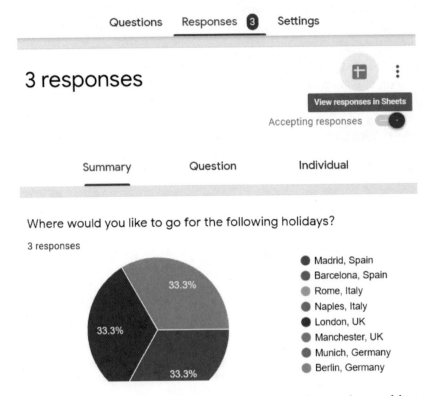

Figure 12.13 – Clicking on View responses in Sheets to open the Google spreadsheet file

By the way, now, the **Responses** page shows a summary of the replies and a few other sections, including **Question** and **Individual**, which are different ways to see people's responses.

Congratulations! You have completed a Google form and prepared it for the Power BI connection. We needed to write our responses to the Google spreadsheet to achieve that. So far, we have learned how to create the form, what the available types of questions are, and how to customize some of the form's settings. In addition, we understood how to share the form via a link and print the responses to a Google spreadsheet. In the next section, we will learn how to link the form itself to Power BI, which will update every time a new user completes it.

Understanding how to publish the dataset

This section will teach us to link the Google spreadsheet to Power BI, which is already mirrored to the Google Form responses. We are talking about a type of connection that will automatically update our charts. *How can we do that?* Let's see:

1. Open the Google spreadsheet created previously. If you can't find it, go to your Google Drive using this URL, `https://drive.google.com/`, and then navigate your drive's folders until you find the Google form or spreadsheet.

2. If you locate the **Google Form** file, open the **Responses** page and click on the green icon in the top-right corner of the main panel. We did the same before. If you have issues, check *Figure 12.10*.

3. Once you have the spreadsheet open, click on **Publish to the web** from the **File** menu, as shown in the following screenshot:

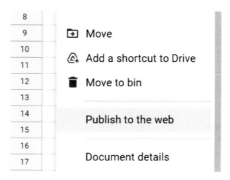

Figure 12.14 – Publish to the web feature

4. Now a new window will pop up. Don't click on the **Publish** button immediately as the window contains a few of the publishing settings we need to set. Let's see what to do to achieve our objective. Expand the **Published content and settings** menu. You will find it just at the bottom of the opened window, as shown here:

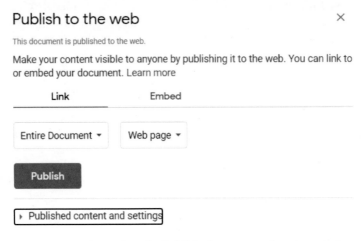

Figure 12.15 – Expanding the Published content and settings section

5. From here, click on the **Entire Document** drop-down list. When the list opens, you'll see two options: **Entire Document** and the name of our form, in my case, **Form responses 1**. Both of these are grayed out.

6. Click on the **Entire Document** option to disable it and then select the form. I know it's weird that we have to deactivate it first to check the second one, but this is how **Google Sheets** works. The following screenshot shows what I just described:

Figure 12.16 – Google spreadsheet publishing settings

7. So, to summarize, click on the **Entire Document** drop-down list, click on **Entire Document** again, and then select **Form responses 1**.

8. Also, make sure to check the **Automatically republish when changes are made** option. This option allows us to start the real-time connection between Power BI and the Google spreadsheet data, and that's exactly what we wanted to do here.

After that, focus on the upper part of this window and set everything as indicated in the following screenshot:

Figure 12.17 – Final options to set inside the Publish to the web window

As you can see, we have to select **Form responses 1** again from the drop-down list that appears on the left of the UI.

9. Then, select **Comma-separated values (.csv)** from the other drop-down list. CSV is a widespread type of format that developers use to exchange data between services, especially when dealing with Excel or Google spreadsheet files.

10. Next, click on **Publish** to complete the task. When you do, you'll see an alert pop up that says **Are you sure you want to publish this selection?**. Click **OK**.

Awesome! Everything is done now. The following window should look like yours:

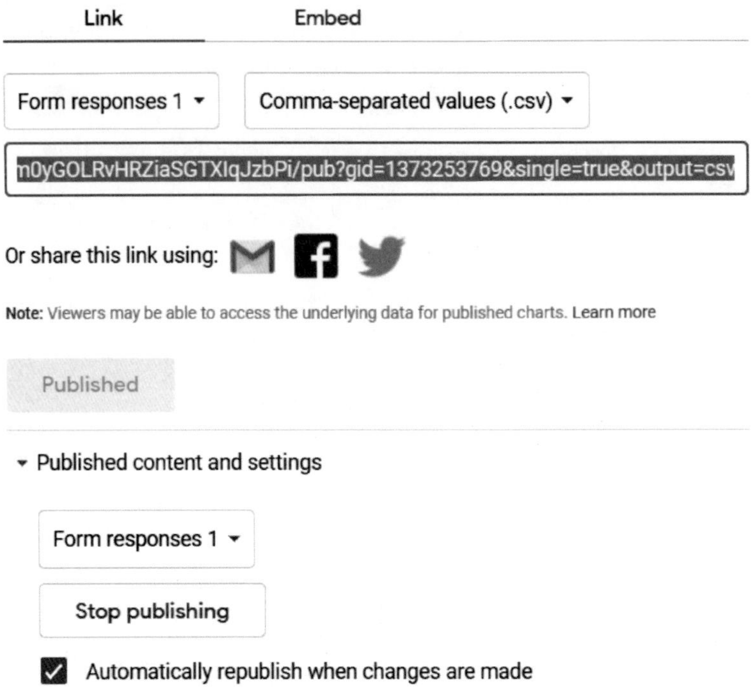

Link	Embed

Form responses 1 ▾   Comma-separated values (.csv) ▾

n0yGOLRvHRZiaSGTXIqJzbPi/pub?gid=1373253769&single=true&output=csv

Or share this link using: M f 🐦

Note: Viewers may be able to access the underlying data for published charts. Learn more

Published

▾ Published content and settings

Form responses 1 ▾

Stop publishing

☑ Automatically republish when changes are made

Figure 12.18 – Publishing settings completed

Copy the link to somewhere where you can quickly find it later.

Before moving on, I would like to comment on this page as I want you to understand what's happening. On the upper side of the window, you'll see a link that we need to copy inside Power BI, and we will do that in a minute. Pay attention to the end of the string. It says output=csv. Every time you repeat this workflow, make sure that the string always ends with output=csv. Things will not work correctly if this option isn't enabled. Also, just below the Facebook and Twitter icons, there is a grayed-out button – **Published**. This means that the data is now accessible publicly from the web, and everything is up and running. One more thing. On top of the **Automatically republish** checkbox, there is another button that allows us to **Stop publishing** the dataset. Keep that in mind in case you need to do so.

Well, we have now completed the setup on the Google spreadsheet *side of things*. Basically, we pulled out some *cables* from the Google Excel-like service, and we want to connect those *cables* to another end, Power BI. Let's find out how in the next section.

Connecting the cables on the Power BI side

We have done a great job so far, and to connect Power BI, we just need to do a couple more things as we have already done most of the job. Here, inside Power BI, we want to set up the link that will allow us to establish a real-time connection. Proceed as follows:

1. Open Power BI Desktop.

2. Click on **Transform Data**. You'll find the button more or less at the center of the top menu.

3. We have now opened **PQE**, the Power BI **Power Query Editor**.

4. Now, click on the pointing-down black arrow of the **New Source** button. It's located on the left of the top menu ribbon. Then, click on **More…**.

5. A new window will appear. Move the cursor inside the textbox in the top-left corner and type web. Then, select its icon from the list to the right of this window, as shown here:

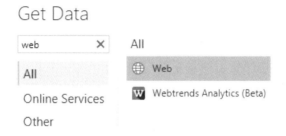

Figure 12.19 – Selecting the web to establish a connection to a web source

6. When you select **Web**, click on the **Connect** button at the bottom right of the window.

7. Now it's time to grab the link we generated previously under the **Publishing** settings of the Google spreadsheet. Grab it and past it inside the **URL** textbox of the new window. Also, double-check that the link ends with output=csv. Then, hit **OK**.

8. You will see a new window appearing. Here we have the chance to specify some technical settings on the CSV format. However, Power BI should have already located the **File Origin** and **Delimiter** options. However, make sure **Comma** is selected under the **Delimiter** option. Then, click **OK** again.

    We're now back inside the PQE. You'll notice that the first column of our table starts with **Timestamp**, but we didn't ask the form to record any timestamp. This is due to the Google Forms default settings. It saves both the date and the time, which is helpful.

9. As we now have a pretty simple dataset, there is no need to format the data or create custom columns as we did in previous chapters, such as in *Chapter 11, Visualizing Data from Multiple Models in Power BI*. Click on the **Close & Apply** button at the far left of the **PQE** menu ribbon to confirm our operation.

10. All set! Power BI is now linked to the Google spreadsheet in real time. Let's now quickly prove that. You don't have to do this, but if you want, you can, of course. Build a few charts on the Google Forms dataset. This is my version:

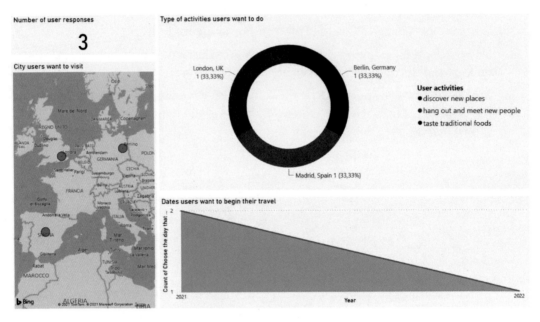

Figure 12.20 – Quick dashboard to check the Holiday Wishes responses

I know this is a simple dashboard, but we can't do much with that data only.

11. Now, let's add another three entries to our Google form. Open the **Google Form** page and click on the **Send** button in the top-right corner. Click on the **Link** icon, copy the link, and paste it into another browser tab. Then, simulate three or more entries.

12. When you have completed it, you need to go back to Power BI and hit the **Refresh** button just next to the **Transform Data** button at the center of the top menu. Power BI takes a few seconds to reload the data, and the magic happens!

Basically, every time you want to check the data, you just open the Power BI file and click on the **Refresh** button. All the connections we established before will do the rest in terms of transferring the updated table values.

The following screenshot shows the updated charts:

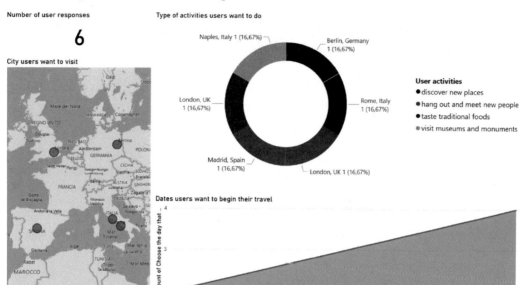

Figure 12.21 – Dashboard updated!

As you can see, the job is done! In this section, we successfully linked the Google spreadsheet to our Power BI file. We learned how to use the PQE to connect the Power BI database to a new source coming from a web service page. Then we demonstrated the real-time connection between those two tools by creating a simple dashboard using the simple **Holiday Wishes** dataset. We now know everything we need to replicate this workflow and find insights using company data, client data, or any type of data we want! We will complete the Google form and use its data to build the dashboard in the next section! *Isn't that awesome?!* Let's go.

Completing the Google form

Now the fun part begins! This section is concise and quick. We just need to complete a form after all. Indeed, I've prepared a Google form and chained it to a Google spreadsheet, and then connected everything to Power BI, as we did in the last section.

Just to be clear, do not enter personal information on the Google form. We just want to have fun creating a dashboard that shows the readers' skills, their job role, their industry, and their country (I don't even ask for the city). As a first question, I will ask you to provide a username by creating a random funny one, such as lovelypanda, bigsalmon, maddog, or something else. The important thing is not to provide personal information. I also removed the field that collected emails from the readers as, again, *this is just a fun experiment. There is no need for personal information.*

Also, it isn't mandatory to complete the form in order to complete the chapter. If you don't want to fill in the form for any reason, feel free to skip to the next section. You will get access to the dataset anyway. I will provide it in a few minutes. Instead, if you want to participate in the experiment, I suggest you fill in the form as it would be nice to see, using Power BI, the data coming from the readers themselves! Completing the form will take no more than a minute, I promise.

Before starting to complete the form, I want to point out just a few rules to follow, so as to keep everything clean and professional:

- I will approve each response before being publicly visible to anyone. I want to avoid bad replies. It is the internet, after all. Who knows what will happen if the form gets into the wrong hands!

- There are two questions about your skills at the start and end of the book to analyze the knowledge acquired. Be honest, don't cheat. It's a fun experiment, and the data can't be linked to you anyway.

- Again, do not provide email addresses, phone numbers, or any other type of personal data. I will remove them during the daily approvals.

- As the book's language is English, I ask you to complete the form in the same language to have a homogeneous dataset. Responses in other languages will be removed. Oh, that sounded merciless, didn't it?

- Have fun! That should have been the first rule, but if I had placed it at the beginning of the list, you wouldn't have read the following ones.

Enough talking. The link to complete the form is the following: `https://cutt.ly/nEruBiL`.

Fill it in and come back!

Thanks for taking the time to complete the form. I hope you enjoyed this type of learning experience as I am no professional book author, and this book took almost a year to complete and the work of 10 people. Now that you have completed the form, let's go straight to the next section, where we will use the publicly available dataset to build some cool-looking charts. Also, your response will not appear on Power BI right now. As I said, I have to approve each answer. Let's start to build the dashboard and then refresh it in a day or two to check your answers and others.

Remember, you now have the Power... BI.

Figure 12.22 – I've got the Power BI!

So, after a day or two, to check your responses, you only need to remember your username to filter the results on Power BI if you want to compare your answers to others. Then, you can keep the Power BI file on your computer and refresh it in the coming weeks and months *to see even more data coming from other readers, hopefully from all over the world!* You can check their skill levels, job roles, industries, and countries!

In this section, we learned how to create a live streaming connection to push data to Power BI, using a Google form and a Google spreadsheet. We understood how to set the **Publish to web** settings to achieve this objective. We learned how to grab the Google services cables and connect them to the Power BI engine. Isn't that amazing! Once everything was up and running, we completed the form and provided the answers. Now it's time to see how to import the dataset in Power BI and create our charts!

Importing the data and creating the charts

We're now ready to complete the last section and create the Power BI dashboards. This section will explore the book readers' live dataset and use it to find some fantastic insights. So we will repeat the workflow we did earlier in the first section, *Building the form*, but here, we won't waste time creating a new Google form as we will use the one I've already prepared. The main goal is to create the charts and focus on Power BI rather than repeating "linking" operations.

Importing the dataset

To import the dataset into Power BI, follow these steps:

1. Open Power BI Desktop.

2. Save the file on your PC.

3. Click on **Transform data** to start the PQE editor, as shown here:

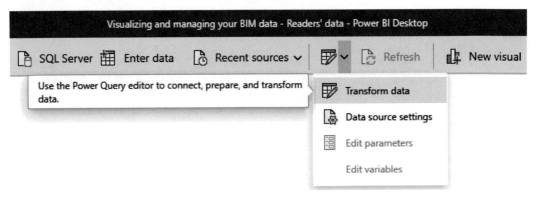

Figure 12.23 – Opening the Power Query Editor

Once you open it, you'll see a new window popping up.

4. Click on the **New Source pointing down black arrow** to expand other options. Then, select **Web** if it is available from the drop-down list. If it isn't, click on **More...** and then type Web to import a dataset from a web source.

5. Now, the PQE is asking for a URL, and as it is slightly long, I don't want you to waste time typing it. I created a shortcut that points to a shared Google Docs file. Inside this file, you'll find the link to paste to the **URL** field. Open this page: `https://cutt.ly/oW9i6xg`.

6. Now, paste the link you found inside the Google Docs file to the **URL** field of the Power BI PQE. As we specified previously, you always want to check that the link ends with `output=csv`. When you paste it, hit **OK** and then **OK** again.

7. When you do, you'll see the PQE with a table full of data. Let's check whether that data needs to be formatted. Select the first column, **Timestamp**, and then click on **Transform** to open the menu, as shown here:

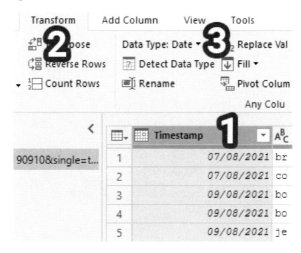

Figure 12.24 – Check the data type of the first column

8. So, after selecting **first column (1)**, click on **Transform (2)**, and then check the **Data Type** value. In my case, it says **Date**, which is correct. If, in your case, it isn't right, select a **Date** data type. However, if, for whatever reason, you experience problems related to this data type change, you can try to change the formatting from the **Model view** panel. Try this as follows (only if you're having issues):

Figure 12.25 – How to fix date formatting issues

9. Now, back in the **Data** view, check all of the other columns on your own.

    The rules are simple. In the case of strings such as the username or the country columns, you should see a **Text** data type. In the case of numbers such as the age or book rating columns, you should check whether the data type is **Whole Number**. You will also see the last column, **approved**, with empty cells. That's OK. I've created two sheets inside that file. One is public, one is not. The data under the approved column is only visible to me. However, you don't need it in any case to create the charts.

10. When you check all of the columns' data types, go to the **Home** tab and click on the **Close & Apply** button. Perfect! From now on, each time we refresh the Power BI file, the PQE will ensure that everything is adequately formatted if we specified that, so we don't have to worry about formatting data that will be created in the future.

OK. Now we have imported the live dataset. We can refresh it whenever we want to see whether new responses have been approved. Refresh it during the creation of the charts. Who knows, maybe I'll approve the responses in a few minutes while you're placing the charts!

Creating the charts

Now we want to place the charts that will compose our dashboard. If you don't like some customization, you can always choose the one that works better for you. Anyway, I won't explain every single chart as you already know how to do that. I will present a few of them. Then I want you to create new chart types and find insights using the dataset provided. Then, share the dashboard with me once you're done. I would love to see what you have achieved. You can reach me on LinkedIn or Twitter.

Now, before placing any chart, I always ask myself a question and give some answers. Please stick with me and do the same. The question is, *What kind of analysis do we want to do with this dataset?* You should always ask something like that before building any type of chart, as it will help you focus on what matters and avoid wasting time placing random charts with less or no sense. Also, each answer will correspond to one or more charts. And, of course, we don't need to give all the answers now. Just type the most important that comes to mind. The other ones will follow during the chart's creation. So, my answers are as follows:

- Check the average age of the readers.
- Understand the male/female gender ratio.
- See which countries have the most readers, and which ones the least.
- Understand the distribution of roles between countries and ages. For instance, how many BIM managers are from Spain under the age of 40? How many architects are under 30 from Germany, and so on?
- See the correlation between the book ratings and the countries or the continents. I mean, which countries liked it the most? Which countries liked it the least?
- Analyze what the correlation is between book ratings and genders.
- Understand the ratio between the number of readers and the start/end skill levels.

- See what the first AEC fields between the readers, and also the last fields are.

- In which months do we have the most completed forms? And in which months do we have the fewest?

- Also, something very technical, what are the coolest usernames? :D

At this point, we have provided a lot of answers. Let's try to design some charts using the previous answers. I want to create three charts. The first one will be the donut, which is quite simple to make and read. The second, a little more complex but nothing to worry about, is the map chart. And the last one, a little more challenging to create than the previous one, is the scatter chart. I picked those three because if you know how to create them, you'll be pretty much ready to make any type of chart in Power BI. Let's start with the donut chart.

Donut chart

We will start with a simple one – the gender ratio:

1. Place a donut chart on the Power BI canvas.

2. Drop the **gender** column on to the **Legend** and **Values** fields. Make sure to choose **Count of gender** as the option for the **Values** field only.

3. Now, let's go to **Formatting panel** and activate just **Detail labels**, **Title**, **Background**, and **Tooltip**.

Then, format the chart as you want—colors, fonts, font sizes, and so on. We won't cover those kinds of customization here, as we did that many times in the previous chapters of this book. However, if you need a refresher on chart formatting options, re-read *Chapter 11, Visualizing Data from Multiple Models in Power BI*, as we covered those subjects there.

The following is a diagram of the recently created donut chart:

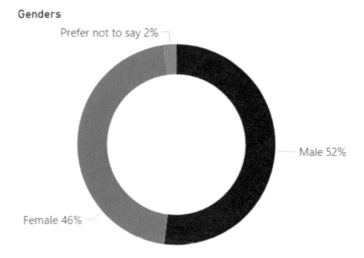

Figure 12.26 – Gender

As you can see, the diagram quickly shows the ratio between readers' genders. We can use it to filter out the results when the dashboard is completed. For instance, if we click on **Female**, all the other charts will update and show just the results corresponding to female readers.

Map chart

Now we want to use the locations and display them on the map. Here, we will deal with a few more parameters than the ones we used in *Chapter 11, Visualizing Data from Multiple Models in Power BI. What if I want to use the country column and get, for example, the continents? Is that even possible in Power BI?* The short answer is *Yes*. And it is pretty simple too. Let's see how:

1. Place a map on the canvas.

2. There is more than one way to create a new column of data to get the continents out of the countries. We will create a custom column and then use **DAX** to achieve our goal. Now, go to the **Data** view. It's the second icon to the left of the UI.

3. Then, open the **Home** tab and click on **New column** inside the **Calculations** group of buttons.

4. Here, open this link: `https://cutt.ly/oW9i6xg`.

5. Scroll down to the second section of the page, **Power BI DAX formula to extract continents from countries**, as shown here:

Link to copy inside the URL field

https://docs.google.com/spreadsheets/d/e/2PACX-1vReSFLyy-w6zrHzHCPSZH_jSj36olg8a
XQ8i3kL52cZX9p0VaEh6cqwSAEQNUr-GfUcdxxnG787FtNI/pub?gid=137090910&single=tr
ue&output=csv

Power BI DAX formula to extract continents from countries

```
calc_continents =
SWITCH(
    'pub?gid=137090910&single=true&output=csv'[country],
    "Austria", "Europe",
    "Albania", "Europe",
    "Belgium", "Europe",
    "Bulgaria", "Europe",
    "Croatia", "Europe",
    "Cyprus", "Europe",
    "Czechia (Czech Republic)", "Europe",
    "Denmark", "Europe",
    "Estonia", "Europe",
    "Finland", "Europe",
```

Figure 12.27 – Power BI DAX formula to extract continents from countries

We are going to use a **DAX** function called **SWITCH()**. The function simply returns different results depending on another value. In the English language, it means that the function checks each value, and if it contains **"Austria"**, for example, it will write **"Europe"**, as shown in the preceding screenshot (*Figure 12.27*). So, copy everything from the Google Docs link, starting with **calc_continents**, to the closing round bracket at the end. I know it's a bit long as a **DAX** formula, but we have many countries on Earth!

6. Now, go back to Power BI, and click on the pointing down arrow at the far right of the formula textbox to expand the section. The following screenshot shows the icon:

Figure 12.28 – Click on the pointing down arrow to expand the formula textbox

7. With the formula textbox expanded, paste everything you copied from the Google Docs file. Once copied, the formula should look like the following screenshot:

```
 1 calc_continents =
 2 SWITCH(
 3     'pub?gid=137090910&single=true&output=csv'[country],
 4     "Austria", "Europe",
 5     "Albania", "Europe",
 6     "Belgium", "Europe",
 7     "Bulgaria", "Europe",
 8     "Croatia", "Europe",
 9     "Cyprus", "Europe",
10     "Czechia (Czech Republic)", "Europe",
11     "Denmark", "Europe",
12     "Estonia", "Europe",
13     "Finland", "Europe",
```

Figure 12.29 – The SWITCH function copied inside the DAX editor

Also, check the end of the formula. It must close with the following lines:

```
    "Suriname", "South America",
    "French Guiana", "South America",
    "Falkland Islands", "South America"
    )
```

The last line doesn't have a comma but a closing parenthesis, and that's correct.

8. When everything is OK, go to the upper-left side of the UI, where you will find two icons, an **X** and a check symbol (✓). Click on the checkbox to confirm the operation. Also, click on the pointing down arrow again (upper-right) to collapse the **DAX** formula textbox.

9. Now, go back to the **Report** view, where we placed the map chart. Drop **calc_ continents** inside the **Location** and **Legend** fields. Then, drop the **country** column into the **Size** field. Make sure to select **Count of country**.

10. Done! Now have fun customizing the map chart. Mine looks like the following:

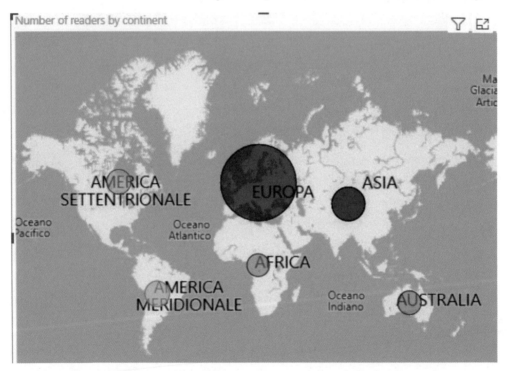

Figure 12.30 – Map chart displaying how many readers per continent there are

Fantastic, the map chart looks really cool! At the moment, Europe wins in terms of the number of readers, but Asia isn't too far behind. However, the data will look utterly different in a few weeks as (hopefully) more and more readers complete the book. Let's now jump to the following chart.

Scatter chart

Hi! The scatter chart is excellent for correlating two sets of data belonging to the same macro-category. I want to use it to see the correlation between continents and book ratings. The question is, *In which continent is the book most appreciated, and in which continent is it appreciated the least?* Let's see quickly how to build that:

1. Place a scatter chart onto the canvas. You can find it next to the **Pie chart** icon.

2. Drop **calc_continets** inside the **X axis** field.

3. Drop **book ratings** into the **Y axis** field and make sure to select **Average of book ratings** after placing it.

4. Then, drop the **countries** column inside the **Size** field and make sure it says **Count of country**.

5. The chart is complete! All you have to do now is to customize its formatting options. I have completed one using light-blue, diamond-shaped symbols, as I think they look lovely!

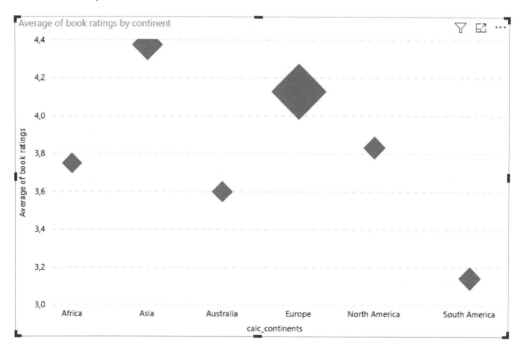

Figure 12.31 – Scatter chart

Perfect! The scatter chart is complete, too. Let's see. It seems that in Asia, the book is more appreciated than in South America, while African, Australian, and North American readers are thinking, "Meh..." with an average score between 3 and 4. But I am happy anyway that those countries' ratings are closer to 4 than 3! And, those are just the starting values for the book ratings, as they will update for sure in the coming weeks (hopefully for the better).

Now I want you to build more charts using the dataset provided. If you'd like to look at my version, you can check it out at the following link: `https://cutt.ly/vEgkRa9`.

Once you open it, pay attention to the bottom center of the page. The report I've created has two pages. You can move back and forth using the black arrow icons. Have fun!

This section taught us how to import the data into Power BI and establish the live connection with the Google services dataset. Also, we learned how to create a few charts using the readers' data. Those three charts gave us numerous insights into the level of appreciation of the book, readers' gender, roles, the industry, and overall ratings.

Summary

Let's now recap what we achieved during the whole chapter. Here we discussed how to build a powerful workflow using Google services and Power BI to stream data collected by the form. As a simple example, we started by learning how to make the Holiday Wishes form. Then we used it to understand how the Google Power BI connection works and set up everything on both sides. Then, we completed the premade form to collect book readers' data and imported that dataset into Power BI to create the charts. Also, we placed three types of charts to start our dashboard – a donut chart, a map chart, and a scatter chart. Now, build the rest of them and ask yourself what the chart's purpose is before making any. If you want, you can get inspiration from the completed report I've shared previously. Now it's time to say congratulations. You've completed the book *Visualizing and Managing Your BIM Data*. I know at some points, the book might have been difficult to grasp, and that's perfectly normal. After all, no pain, no gain. To be honest, we covered many subjects for one book, and my goal was to give you all the tools to start building your new skills on your own. You are now familiar with computer science subjects such as what a data center is and how it all began, how the cloud works, how data is structured, and how a company uses it to do business in today's world. We talked about hybrid jobs and how they will be more and more critical in the future.

Theory aside, we covered other subjects, including the fundamentals of computer science. We learned how to work with numbers, strings, elements, and lists and create various Autodesk Dynamo data-gathering scripts, and we learned how to manage, organize, and export that data to Excel, taking advantage of the regular expression functions. Then we understood how to grab data, not from one single Revit model, but from many of them simultaneously. And throughout the whole book, we touched on Power BI several times, and each time we added a brick to the wall we were building. Now the wall is complete, and you have all the skills needed to consider yourself a hybrid worker! My goal wasn't to teach every single little detail about the tools. I wanted you to be curious about that stuff. If you are now, it's a win!

Tools are not the main thing: the logic behind them is. This is a quote I like a lot. The first time I heard it was from an esteemed and brilliant colleague, *Sol Amour*, now product manager at Autodesk, working every day to always provide us with the best tools and features on Autodesk Dynamo. During the Autodesk University event in London in 2019, he said that we should learn the logic behind the tools rather than the tools themselves, and that quote says it all. *It's time for you and me to now embark on some new, exciting, and fantastic adventures! Best of luck!*

Figure 12.32 – Good luck with your new adventures!

Henceforth, I wish you the best in your career and an extraordinary and beautiful life. Ciao!

Packt.com

Subscribe to our online digital library for full access to over 7,000 books and videos, as well as industry leading tools to help you plan your personal development and advance your career. For more information, please visit our website.

Why subscribe?

- Spend less time learning and more time coding with practical eBooks and Videos from over 4,000 industry professionals

- Improve your learning with Skill Plans built especially for you

- Get a free eBook or video every month

- Fully searchable for easy access to vital information

- Copy and paste, print, and bookmark content

Did you know that Packt offers eBook versions of every book published, with PDF and ePub files available? You can upgrade to the eBook version at packt.com and as a print book customer, you are entitled to a discount on the eBook copy. Get in touch with us at customercare@packtpub.com for more details.

At www.packt.com, you can also read a collection of free technical articles, sign up for a range of free newsletters, and receive exclusive discounts and offers on Packt books and eBooks.

Other Books You May Enjoy

If you enjoyed this book, you may be interested in these other books by Packt:

Increasing Autodesk Revit Productivity for BIM Projects

Fabio Roberti, Decio Ferreira

ISBN: 978-1-80056-680-4

- Explore the primary BIM documentation to start a BIM project
- Set up a Revit project and apply the correct coordinate system to ensure long-term productivity
- Improve the efficiency of Revit core functionalities that apply to daily activities
- Use visual programming with Dynamo to boost productivity and manage data in BIM projects
- Import data from Revit to Power BI and create project dashboards to analyze data
- Discover the different Revit plugins for improved productivity, visualization, and analysis
- Implement best practices for modeling in Revit

Learn SOLIDWORKS 2020

Tayseer Almattar

ISBN: 978-1-78980-410-2

- Understand the fundamentals of SOLIDWORKS and parametric modeling
- Create professional 2D sketches as bases for 3D models using simple and advanced modeling techniques
- Use SOLIDWORKS drawing tools to generate standard engineering drawings
- Evaluate mass properties and materials for designing parts and assemblies
- Understand the objectives and the formats of the CSWA and CSWP exams
- Discover expert tips and tricks to generate different part and assembly configurations for your mechanical designs

Packt is searching for authors like you

If you're interested in becoming an author for Packt, please visit authors. packtpub.com and apply today. We have worked with thousands of developers and tech professionals, just like you, to help them share their insight with the global tech community. You can make a general application, apply for a specific hot topic that we are recruiting an author for, or submit your own idea.

Hi!

I am Ernesto Pellegrino, author of Managing and Visualizing your BIM Data. I hope you enjoyed reading this book and found it helpful in increasing your BIM data management and visualization skills. The book also has chapters written by friends and brilliant colleagues worldwide, Manuel Andrè Bottiglieri, Luisa Cypriano Pieper, Gavin Crump, and Dounia Touil.

It would help me (and other potential readers!) if you could leave a review on Amazon sharing your thoughts on Managing and Visualizing your BIM Data.

Your review will help me understand what's worked well in this book and what could be improved upon for future editions, so it really is appreciated.

Best Wishes,

Ernesto Pellegrino

Manuel André Bottiglieri

Dounia Touil

Gavin Crump

Luisa Cypriano Pieper

Index

P

Q

R

V

W

Made in the USA
Middletown, DE
28 December 2021